# Fundamentalist World
## The New Dark Age of Dogma

**Stuart Sim**

Icon Books UK  Totem Books USA

Originally published in the UK in 2004 by Icon Books Ltd.

This edition published in the UK in 2005
by Icon Books Ltd., The Old Dairy,
Brook Road, Thriplow, Cambridge SG8 7RG
E-mail: info@iconbooks.co.uk
www.iconbooks.co.uk

This edition published in the USA in 2004
by Totem Books
Inquiries to: Icon Books Ltd.,
The Old Dairy, Brook Road, Thriplow
Cambridge SG8 7RG, UK

Sold in the UK, Europe, South Africa
and Asia by Faber and Faber Ltd.,
3 Queen Square, London WC1N 3AU
or their agents

Distributed to the trade in the USA by
National Book Network Inc.,
4720 Boston Way, Lanham,
Maryland 20706

Distributed in the UK, Europe, South Africa
and Asia by TBS Ltd., Frating Distribution
Centre, Colchester Road, Frating Green,
Colchester CO7 7DW

Distributed in Canada by
Penguin Books Canada,
10 Alcorn Avenue, Suite 300,
Toronto, Ontario M4V 3B2

This edition published in Australia in 2005
by Allen & Unwin Pty. Ltd.,
PO Box 8500, 83 Alexander Street,
Crows Nest, NSW 2065

ISBN 1 84046 628 6

Typesetting by Hands Fotoset

Printed and bound in the UK by Cox and Wyman Ltd

# Contents

# Acknowledgements

Thanks go to my editor at Icon, Duncan Heath, for his invaluable support and guidance from the very start of this project. As always, Dr Helene Brandon was a calming influence at critical times.

# About the Author

Stuart Sim is Professor of Critical Theory in the English Department at the University of Sunderland. He is the author of *Derrida and the End of History*, *Lyotard and the Inhuman* and *Irony and Crisis: A Critical History of Postmodern Culture*, all published by Icon. His work has been translated into nine languages, and he is a Fellow of the English Association.

## CHAPTER ONE

# Introduction: The Wilderness of Fundamentalism

The philosopher Jean-François Lyotard dramatically announced to the world in 1979, in his book *The Postmodern Condition*, that the day of 'grand narratives' was now past.[1] They had ceased to merit our support, and we had entered into a brave new postmodern world where institutional authority would no longer hold us under its spell as it had done throughout most of the modern era. The old socio-political order was dying out and the future would be libertarian. By 'grand narratives' Lyotard meant universal theories in the style of, for example, Marxism: that is, theories which claimed to be able to explain, and in large measure to predict, whatever took place in the world of human affairs – whether a political crisis, a stock market crash, or a sociological trend. We could assume that religions fell under the heading of grand narrative too, and that their influence, already much reduced in Western society – in Europe, certainly – would continue steadily to decline. Not only was the future to be libertarian, the future was to be secular. At best, religion could be expected to occupy a residual presence on the margins of daily existence: a ghost from the past as far as most of us were concerned.

Over the course of the 1980s, Lyotard's words came to seem highly prophetic as the Soviet empire proceeded to collapse, an event that paved the way for the reunification of Germany and left in its wake a motley collection of other states, some old and some new, to make their accommodation with the Western political order as best they could. Universal political theories did indeed seem to be falling into terminal disrepute, with previously totalitarian regimes withering away in the face of mass public indifference. A new world order loomed, free from the sterile ideological assumptions of the past. Marxism patently had lost its force in Western culture. As far as the East went, if Marxism continued to be the official doctrine of the Chinese state, it was surely Marxism in name only. Far from propagating the doctrines of Marxism's founders, the Chinese Communist Party, self-appointed guardian of the political interests of a quarter of the world's population, was enthusiastically embracing capitalist economic methods. The Chinese masses were being urged to become entrepreneurial and to become rich, with the Party even arguing that becoming rich was a duty one owed to one's society. Marx, Engels, Lenin and Mao, one could only imagine, were collectively turning in their graves at such a distortion of the communist creed. Although North Korea and Cuba continued on the communist road, they cut rather sad and marginal figures in the world – Marxism as dead end rather than hope for the future.

As a political theory, Marxism had fallen off the radar screen: this was the age of pragmatism, the age of the free market triumphant. For a host of commentators, led by the American political scientist Francis Fukuyama, the Western democratic system had won, and the messy history of clashing civilisations had come to a welcome end.[2] According to Fukuyama, all the world's political ideologies were destined to converge on the Western liberal democratic ideal, and it would be only a matter of time before this occurred. This was where all history inexorably was leading. So complete did the victory appear to be that some thinkers could even bemoan the lack of any real opposition in the new political dispensation, the state of 'living without an alternative', as the sociologist Zygmunt Bauman dubbed it, in which, with communism vanquished, the West seemingly was free to do whatever it wanted without hindrance.[3] As Bauman went on to concede, this was not an age in which to be a critic of the prevailing order: you just felt in limbo, bereft of any meaningful constituency listening to you or expecting a lead from you.

A post-Marxist movement emerged around this period, dedicated to carrying on the work of Marx in a new cultural climate, even if that amounted to doing no more than invoking his spirit in the struggle against political injustice and economic exploitation. Ernesto Laclau and Chantal Mouffe were in the vanguard of this movement, and they created something of a stir within the Western Marxist establishment with their call to support the many new protest movements that were springing up around the globe. This was the way, they argued, to combat social and political oppression in a rapidly changing world that no longer seemed to conform to Marxist schemes. But post-Marxism had a limited impact in the wider public arena, spending much of its time squabbling with fundamentalist Marxist thinkers who were unwilling to admit that they had lost their power base. This seemed further evidence of the triumph of the new, free market-based, Western-controlled, global political order. There really did appear to be no alternative to turn to in our post-communist world. Liberal democracy could be considered humankind's destiny.

## The Return of Grand Narrative

Looking back on this period from the vantage point of the new century, one can only wonder what went wrong – or why the cultural signs of the times were so drastically misinterpreted. As of that fateful event 9/11, grand narratives are back on the global political agenda – 'with a vengeance', we might entirely appropriately say. Fundamentalism has replaced communism as the spectre haunting the Western consciousness: a spectre that looms ever larger in the aftermath of 9/11 and the apparent inability of the Western powers to eradicate the secretive and mysterious Al-Qaeda network that lay behind that terrorist attack. Even more ominously, it has become evident that fundamentalism runs much deeper in our culture than just matters of religion. As Islamic fundamentalism clearly signals to us, religious fundamentalism is inextricably implicated in politics. Contemporary American Christian fundamentalism tells us the same story (note its influence on the 'Christian Right', for example, with its strong power base within the Republican Party); as do the Jewish and Hindu varieties. The Middle East is a mess, with Judaic and Islamic societies locked into what certainly looks like a clash of civilisations with incommensurable objectives. Even if a peace deal were signed there tomorrow, few of us would believe in its long-term prospects, so far apart are the two sides on all the critical issues. Meanwhile, the authorities in India have on several occasions in recent years turned a blind eye to the persecution of Muslims by Hindu nationalists, with riots, kidnappings and murders being reported. Religion and politics are natural bedfellows, no matter how much some of us may deplore the fact and wish it were not so (those of us who lack the 'religion gene'). Perhaps what we are having to come to terms with, belatedly, is what sociologists have dubbed 'the myth of secularisation':[4] the realisation that religion is by no means either dead or dying, as so many of us had come to believe.

Picture yourself in the Afghanistan of the Taliban, with almost all evidence of modern life, other than guns and armoury, abolished. No television, films, CDs, alcohol, or Western clothing or publications allowed. Mandatory dress codes in operation for both sexes, rigidly enforced by zealous, gun-carrying militiamen in no mood for debate. Relations with the West effectively severed. Terrorist organisations such as Al-Qaeda welcomed into your midst. Women more or less barred from public life, and confined to the family home. The economy, already ravaged by the long-running war of liberation against the Russians, operating at bare subsistence level; the Taliban leadership (Mullah Muhammad Omar and his colleagues) being more interested in theological purity than economic revival. More interested in theological purity, too, than in preserving the country's historical heritage: hence the destruction of the ancient Buddhist statues in Bamiyan, despite protests from the West. All in the name of Islam, as interpreted by fundamentalists trying to create the Muslim 'utopia' here on Earth, having expelled the heathen Russians and their puppet Marxist government. Secularisation really was a myth in this instance. Ayatollah Khomeini's Iran in the aftermath of the overthrow of the Shah's regime presented a similar picture, with a campaign waged by the new Islamist government against modernisation. Islam is an increasingly important force as well in many of the ex-Soviet republics in Central Asia; states, as one commentator claims, 'now ripe for social, political, and economic upheavals of one sort or another', which 'will be exploited by the best-organized opposition in the region – the Islamic militant parties'.[5] Religion is still a potent force in our world, capable of establishing political control over significant sections of the world's population. The Taliban may have gone, but their legacy lives on in global politics, with relations between Islam and the West at their lowest point for generations.

Fundamentalism in the political arena is soon embroiled in issues of economics, not to mention nationalism and ethnic strife. It spreads like a ripple. If we look around us, fundamentalist principles can be found at work in all spheres of life. Market fundamentalism, as a case in point, is a well documented phenomenon in global culture (the term being coined by the international financier George Soros), and for some commentators the International Monetary Fund (IMF) and the World Bank pose as great a threat to global peace and harmony as any Islamic fundamentalist movement. The Islamic scholar Akbar S. Ahmed was one of the first to draw attention to the adverse effects of IMF and World Bank policies towards the Third World, and even establishment Western economists such as Joseph E. Stiglitz, erstwhile adviser to the Clinton presidency, have come to express grave misgivings about these institutions of late.[6] These misgivings aren't surprising, given the many failures that the IMF and World Bank have been associated with in the last decade or two. Africa, Russia, South-East Asia and Argentina all bear witness to what can happen when free market economics, as practised in the most advanced nations of the West (admittedly with varying degrees of rigour, depending on local cultural factors), are imposed on countries lacking the requisite social and political structures to make these work.

As I write, the Argentinian economy is in ruins, in what can only be called the political equivalent of bankruptcy. If it were a business, Argentina would have been closed down altogether by now, or taken over by one of its competitors at a rock-bottom price. The country's banking system has collapsed, taking with it most of the population's savings and reducing huge numbers to penury – the professional classes no less than the traditionally vulnerable working class. Barter has become the main means of economic transaction – a particularly humiliating experience for any nation in the modern world, never mind one with the extensive natural resources of Argentina, as well as its carefully cultivated self-image of being the most developed and sophisticated of South American countries. Even rubbish has become a political issue in such a desperate situation, its ownership disputed: 'Squatters, piqueteros and even the cartoneros – the armies of scavengers who comb through garbage looking for cardboard to sell – are under siege. According to the former owner of Buenos Aires's largest privatised garbage company, now running for mayor on a platform of "Let's take back Buenos Aires", garbage is private property and the cartoneros are thieves.'[7] One suspects the IMF and World Bank, with their intense market consciousness, would probably be in agreement with this assessment.

Argentina's political history is a chequered one, with rampant inflation and corrupt government practically the norm, but it's only since it came under the wing of the IMF and World Bank that it has ceased to function at all. Squabbles over rubbish ownership have to be a low point for any country to experience. IMF/World Bank policies have made a bad situation far worse, and succeeded in driving Argentina to the wall – all in the name of market fundamentalism (and behind that, as we'll see, lie globalisation and corporate fundamentalism, further pressures on the vulnerable). Yet the IMF and World Bank stand by their policies for ailing economies, and see no reason to change them. Another Argentina is an altogether too likely occurrence, as Joseph Stiglitz has warned. Somehow one doubts if even that would dent the confidence of the market fundamentalists. If hope springs eternal, so does their faith in free market capitalism (as well as the 'one size fits all' approach).

Religion, politics, economics: it's not too fanciful to suggest that when you step outside the door in the morning, you step into a fundamentalist world, a new dark age of dogma. How can you negotiate your way through this potential minefield?

We live in a fundamentalist world because fundamentalists exert such a powerful influence on so many of our institutions – religious, political, and economic. This is not to say that there is a global conspiracy of fundamentalisms. Fundamentalists in one area don't necessarily agree with fundamentalists in another: in practice, they are more likely to disagree with each other, often quite violently. This is particularly noticeable in the sphere of religion: Christian fundamentalists reject the claims of Islamic fundamentalists, and vice versa. Each side asserts that it's in possession of 'the truth', that it was revealed to their prophet and their prophet alone. There can be no dissent from this article of faith: by definition, monotheistic religions can't countenance competition. More than one monotheism in operation is an offence to one's faith. Religious fundamentalism is exclusion-minded: you're either in the charmed circle of believers or you're the enemy – there's very rarely any middle position offered for you to adopt. Contemporary political thought differentiates between 'antagonistic' and 'agonistic' relationships between competing groups or movements. In the latter case, differences are accepted by all sides and competition is marked by mutual respect; in the former, at least one of the parties refuses to accept the legitimacy of the others and accords them no respect whatsoever. Religious fundamentalism is unashamedly in the antagonistic camp, actively encouraging its followers to believe that, in the words of the American political theorist William E. Connolly, they are 'under an absolute imperative to eliminate' all other competitors.[8] As we know from 9/11, this injunction can be taken to extreme lengths: 'eliminate' is no mere metaphor.

An antagonistic orientation means that religious fundamentalism frequently clashes with other forms of fundamentalism. Market fundamentalism may be acceptable to many Christian fundamentalists, particularly in their American heartland (the Christian Right might just as easily be dubbed the Christian Capitalist Right), but not to Islamic fundamentalists – or Marxist fundamentalists either. Their economic theories are diametrically opposed to market fundamentalism on a range of issues, such as interest rates and profits; Muslims regarding the former as against the doctrines of the Koran (Christians had similar scruples at one time, but have long since managed to overcome them), Marxists the latter as a form of theft from the working class. We aren't likely to find accommodations being made on such fundamental topics, and indeed the new Islamic fundamentalist movements are showing remarkably little concern with economic matters. According to the journalist Ahmed Rashid, they 'are not interested in transforming a corrupt society into a just one, nor do they care about providing jobs, education, or social benefits to their followers'.[9] It is theological purity, and the power that derives from enforcing this, that drives them instead. Nationalism can confuse the issue even further. For many in Western Europe, Islam represents the antithesis to traditional conceptions of national identity, and Hinduism is nearly as suspect (if less obviously a terrorist threat to the European way of life). It's not so long ago that Judaism was considered to be just as alien to European culture, with horrific consequences the aftermath of which still affects our political life very profoundly. Suspicion and fundamentalism can be cited as another pair of natural bedfellows.

Even in the more liberal countries of Europe, we can find disquiet being expressed about the long-term implications of immigration from the Third World on the national way of life (with religion clearly one of the complicating factors). In Holland, Pim Fortuyn constructed a meteoric political career out of playing on such fears, and his assassination in 2002 ironically enough helped to propel his party, Pim Fortuyn's List, into power as part of a coalition government. Admittedly, without their charismatic leader they have since faded from view, and latterly from government, but Fortuyn's ideas manifestly had struck a chord with a significant section of the traditionally liberal-minded Dutch electorate. This despite the

Dutch authorities having devoted considerable time and effort to making multiculturalism work, and with cities such as Amsterdam appearing to be multicultural success stories that the rest of Europe could copy. Fortuyn's demand that all immigrants should uphold Dutch values cut right across the multiculturalist ideal.

The history of Jean-Marie Le Pen and his National Front party in France in recent years is further evidence of the appeal that nationalist fundamentalism can exert. Anti-immigration is the core of Le Pen's political philosophy, which claims that French national identity is under threat because of the influx of economic refugees from the Third World (particularly Islamic refugees, for whom Le Pen has a special dislike). Le Pen won through into the second round of the French presidential elections in 2002, eliminating his socialist rival in the process, and although he was then soundly defeated by the Gaullist candidate Jacques Chirac (socialist voters backing their despised opponent Chirac in a tactical move to block the even more despised Le Pen), he had made his point about how much opposition there was to multiculturalism throughout France. The National Front party also polls well in local politics, and has controlled several city and town councils. Le Pen continues to be a formidable presence in French political life, the public voice of a large constituency with a deep dislike of the multiculturalist ethos. Jörg Haider's Freedom Party in Austria has exploited the same kind of fears about national identity, and with even greater success than Le Pen, finding, as with Pim Fortuyn's List, that they provided an entry into national government. Intolerance can pay political dividends if it's packaged in the right way.

Then there is the American militia movement, an intriguing, and worrying, blend of nationalism, politics and religion. The movement pictures itself as an embattled minority within the United States, striving to defend the constitution from those who would seek to amend or overturn any of its basic principles, such as, crucially, the right to bear arms. Nothing seems to be more fundamental to this group's sense of identity than that particular right, which must never be infringed; their self-definition seems to depend on it. Ranged against the movement, in their interpretation, is a conspiracy which includes their own government, and quite possibly the United Nations. The American way of life is under threat from this conspiracy, which for militia supporters justifies acts of terrorism being perpetrated within the United States by disaffected rogue individuals such as Timothy McVeigh, who was executed for bombing a government building in Oklahoma City in 1995 with considerable loss of life. The American government was the enemy in his view, and he has become a martyr figure within the militia movement in consequence. When it comes to groups like Aryan Nations, we find race coming onto the scene, with white supremacist policies even extending to their religious practice. The writer Malise Ruthven reports visiting the Church of Jesus Christ Christian-Aryan Nations compound in Northern Idaho, signposted 'Whites Only' on its entry checkpoint just to make sure there's no ambiguity about their mission, and finding a portrait of Hitler hanging in the chapel.[10] We must assume that God has fascist leanings. Tolerance of the outside world is in very short supply in this claustrophobic movement, which sees fundamentalisms to be defended wherever it looks – and defended by the gun preferably.

The lack of tolerance to perceived outsiders is a characteristic trait of fundamentalism, which has little time for any but its own. In the uncompromising words of a contemporary Baptist churchgoer in Texas challenged on the rigidity of his beliefs: 'Either we're going to be in heaven, or we're going to be in hell. Forget about Islam, forget about Buddhism, forget about religion. Jesus Christ says there's only one way to heaven, and that's through Him, OK?'[11] One hardly knows where to start in countering such dogmatic sentiments. 'The truth' is not an elastic concept to this kind of believer, not something up for negotiation or debate on agonistic principles. (The Muslim equivalent would be the words of the 'two-fold creed' from the 'Pillars of Islam': 'There is no god but God, and Mohammed is the messenger of God'; again, this admits of no counter-argument.) The fundamentalist mind does not like difference, it does not like dissent. What it really likes is submission to the system, and uncritical adherence to the creed. For those of us committed to the principles of liberal democracy (for all its flaws), or sympathetic to the idea of postmodernity and its campaign against authoritarianism in public life, this is a dangerous state of affairs. Living in a fundamentalist world means being under pressure to conform to a totalitarian mind-set which brooks no opposition. To oppose is to be seen to join the conspiracy that fundamentalists, with their essentially Manichean world view – in which good and evil are lined up against each other in universal conflict – feel is ranged against them at any one point. If it's not your desire to conform or submit, if you think authority is there to be challenged rather than blindly obeyed, then it's time to come to know your adversary better.

## The Fundamental Things Apply

Fundamentalist attitudes can be found throughout human history, with most religions exhibiting them at some point or other in their development, and increasingly so as they gain power, but the term itself is of surprisingly recent origin. Its first recorded use is in 1920, to describe the doctrines put forward by hard-line Protestant theologians in America determined to halt what they regarded as the drift towards liberalism in religious belief in their society. Little did they know the diverse uses to which the term subsequently would be put, or just how contentious it would become (the Islamic world generally denying that the fundamentalist tag should be applied to it at all, given its Christian heritage).[12] The major fruit of their efforts was a multi-authored series of pamphlets called *The Fundamentals* (1910–15), which, under the editorship of A.C. Dixon, aimed to establish the basic principles of Christian faith in an increasingly sceptical modern world.[13] There were five such principles, or 'fundamentals', and a fundamentalist was a believer who, as the journal editor and coiner of the phrase Curtis Lee Laws put it, was willing 'to do battle royal for the Fundamentals'.[14] The fundamentals have been summarised by the historian George M. Marsden as follows: '(1) the inerrancy of Scripture, (2) the Virgin Birth of Christ, (3) his substitutionary atonement, (4) his bodily resurrection, and (5) the authenticity of his miracles.'[15]

At the centre of the enterprise lay the belief in the inerrancy of the Bible, and it was on such issues that fundamentalists differed from evangelicals. Evangelicals emphasised the personal aspect of religious belief (culminating in the 'born again' movement), and were enthusiastic readers of the Bible, but they stopped short of regarding it as beyond interpretation. For fundamentalists, however, the Bible was literal, revealed truth, the 'absolute transcript of God's mind' as one supporter claimed.[16] This meant that it could not, and should not, be questioned in any way: dogmatism took precedence over debate. To this day, Christian fundamentalism holds fast to this central tenet, which justifies, amongst other things, the continuing championship of creationist doctrines within so many Protestant sects (evangelicals can be more pragmatic about such things, more willing to interpret them metaphorically). Creationism holds that the Earth was created in a very short time span just a few thousand years ago, and repudiates the doctrines of Darwin as well as any of the sciences which trace the existence of the Universe back through billions of years. Evidence which appears to back up the claims of these theories, fossil remains, for example, is discounted by a variety of ingenious arguments – God testing our faith, etc. Officially sanctioned to be taught in the school system of several American states, creationism has crept into the British educational system as well, with some privately funded institutions introducing it onto the syllabus, and the government apparently turning a blind eye in the spirit of involving private enterprise in the public domain.* Once again, we see how religious fundamentalism spills over into the political arena, this time into educational policy and practice.

Paradoxically enough, the postmodern insistence that truth is plural and indeterminate has helped to endow creationism with a certain degree of respectability. The argument goes that Darwinism is one way of explaining the evolution of mankind, creationism another, and that within their own terms of reference each makes sense. If there is no ultimate truth we can appeal to, or even criteria by which to establish what would count as ultimate truth, then creationism has as much right as Darwinism to make its case and to induct the young in its own version of 'science'. As Malise Ruthven has observed of creationism's reception in America, such a claim 'appeals to a natural American sense of fairness. It makes the evolutionists – who reject it – look like doctrinaire spoilsports.'[17] There is no easy rejoinder to this line of argument from within the

---

* As in the case of Emmanuel College in Gateshead in northern England, funded by the Vardy Foundation as part of the government's city academies programme for improving inner-city schools. City academies are jointly funded by government and business, with the business sponsor granted a controlling role in the enterprise. The Vardy Foundation has plans to open six new schools. Leading scientists such as Richard Dawkins have been very critical of the Foundation's support for creationism.

postmodern camp: a combination of inerrancy and indeterminacy makes for a formidable opponent. Extremism can be subtle on occasion, taking advantage of pluralism in order to fight the battle against pluralism.

## The Personal and the Political

This book will be defending the right to dissent, since this is what is most at risk from the spread of fundamentalism. We have to recognise just how insidious and pervasive the fundamentalist threat is. Religious fundamentalism may be the best-known type, but there is a series of fundamentalisms operating in our world, in the realms of economic policy, politics, thought in general. They may not form a conspiracy, they may reject each other's claims quite categorically and even despise each other intensely, but they are linked together in interesting ways that create a fundamentalist world where dissent and difference are marginalised. Not every fundamentalist is a terrorist, but every fundamentalist is a dogmatist, and that is reason enough for the rest of us to worry; especially when dogmatism generates a desire to suppress all other viewpoints. The current cultural climate seems particularly conducive to the growth of fundamentalism. As one historian of American fundamentalism has noted of the phenomenon's resurgence: 'Once again, H.L. Mencken's quip seemed apt: "Heave an egg out a Pullman window, and you will hit a Fundamentalist almost anywhere in the United States today."'[18] We need to reflect on why fundamentalism has come into its own again in so forceful a fashion, and what this says about us as a species; why certainty attracts so many more followers than doubt does. John Bunyan's famous allegory *The Pilgrim's Progress* begins with the narrator describing himself as engaged in a journey through 'the wilderness of this world'.[19] It's time to venture forth into what for postmodernists is the wilderness of fundamentalism, to discover just what it is we are up against.

In a book of this kind the author has to decide what his or her role is, and to what extent to reveal himself or herself, innermost feelings and all, to the reader. The author in this case is an academic, and academics are taught to write in certain ways to abide by prescribed academic conventions of critical debate. Those conventions dictate that the author adopts a dispassionate, impersonal tone as much as possible, and avoids direct intervention into the text. The personal is to be suppressed in order to ensure that the argument, not the arguer, is the focus of attention. Agonism rather than antagonism is the ideal. It may be a fiction (academics are as capable of being antagonistic as anyone else), but it's a fiction that most of the profession adheres to most of the time. Maintaining that fiction will be all the harder here when we are going to be delving into such delicate areas as one's spiritual and political beliefs. Readers have the right to expect something more than an assumption of consensus in such cases, hidden behind an objective academic style. So let's put the conventions aside in this instance and introduce the author directly into the text, to let the reader know why the author finds the topic important and, more to the point, what ideals, beliefs and, yes, prejudices the author brings to the project.

This need not be embarrassingly confessional. My political position is, broadly speaking, post-Marxist; which means that I have a residual respect, and even nostalgia, for the Marxist world view while having come to recognise, and reject, its totalitarian and authoritarian character as it has expressed itself over the course of the 20th century. A Marxist line on the topic of fundamentalism would be easy to construct: religion, capitalism, and nationalism are standard Marxist targets, and fundamentalists in these areas can only be regarded as the enemies of human progress with the various 'opiates' they are offering the masses. I am just as concerned to confront these enemies: so assume an anti- disposition on my part in each case, with some qualifications which will be outlined as we go. I will be more sceptical, however, about the notion of progress – at least as conceived of by any of the modern world's universal political theories (a phrase I will tend to prefer to the more academic 'grand narrative' from now on). Post-Marxists are Marxists who have been bitten by the postmodernism bug (a desirable infection in my view). They are committed, therefore, to challenging authority in its various guises, including the authority emanating from Marxism, that grandest of universal theories with its belief in the ultimate perfectibility of the human race. Marxism is capable of being just as fundamentalist as any religion in protecting its doctrines from critics and non-believers. I recall only too vividly delivering a conference paper a few years ago criticising Marxism for its authoritarian tendencies, only to be told by a particularly testy member of the audience during the discussion period after- wards, that if I would only 'go and read some fucking Marx' I would discover just how wrong I was in my opinions.* The clear implication was that Marx's works were every bit as inerrant as Christian fundamentalists took the Bible to be; that they constituted yet another 'absolute transcript' beyond questioning by mere mortals. There were no failings to be reported; the fault lay in humanity, not in the ideas. As we'll come to discover, that is a quintessentially fundamentalist attitude.

Rather than absolutist, totalising theories such as Marxism (or the bulk of world religions), which converge on a central truth, postmodernists want to press the case for difference,

---

* I seem to have a talent for upsetting fundamentalists. Another conference paper of mine some years ago, applying postmodern theory to John Bunyan's fiction, inspired a member of the audience to declare that I would surely be damned for my irreverence.

diversity, scepticism and multiculturalism.[20] Progress is to be understood in a different way from the 'victory' of an over-weening ideology. And that's where the first problem arises. How far can one defend multiculturalism when it involves religions that refuse to recognise difference, diversity and multiculturalism in their turn? Immediately we find ourselves plunged into tortuous discussions about the role and position of women in Islam (to veil or not to veil?); the treatment of minorities by almost all world religions; the anti-gay agenda of almost all theological discourse. Pim Fortuyn was notorious for being openly anti-Muslim in a society officially committed to multiculturalism; but he was anti-Muslim because Islam, particularly fundamentalist Islam, discriminates harshly against women and gays. Do we criticise his lack of tolerance, or applaud his liberalism? The fact that Fortuyn was assassinated for being anti-Muslim by a Dutch animal rights activist shows just how confusing the whole issue is capable of becoming.

As Fortuyn's case suggests, a subsidiary problem to emerge from this debate is whether calling for an end to such oppressive practices is tantamount to imposing a Western scheme of values on other cultures. If that is so, then one runs the risk of becoming, at least implicitly, *anti*-multicultural. Multiculturalism argues against universal values, and what else is equal rights for women, as a particular case in point, but a universal value? A universal value that, as we know, is not being universally respected, with the Muslim world currently the worst offenders. In their desire to project an image of tolerance, anti-fundamentalists on the left can tie themselves in knots over such questions.

Putting the issue aside for the time being, there are certain commitments that a post-Marxist socialist like myself feels obliged to uphold regardless of cultural circumstances. Prominent among these would have to be equality of opportunity, an end to cultural oppression and the tyranny of tradition (religiously inspired or otherwise), and the eradication of discrimination on the grounds of gender, ethnic group, social position or sexual preference. No doubt these are somewhat predictable, and, I hope, to most of my audience entirely unexceptionable also. Yet the forces of discrimination, tyranny and cultural oppression are currently flourishing around the globe, in the West as well as in the Third World, and, more depressingly for us socialist-minded sceptics, apparently can claim very considerable support for their programmes. Again, conspiracy theory will not take us very far when there is such willing commitment 'to do battle royal' for the various fundamentalist causes: zealots aren't hard to find. Fundamentalism thrives because there is a ready market for it; it appeals to something within human nature that we need to confront. Whether or not we agree with such concepts as the 'authoritarian personality' (see next chapter), it has to be acknowledged that many individuals feel more secure within authoritarian systems of belief.[21] The more optimistic postmodern theorists may think that we live in a postmodern world where grand narratives are in irreversible decline, but in reality we inhabit a fundamentalist world where those narratives are in rude health. What is the sceptic to do under such inauspicious circumstances, when a new dark age of dogma seems to have taken hold? Well, he can start by identifying the scale of the problem. Our journey through the wilderness of fundamentalism begins.

## CHAPTER TWO

# Back to Basics: The Fundamentalist Mentality

What drives the fundamentalist mentality? Why can fundamentalism still prove to be so attractive a proposition to so many, in a cultural climate in which authority is being subjected to more sustained challenge than almost ever before? Postmodernists have been in the forefront of this challenge, building on generalised public distrust of politicians, political systems and political ideologies extending from the late 20th into our own century. And not just political systems and ideologies, but traditional institutions, such as the British monarchy, which now finds itself confronted by a growing republican movement oblivious to its traditional aura (what we might call a 'battle anti-royal' is developing on this issue). I take postmodernism in this respect to be a theorisation of what is already happening at grass-roots level in society, and at that level, in the West at any rate, authority's star certainly appears to be on the wane. Why does fundamentalism seem to be bucking that trend, and to what ultimate purpose?

That is part of the answer, of course: that the challenge to authority, the rise of libertarianism, has generated a counter-reaction because so many individuals feel threatened by the insecurity that the breakdown of authority brings in its wake. One person's liberation from oppression is another person's descent into anarchy. The fundamentalist mentality is a search for security in a period of bewildering cultural change; at least in part it's a siege mentality, and we can sympathise with this to some extent. Technological change has speeded up considerably of late, and its intrusiveness in our daily lives can be very alienating – and not just to technophobes. As an example of just how alienating it can be, theorists have seriously broached the notion of cyborgs, suggesting that the future lies in some form of hybrid between humans and technology. Some find this prospect exciting and liberating, arguing that it will extend human capabilities by entering into partnership with machines, especially with computer technology.[1] Others find the idea of altering both the human form and human nature as radically as this deeply disturbing, and fear that the machine side will in time take over to eclipse the human altogether. An 'inhuman' future holds either promise or threat. It's against such a cultural backdrop, with its wholesale rejection of history and tradition, that movements like religious fundamentalism have developed. Putting the most positive spin on it, fundamentalism is a desire for the retention of traditional values; for a tried and tested belief system in a period when belief systems seem to be crumbling all around. Order confronts anarchy for this constituency.

The fundamentalist mentality is also a search for the power and control that the dominance of your system of belief brings, whether in the sphere of religion, economics or politics; as well as for self-definition in the face of the spread of multiculturalism. Going 'back to basics' is an attempt, however misguided, to hold radical change at bay and, if possible, to turn back the clock to a time when the world, apparently at least, conformed to your value system. In religion, to a time when all were believers of the same creed and theocracy was in force; in politics and nationalism, to a society before pluralism and multiculturalism became complicating features on the cultural landscape; in economics, to something like the free market system found in 19th-century England, when *laissez faire* practices ruled and the state followed a non-interventionist policy towards the national economy. It's little better than nostalgia in each case, and misplaced nostalgia at that: fundamentalists almost always see the past as simpler than it was in reality. But all of us are capable of exhibiting this kind of behaviour, no matter how open-minded we may be – or think we are. The fundamentalist mentality is part of human nature: that's why it requires such careful monitoring. Like all aspects of human nature, it can be encouraged or discouraged. It's in the sceptic's interest to provide as much discouragement as possible, to show that we need not give in to this impulse. The disposition towards authoritarianism and dogmatism may lurk within us, but that's no reason for allowing it to dominate and thus set the tone, and the values, of our society.

## The Authoritarian Personality

The notion of the 'authoritarian personality' was put forward in a book of the same name published in 1950, to explain the widespread success of fascism in Europe during the earlier 20th century. The authors were a group of philosophers and social scientists led by the German philosopher Theodor W. Adorno, one of the key figures in the influential Frankfurt School (well known for their Marxist-oriented analyses of Western culture). Writing in the aftermath of the Second World War and the Holocaust, their collective assessment was that prejudice was one of the most pressing problems of the age, a blot on Western civilisation and its professed ideals. Adorno and his collaborators sought to pin down the psychological causes of this phenomenon so that it could be addressed and countered in the new society emerging in the post-war era: 'it may be hoped that knowledge of what the potential fascist is like ... will make symptomatic treatment more effective.'[2] For the authors, that fascist potential was still there under the surface in Western society even after the defeat of Nazism, and they warned that we 'would be foolish to underestimate' it.[3]

What the authors found most problematical about the authoritarian personality was its ability to be swayed away from reason, despite a relatively sophisticated cultural background: 'In contrast to the bigot of the older style he seems to combine the ideas and skills which are typical of a highly industrialized society with irrational or anti-rational beliefs. He is at the same time enlightened and superstitious.'[4] From the authors' perspective, the former trait should have ruled out the latter. These were deep waters psychologically, the more so since almost all of us are capable of anti-rational or superstitious beliefs at one time or another in our lives (often quite a lot of the time). The authoritarian personality holds no monopoly on this apparently paradoxical combination. Religious belief consistently makes anti-rational demands on us, agreed, but it seems a bit sweeping, even for someone lacking the religion gene like myself, to dub everyone who follows a religion an authoritarian personality. Or, for that matter, everyone who holds irrational or superstitious beliefs a bigot. Think of the considerable numbers of people in the West who believe in astrology (or are at least prepared to give it the benefit of the doubt), for which there is certainly no rational foundation. The vast majority of them seem to lead otherwise rational lives, and don't as such constitute any threat to the common good (although some extreme rationalists like Richard Dawkins might disagree with that optimistic assessment).* As the science writer John Horgan has put it, 'we all have many minds. ... I have other minds. One glances at an astrology column now and then, or wonders if maybe there really *is* something to all those reports about people having sex with aliens' (and in his science writer mind, Horgan is a sceptic).[5] 'Enlightened' and 'superstitious' are very loaded terms anyway: Enlightenment is anti-spiritual to the religiously minded, all religion is superstition to the more militant followers of the Enlightenment.

*The Authoritarian Personality* is an exhaustive analysis of the attitudes and beliefs of a cross-section of the American population (2,099 respondents in total) conducted by means of questionnaires. The concern was to isolate the psychological characteristics and personality traits of the potentially fascist, or 'antidemocratic' individual; the contention being 'that individuals who show extreme susceptibilities to fascist propaganda have a great deal in common', that they share a 'syndrome'.[6] There was a definite type to be identified, in other words, although the authors had no magic solution to offer on how to deal with this group. They concluded that psychotherapy would probably have little impact on the problem, and that although more sensitive child-rearing was highly desirable, it was difficult to guarantee if the parents already had developed authoritarian personalities of their own. We had to recognise that potential fascists 'are products of the total organization of society and are to be changed only as that

---

* Dawkins sees astrology as part of an anti-science strain in our culture, and thus as inviting attack from rationalists like himself: 'We have an appetite for wonder, a poetic appetite, which real science ought to be feeding, but which is being hijacked, often for monetary gain, by purveyors of superstition, the paranormal and astrology. ... Astrology ... is an aesthetic affront.' (Richard Dawkins, *Unweaving the Rainbow: Science, Delusion and the Appetite for Wonder*, Penguin, 1998, pp. 115, 118.) In Dawkins, there speaks a true product of the Enlightenment project.

society is changed'.[7] While we could take hope from the fact that most of the population did not have this personality, those who did nevertheless constituted a threatening minority who would always be drawn to extreme fundamentalist theories such as fascism; their superstitious side triumphing over their enlightened. The non-superstitious enlightened had their work cut out for them.

## Fundamentalism: The Rational Choice?

There are those who would argue that belief in fundamentalism is not irrational, however, and that in its own way it represents a rational choice by individuals who are assumed to have weighed up all the available evidence and then come to a personal decision on what system of belief to commit themselves to. Clyde Wilcox is one such commentator, and he rejects all personality-based explanations of fundamentalism's attraction. Thus he can defend the fundamentalist-oriented Christian Right in America as follows:

> Support for the Christian Right is *rational* in at least two senses of the word. ... [1] It does not result from pathological psychological forces. ... [2] It is rational in the sense used by political scientists to explore vote choice – citizens are supporting groups that espouse their values and beliefs.[8]

This can make fundamentalism sound quite unthreatening; just one more participant in a pluralist society that welcomes competing opinions about important social and political issues. In Wilcox's reading, Christian Right fundamentalism appeals to a selection of personality types. What is critical is that they have ideological objectives, rather than character traits, in common, and they seek out organisations which promote those objectives. Conservatism is a character trait most would identify with the Christian Right, but, as Wilcox notes, that's not necessarily enough to establish a Christian Right 'type': 'Social-issue conservatism does not always go hand in hand with conservatism on foreign and economic policy.'[9] It's the ideological objectives, and the values and beliefs underpinning them, that we should concentrate on, therefore, if we wish to understand Christian Right politics. There's no point simply demonising fundamentalism – we need to counter it at an intellectual level, granting it respect as a legitimate system of belief entitled to its world view and the means to propagate it. Darwinians, presumably, must engage creationists in debate rather than dismissing them as irrational and unscientific and thus beyond the pale – although the average Darwinian most likely will be horrified by such a suggestion (Richard Dawkins, for example, is vitriolic on the subject of creationism, which he accords no intellectual respectability whatsoever).

Similar points have been made about Islamic suicide bombers: that there's no specific personality type attracted to this activity either, and that it's not to be considered an irrational choice for the individual to make. Instead, a range of social and economic factors combine to create a situation in which suicide terrorists emerge because there's a demand for their sacrifice, and the individuals concerned can see the logic of that demand. Suicide bombing is part of a political campaign (the Palestinian cause in the Middle East, for example, with the Israeli population the target), and it's rational in terms of the objectives sought: the destabilisation of the enemy such that they are forced to negotiate with the revolutionary organisation directing the suicide attacks, or at the very least to reconsider their policy towards them. 9/11 was a carefully calculated exercise in which all the participants had a clearly defined role to play: it was no mere nihilistic gesture on the part of some psychologically disturbed individuals (if any-thing, that makes it even more worrying). The terrorists see advantages both for themselves and for their families in the sacrifice they make for the cause. They are guaranteed a place of honour in the history of their people, no small matter in such traditionalist cultures, and even promised a place in heaven. Their family generally also receives some form of financial compensation from the political organisation in question (Al-Qaeda, Hamas, Hizbollah, etc.). If we want to understand suicide terrorism, therefore, we have to look at the wider socio-political context in which it takes place. Cultural background is more important than psychological type in explaining why individuals can be willing to do such things. As Wilcox argues with regard to Christian Right politics, it's the values and beliefs that we need to engage with, rather than become side-tracked by issues of personal psychology. *What* people believe is of greater importance than *why* they believe it. We can take action on the former, but not really on the latter (or only with far greater difficulty). We'll be returning to the issue of suicide terrorism in Chapter 4.

Wilcox assumes 'a sizable untapped constituency for the Christian Right', although he concedes that the movement may not be able to take full advantage of this: 'until conserva-tive Protestants can resolve their religious rivalries, a unified Christian Right is unlikely.'[10] (Such divisiveness is a historical tendency within Protestantism, and we shall be exploring it in Chapter 3.) Using a wide range of surveys, he points up the differences between the various organisations on the Christian Right spectrum (the Moral Majority, the Christian Coalition, the John Birch Society, the Christian Anti-Communism Crusade, and Christian Voice, for example), although in general it's only the degree of their conservatism that separates them. To outsiders, there is, in general, more to unite than divide them in their beliefs. Wilcox cites a particular survey of

Florida churchgoers that finds 'authority mindedness' amongst Christian Right supporters, and suggests that this may derive from their attitude to the Bible: 'the fundamentalists' commitment to the inerrancy of the Scriptures as an authority on all matters may lead them to support political movements that promote conformity to biblical values.'[11] In other words, the 'personality disorder' explanation is to be discounted in favour of rational choice:[12] one belief rationally disposes you to espouse another (whether belief in the inerrancy of Scripture is itself a rational choice is a more vexed question, but we'll let that pass for now).

The problem with Wilcox's approach is that fundamentalists don't respect the rational choices of their opponents. They don't see themselves as equal partners in a pluralist debating forum (except when it's tactically necessary for them to do so, as in the case of defending creationism within the education system), but as upholders of the truth whose duty it is to demolish contrary viewpoints. Any pluralist would accept fundamentalists' right to their beliefs, but not their right to prevent any others from being expressed. The beliefs may be rational, the objectives may be rational, but not the means taken to impose their system on others – the 'elimination impulse' as we might call it. It's not so much dogmatism that is the problem, as what dogmatism makes people do. Over the course of history, dogmatism has made people do some very nasty things indeed to their fellow human beings, generally in the name of either religion or politics. The communist movement has a particularly sorry record in this respect, with the lives of millions sacrificed over the course of the 20th century in its pursuit of the perfect society minus difference and dissent. Dogmatism plus conviction makes for a formidable combination in a political opponent, and one that tests the pluralist ethos to its limits. How far do you, how far can you, tolerate intolerance in order to prove how tolerant you are? The left in the West has a problem with this; postmodernists have a problem with this; *we* are going to be wrestling with this from now on as we engage with the ideas and personalities of the fundamentalist world.

## Beyond the Authoritarian Personality

The concept of the authoritarian personality can take us only so far in the study of fundamentalism, therefore, and we shall have to accept that the beliefs involved can be seen as rational in terms of their objectives and don't necessarily involve superstition. They would be easier for the sceptic to counter if they were, but the situation is much more complex than that: there is at the very least a grey area where religion and politics meet, the area where 'authority mindedness' comes into play. We need to move beyond the authoritarian personality as an explanation for the continuing appeal of fundamentalism in our day. What fundamentalism involves above all else is a desire for certainty and for the power to enforce that certainty over others. Fundamentalists like order, conformity, and the absence of opposition, and they are willing to do battle royal to achieve this state of affairs in their culture. We shall observe that desire at work in the various forms that fundamentalism can take in the contemporary world: religious, political, economic, nationalistic, and so on – the steps that activists take to protect their position prove to be strikingly similar. Different personality types can be attracted to the fundamentalist cause, but what they share is a burning conviction of the rightness of their beliefs and the necessity to impose them on the rest of us. And they can be indefatigable in the pursuit of their goals: fundamentalists don't lose heart easily, and can always find the will to regroup after setbacks occur. Neither contradiction nor paradox within their belief system will deter them. Sometimes those beliefs can be admirable, even to a sceptic, but not the methods used by fundamentalists to ensure their dominance. Those methods will be coming under close scrutiny for the rest of this book.

## CHAPTER THREE

# Fundamentalism in History

Fundamentalism may have been coined as a term as recently as 1920, but the phenomenon itself can be traced back into history well before the formal establishment of any fundamentalist movement as such. Most major world religions have tended to conceive of themselves as the only 'true' religion, and have proved to be highly intolerant of each other in consequence. 'Holy' wars have a prominent place in world history, and they can make grim reading for the religious and non-religious alike in terms of what human beings are prepared to do to their fellows in the name of belief: massacres, hideous tortures, burning at the stake – there seems no limit to the cruelty that can be meted out by religious zealots. Intolerance of other cultures is intensified when religion is part of the equation; the Crusades being an example of a fundamentalist response to Islam when the latter occupied Christian holy sites. (One of George Bush's most notable gaffes in the aftermath of 9/11 was to proclaim a 'crusade' against terrorism, thus further alienating the Islamic world in general, and the Arab in particular, for whom the term has a long, and very negative, historical resonance.) The Reformation, for all its reforming instincts (which, if I may declare myself a Protestant atheist, I would wish to defend, if not its subsequent history), also had a fundamentalist aspect to it, with its demand that the Christian Church be returned to its original state of doctrinal purity. With that aim to the forefront, Protestantism, particularly in America, has gone on to become the heartland of Christian fundamentalism. In the Western world, Christianity, especially when it has become a state religion, has tended to be authoritarian and anti-dissent. Religion and politics have always gone together naturally. It was just such fundamentalist attitudes that the Enlightenment set out to challenge, and we will look at its rejection of the 'back to basics' ethos in the first part of this chapter.

We can also identify various forms of political fundamentalism in the 20th century; in particular the totalitarianism espoused by both communism and fascism, in which there was rigid adherence to certain basic doctrinal principles – the dialectic of history, or racial or nationalist superiority, for example – and all other ideologies were dismissed as invalid. Mass politics is being 'fundamentalised' in each instance. Communism may have gone into steep, possibly terminal decline, but fascism continues to undergo periodic revivals within Europe, to the continued despair of the political left and centre everywhere. The success of Jean-Marie Le Pen's National Front party in France, where it regularly polls several million votes in the national elections, is proof that political fundamentalism is still capable of exerting mass popular appeal. In fact, the far right is currently thriving throughout Europe, often self-consciously building on the historical legacy of fascism.

It is to the historical record of religion that we turn our attention first, however, given that it provides such a rich source of examples of the fundamentalist ethic in action. Religion has led the way in encouraging the development of fundamentalism, and has proved a congenial home for the fundamentalist temperament through the ages. Little wonder that it was to come under such intense scrutiny during the Enlightenment period.

## Light on Religion

One of the primary objectives of the 18th-century Enlightenment movement was to set humankind free from superstition, and for the more radical thinkers of the time, nowhere was superstition more prevalent than in the area of religion. Voltaire, la Mettrie and d'Holbach, for example, all strongly attacked organised religion, d'Holbach arguing that we should remove religion from our lives altogether. Views such as these have led historians like Peter Gay to see the Enlightenment as the source for what he calls 'modern paganism' ('the *philosophes*, in a phrase, were modern pagans').[1] From this perspective, the Enlightenment project is a strongly secularising influence in Western culture, and secularisation is to be applauded. In fact, opinions vary amongst modern historians as to how central the debate over religion was to the Enlightenment, but it's generally acknowledged that in Western Europe there was a change in perception of religion's place in society over the course of the 18th century. Dorinda Outram has outlined the range of perceptions involved as follows:

> ... the Enlightenment produced a wide variety of responses to organised religion, ranging all the way from violent Voltairean hostility to religion, through to attempts to bolster orthodox belief by demonstrating its rationality and accordance with natural law. The century can also be seen as one of great religious creativity, even creating the characteristic and new religious idea, that of toleration, which was possibly its most important legacy to succeeding centuries.[2]

Reason could be used on behalf of religion, therefore, but only if religion itself could be shown to be rationally based (one of the major influences on Enlightenment thought, the 17th-century English philosopher John Locke, wrote a treatise entitled *The Reasonableness of Christianity* in 1695). The days of confrontation are assumed to be over. Admittedly, practice could often lag behind theory on the issue of toleration (as Catholics in Protestant countries and Protestants in Catholic could readily attest, never mind Jews almost anywhere), but in principle Enlightenment thought encouraged the development of a pluralist perspective.

For the radicals, however, reason was in direct conflict with religion, and they wanted at the very least to downgrade religion's importance in the intellectual realm. The French scientist Pierre-Simon Laplace is reputed to have replied to the Emperor Napoleon's query as to the place of God in his cosmological system (as outlined in Laplace's monumental *Celestial Mechanics*): 'Your Highness, I have no need of that hypothesis.' That could be seen to sum up the more extreme – that is, French – Enlightenment attitude to religion in general: an unnecessary notion that could, and rationally should, be dispensed with at the earliest possible convenience. (Even modern-day scientists can still feel compelled to explain the redundancy of the 'God hypothesis', as in the remarks of the eminent particle physicist Steven Weinberg: 'we can hope that we'll find something like a concern for human beings, say, or some guiding divine plan built into the fundamental rules. But when we find out that the fundamental rules of quantum mechanics and some symmetry principles are very impersonal and cold, then it'll have a demystifying effect. At least that's what I'd like to see. ... I see it as part of the growing up of our species, just like the child finding out there is no tooth fairy. It's better to find out there is no tooth fairy, even though a world with tooth fairies in it is somehow more delightful.')[3] *Philosophes* like d'Holbach argued that it was particularly irrational to believe in miracles, and as Dorinda Outram has pointed out, even '[a]ttempts to construct a "reasonable" or "rational" Christianity caused as many problems as they solved'.[4] Reason and religion made at best uneasy collaborators, and it became increasingly difficult to square religious belief with Enlightenment ideals. The two were diverging by the end of the 18th century, and essentially were to remain so from then onwards into our own time. And the more they diverge, the greater likelihood there is of the development of a 'back to basics' movement within the ranks of the religious to protect their belief.

## Holy Wars

Holy wars have been a regular feature of human history, especially since the rise of the major monotheistic religions: Judaism, Christianity, and Islam. The last two in particular have a long record of conflict with each other which shows no sign of abating. We have all become very familiar recently with the concept of *jihad*, which the Al-Qaeda leadership has been calling for against the West with monotonous regularity. *Jihad* figures prominently in Islamic life, and for many in the West it's one of the defining, and depressing, features of the faith that it's so easily oriented towards holy war (although apologists will always point out that *jihad* need not be interpreted as violent struggle – it can also, somewhat more innocuously, mean struggle within oneself). Yet we need to remember the West's history here too; as Roland Jacquard has pointed out: 'Violence in the name of religion – of all religions – is as old as history.'[5] Christianity has at least as bad a record in the holy war stakes, and some commentators take its attitude to be even more hard-line than Islam about non-believers. Malise Ruthven, for example, contends that 'the doctrine of jihad is a good deal more humane than papal bulls urging the extirpation of heretics'.[6] Ruthven was writing before 9/11, and we may want to question that assessment now in the light of that and other subsequent terrorist events, but it's salutary nonetheless to remember Christianity's substantial heritage of violence both within and without Christendom.

The Crusades are the primary example historically of the clash between Christendom and Islam. For the Christian side this was the holiest of holy wars, its goal to bring the major sites of biblical Christianity back under Christian control:

> A crusade was a holy war fought against those perceived to be the external or internal foes of Christendom for the recovery of Christian property or in defence of the Church or Christian people. As far as the crusaders were concerned, the Muslims in the East and in Spain had occupied Christian territory, including land sanctified and made his very own by the presence of Christ himself, and they had imposed infidel tyranny on the Christians who lived there.[7]

The land sanctified by Christ was also land sanctified by the Prophet Mohammed, so any attempt to displace the Muslim presence generated a holy war in return. Neither side was willing to concede supremacy to the other, and the conflict over the disputed lands was to go on for several centuries. In our own day, control over the holy sites in Jerusalem is still being contested; this time between Jews and Muslims.

The Christian holy war of the First Crusade began with spontaneous pogroms against those perennial targets of Christian vengeance, the Jews. So violent were these, throughout Germany and Central and Eastern Europe, that the historian Jonathan Riley-Smith has referred to them as 'the "first Holocaust" of European Jews'.[8] A further massacre of Jews took place when Jerusalem was captured by the crusaders in 1099, the city itself being sacked. When Saladin recaptured the city for Islam in 1187, he was notably more merciful towards the inhabitants, many of whom were allowed their freedom in exchange for a ransom. Christian ire could even be directed against their co-religionists, the Greek Orthodox believers of the Byzantine empire, whose capital city, Constantinople, was sacked with particular ruthlessness and brutality by the forces of the Fourth Crusade in 1204. Holy war clearly impressed itself deeply on the psyche of both sides, and was to continue in some form or other between them for hundreds of years, as the Ottoman empire kept edging into Eastern and Central Europe. Countries such as Austria and Hungary saw themselves in the front line of a seemingly endless holy war against the forces of Islam.

The campaign to drive the Moors out of Spain, and thus to expel Islam from Western Europe, was another critical episode in the Christian–Islamic holy war. The Moors had conquered Spain from North Africa in the 8th century, but from the 11th century onwards Christian forces were engaged in what came to be known as the 'Reconquest' (*Reconquista*) of the Iberian Peninsula. In the words of a 13th-century Castilian: 'there is war between the Christians and the Moors, and there will be, until the Christians have got back the lands which the Moors took from them by force.'[9] Europe was to be identified with Christendom, and Christendom had no place for other monotheisms (although after the fall of Constantinople in 1453, large parts of Eastern Europe were to remain in Ottoman hands for several centuries more, and Christians fared rather better there than Jews and Muslims had in Christian Spain).

Spain was not content just with expelling the Moors and Islam; it then turned its attentions on the Jews, who had formed a significant minority under Muslim rule. The holy war against Islam was soon transformed into a holy war against Judaism, prosecuted with particular cruelty. Jews were faced with a choice between forcible conversion to Christianity (becoming *conversos*, as they were known) or imprisonment and death. Many fled the country, or pretended conversion, but many also were massacred or burned as heretics in *autos da fe* by order of the Inquisition. The Inquisition was in fact originally established to test the faith of *conversos*, whose Christian commitment was always to remain suspect. Religious pluralism was not an option for the Catholic authorities, and the Jews bore the brunt of the militant Christianity developed to combat the Moors. The historian Jill Kilsby has argued that '[h]atred by "old" Christians for the Muslims was nowhere near as violent as that experienced by Jews and *conversos*', pointing out how '[i]n Seville alone between 1480 and 1488 over 700 *conversos* were burned and many thousands received other punishments. In total between 1483 and 1498 approximately 2,000 people were burned'.[10] Christianity's reputation emerges from such events considerably tarnished.

## Catholicism: The Original Fundamentalism

Catholicism has been engaged in something like a holy war for most of its history. Heretics abounded in the medieval period (Cathars, Waldensians, Free Spirits, etc.), and were invariably harshly dealt with by the Church authorities, who permitted no challenge whatsoever to their power base. (Catharism, or Albigensianism, which flourished in the south of France from the 11th to the 14th centuries, even became the subject of a full-blown, and ultimately successful, crusade against its domain.) Then, in the early 16th century, the Reformation came on the scene, setting in motion a long-running conflict with the Protestant movement: a conflict which continues, if only rarely in violent form (as in Northern Ireland), into our own century. (Each side is still competing with the other for converts, with American Protestant evangelicalism latterly making inroads into traditional Catholic strongholds in South America.) The Reformation generated a Counter-Reformation on the part of Catholicism, which was reasonably successful in stemming the advance of Protestantism throughout Europe, and even winning back territory from Protestant control (France reverting to Catholicism after being on the brink of going Protestant, as a case in point). Having weathered the crisis, Catholicism consolidated its position as a major world religion with an aggressive recruiting policy and a practised ability to exercise tight control over the lifestyles of its adherents: 'Once a Catholic always a Catholic', as the popular saying goes.

Despite the development of Protestantism, Catholicism continues to regard itself as not just the only true Christianity, but the only true *religion* (universal theory comes no more universal). Over the years it has amassed a battery of doctrines to reinforce its claims to this exalted status. Papal infallibility is a latter-day addition to its authority, although the Church hierarchy had never been in much doubt over the rightness of its actions before (as Jonathan Riley-Smith has drily noted, '[f]or most of its 2,000-year history the papacy has not been in the forefront of reform').[11] Vatican pronouncements are handed down as law, whether on the subject of contraception, priestly celibacy, or women priests – to name some of the most contentious issues on its current agenda. While a certain amount of debate is permitted to take place on such topics, it's at a rarefied level in the hierarchy where the laity have little input and decisions tend towards the very conservative. Catholicism has a very strong sense of history, and is more concerned to preserve traditional authority than to respond to cultural change. Considerable pressure has been exerted over the issues mentioned above – contraception, priestly celibacy, women priests – but so far to little avail. As far as the hierarchy are concerned, these are matters of dogma on which only they have the right to pronounce, and they expect their pronouncements to be followed to the letter. Doctrine wins out over the social cost of the Church's ban on birth control in poorer areas of the world (South America, for example), even though the improvement in the quality of life that a change in policy would bring seems obvious to everyone except the Catholic authorities. Although Christian fundamentalism is traditionally associated with Protestantism, it's worth remembering that it has no monopoly on that attitude.

## Back to Christian Basics: The Reformation

It could be argued that Protestantism has been fundamentalist in character right from the very beginning, in that its concern was to purge the Catholic Church of practices which the reformers, from Martin Luther onwards, felt had betrayed the original purity of Christian doctrine (the selling of indulgences, for example). Reform meant a return to the fundamental spirit of Christianity, lost sight of as the Catholic Church grew into a large and powerful institution at least as interested in politics and social control as religion; a return to a simpler form of worship, and a more direct relationship between the believer and God. As the historian G.R. Elton has put it, 'the cause of Luther was the cause of the gospel, and the cause of the gospel involved cleansing the Church of all the means of power and government which the papacy had created in the previous 500 years'.[12] Protestantism emphasised individual faith, and was critical of the notion that the Church could intercede on the believer's behalf. The idea that buying some holy relic could ease one's way into heaven was anathema to the reformers, who thought faith alone (*sola fide*) was what counted. Religion became a much more personal experience under Protestantism, hence the growing encouragement given to individual study of the Bible and to the development of an individual conscience. The socially subversive quality of reform soon becomes apparent.

It's ironic that a movement which set out to combat the totalitarianism of medieval Catholicism became the natural home of a fundamentalism capable of being no less totalitarian in its turn. Perhaps this is only to be expected from a reform movement, which has to assert itself against an entrenched establishment unlikely to be receptive to the idea of change – and the Catholic Church certainly was not prepared to change in this instance, treating Protestantism as just another in a long line of heresies it had been forced to combat over the course of its history. A sense of the rightness of one's position is an almost inevitable corollary of such a power struggle, and Protestantism has never lacked that, even if it has meant having to distance oneself from fellow reformers who have not been quite rigorous enough in outlining the fundamentals of Christian belief. Christian doctrine notwithstanding, there will be little forgiveness of sins if those sins concern the fundamentals of belief. Protestantism in consequence has always tended towards division. The eminent historian of millenarianism, Norman Cohn, has remarked of the early reform movement that 'the Reformers appealed to the text of the Bible. But once men took to reading the Bible for themselves they began to interpret it for themselves; and their interpretations did not always accord with those of the Reformers.'[13] As reform spread throughout Europe it soon took several different forms: Lutheran, Calvinist, and then various other smaller sub-divisions, until there was a whole raft of Protestant churches to choose from, each with its own distinctive theology and sense of its elect status in God's eyes. It's a trait that Protestantism has retained right through into our own time. Recent scholarship tends to emphasise the diversity of reform (which includes the Catholic Counter

Reformation as well, of course), with the theological historian Carter Lindberg insisting that we should speak of 'Reformations' rather than 'the Reformation': 'I view the Reformation era as a time of plural reform movements.'[14] Plural they may have been, but that doesn't mean they were pluralist in character: each had a powerful sense of the rightness of its own interpretation of reform.

In Jean Calvin's case, this sense of rightness extended to attempting to turn the city of Geneva, where he eventually established his base, into a theocracy, with various Church bodies set up to keep close watch over the morals of the populace.[15] The highest of these bodies, the Consistory, carried out its duties with an enthusiasm which for Lindberg sometimes 'approximated a moral reign of terror'.[16] Opinions are divided as to how successful Calvin was in controlling the lives and behaviour of the Genevan citizenry, but his efforts moved the Scots reformer John Knox to describe the city as 'the most perfect school of Christ that ever was in this earth since the days of the Apostles'.[17] Again, we note that desire to recapture the purity of the original doctrine – the true mark of the fundamentalist temperament. The Geneva Church soon gained a reputation for the resolution of doctrinal disputes within the reform movement, 'a kind of Protestant Vatican' eminently qualified to pronounce on theological basics.[18] It was in the nature of Protestantism that those disputes just kept on arising.

## A Walk Through the Wilderness: 17th-Century England

If we want to observe Protestant fundamentalism at its most divisive and least forgiving, 17th-century England provides an excellent case study. Protestantism's tendency to fragment into competing groups, each claiming to be the correct interpreter of Christian doctrine, is nowhere more graphically illustrated than in this turbulent historical period. Religion was not the sole cause of the Civil War of the 1640s, but it was a major contributory factor, religion and politics being almost inseparable in that culture. As long as there is a state religion, as there was with Anglicanism, then that is likely to be the case. The Anglican Church was an uneasy compromise between Protestantism and Catholicism, its foundation inspired by political rather than doctrinal imperatives, and thus it was always capable of being pushed in one direction or the other by militants within the organisation. Whereas Protestant ideas drawn from continental reformers like Calvin were highly influential in the late 16th and early 17th centuries (the 'Puritan' movement, so called), there was an attempt to move back towards Catholicism in the 1630s under the auspices of the then Archbishop of Canterbury, William Laud. Laud reintroduced many of the ceremonial aspects of Catholic worship, alienating much of the Anglican clergy in the process (especially those of Puritan leanings), as well as significant sections of the public at large. John Milton's poem *Lycidas* (1637) expresses the anger of many at the time at the Anglican Church hierarchy's obsession with ceremonial at the expense of more important doctrinal matters:

> The hungry sheep look up, and are not fed
> But swoln with wind, and the rank mist they draw,
> Rot inwardly, and foul contagion spread;
> Besides what the grim wolf* with privy paw
> Daily devours apace, and nothing said.[19]

---

* As Douglas Bush notes, 'wolf' was 'a traditional term of abuse in anti-Catholic writings'. (John Milton, *Poetical Works*, ed. Douglas Bush, Oxford University Press, 1966, p. 146.)

King Charles I's own sympathy towards Catholicism didn't help matters (his wife, Henrietta Maria, being Catholic already), and theological disagreements fuelled anti-regime feeling in the country. By the early 1640s, with Parliament recalled to provide a focus for this general discontent throughout the political nation (it had been in suspension since 1629 by royal decree), the divisions had become so wide that civil war broke out, ultimately with disastrous consequences for the Stuart monarchy.

Religion remained a source of contention throughout a century which featured yet another national upheaval in the 'Glorious Revolution' of 1688–9, when a Catholic king – James II – was driven from the throne (anti-Catholicism being one of the few things that competing Protestant sects could manage to agree on). As the national, established Church, Anglicanism jealously guarded its power which it had no intention of sharing, but there was a steady stream of breakaway groups as the century progressed: Presbyterians, Muggletonians, Particular Baptists, General Baptists, Independents, Quakers, Fifth Monarchists – the list could go on for quite some time. If these breakaway sects opposed Anglicanism and its compromise theology, they also opposed each other, often with just as much fervour. There was little love lost between them, and not much respect for each other's position: antagonism was definitely the order of the day. Thus the Baptist John Bunyan could wade into the Quakers, in an exchange of pamphlets, because they held a different position than he did regarding the relationship of body and spirit in Christ: 'He that confesseth not that Jesus Christ is come in the flesh is Antichrist, and is of Antichrist.'[20] This is antagonism taken to its theological limits, Antichrist being the worst insult one could use in such a situation: one could stray no further from 'the truth' than that (one modern equivalent would be 'fascist'). Each sect was striving to get back to the fundamentals of Christian belief, as it understood them, and that tended to promote deep suspicion of all competitors: although, as observed, they could unite against Catholicism readily enough (if there was unity in Protestantism in the period, then that's where it lay).

One can observe a similar tendency on the political left in the 20th century, particularly the Western European far left, where we find factions subdividing into even smaller factions over fine differences of doctrine that outsiders could hardly recognise existed. If you were a communist in Britain in the 1970s, for example, you could choose between the Communist Party, the Socialist Workers' Party, the Revolutionary Communist Party, and then various other fringe groups – some extremely fringe and extremely small (one joke of the time in university circles was that local chapters held their meetings in telephone booths). The differences between these factions were enough for them to make free use of the term 'class enemy' with each other, however, class enemy carrying much the same abusive charge as Antichrist did for 17th-century sectarians. As much energy could be expended in fighting each other as in fighting the established political power in one's country, with predictably depressing consequences for the left's electoral prospects.

The Civil War led to a proliferation of Protestant sects in England as central political authority collapsed over the course of the 1640s. By the standards of the time there was effectively religious freedom then, with no central government to impose conformity to the established Church on the populace. The more freedom there was, the more sectarian activity there proved to be, with each sect competing for adherents. There was much jockeying for position in the religious market place as the monarchy gave way to a republic after the execution of Charles I in 1649. Indeed, it was very much a buyers' market, individuals often trying out several churches in turn in search of religious truth (they were called Seekers, and as Christopher Hill has pointedly remarked of their quest for the right church, sometimes they 'were satisfied with none').[21]

The more militant sectarians complained that there was not as much religious, or political, freedom as they had been led to expect there would be under the Commonwealth government headed by Cromwell in the 1650s, but that began to seem a golden age once the Restoration of the Stuart monarchy was brought about in 1660. The regime of Charles II had promised to guarantee religious freedom, to 'tender consciences' as it was put in the days just before the king's return from exile on the continent;[22] but in the event it failed to do so, and the Anglican Church soon had its former power and privileges restored to it. A series of parliamentary acts, known collectively as the Clarendon Code (1661–5), prohibited worship outside the Anglican Church as the regime sought to turn the clock back on religious freedom in England and reimpose conformity on the nation. Predictably enough, this merely stimulated the sizeable non-conformist community to resist, despite the harsh penalties meted out to anyone failing to uphold the requirements of the Clarendon Code. John Bunyan, for example, was imprisoned for twelve years for refusing to cease his lay-preaching activities in the Baptist movement (lay preaching being expressly forbidden by the Code). On his release he simply continued as before, however, becoming known as 'Bishop Bunyan' for his ability to draw huge crowds to hear him.

Protestant sectarianism has never been short of resilience, and as Bunyan's example proves, considers itself as engaged in its very own private holy war. Bunyan was to write an allegorical work of fiction called just that, *The Holy War* (1682), in which 'Mansoul' (pictured as a town) is repeatedly assailed by satanic forces, the aptly named Diabolonians, trying to wrest it away from God's protection and the hope of salvation. It takes several cycles of bitter conflict, with many casualties on both sides, before Mansoul is confirmed in God's graces and guaranteed its place in heaven after death: 'And there shalt thou, O my Mansoul, have such communion with me, with my Father, and with your Lord Secretary, as is not possible here to be enjoyed.'[23] In Bunyan's best-known work, *The Pilgrim's Progress* (1678), the everyman figure of Christian is similarly beset by an unsavoury bunch of characters – by their sentiments identifiable as followers of the Anglican Church, as well as of other competing sectarian movements of the time – collectively bent on preventing him from completing his journey from his home in the City of Destruction to the Celestial City, where he will attain salvation amongst God's elect. Christian's single-mindedness in reaching his objective is that of the committed fundamentalist, utterly convinced of the truth of his cause no matter what the rest of humanity may think. In prototypically fundamentalist fashion, Christian's standard tactic when engaged in theological debate by anyone he encounters on the road (as he is repeatedly) is to unleash a string of biblical quotations, carefully annotated in the margins by his author, the very voicing of which serves to demolish his opponent's position and reaffirm Christian's faith in his pilgrimage. Inerrancy always wins the day. It's the 17th-century sectarian experience in essence, and it points the way forward to 20th- and 21st-century Christian fundamentalism too. The beleaguered individual, inerrant text dutifully committed to memory, strides fearlessly on his way, endlessly willing to do battle royal for the fundamentals of his belief against all comers. Onward Christian fundamentalist soldiers!

One optimistic message that we might take away from the 17th century is that the more religious division there is, then the less chance there is also of any one group of fundamentalists coming to dominate. As Norman Cohn observed of Protestant reform, once individual interpretation of Scripture starts, it's hard to control the direction it will take, and the likeliest result is the production of more and more self-contained factions. Excessive factionalism, as the far left has found to its cost in our own time, tends to be self-defeating. What the period called 'enthusiasm' (more or less a by-word for fundamentalism from our 21st-century perspective) eventually created a backlash, as sectarian groups multiplied, each claiming to be the sole repository of the true interpretation of the Bible, all others being at best misguided, at worst agents of Antichrist. There was a general move away from enthusiasm after the Glorious Revolution, although it was to resurface in the English-speaking world (to include America as well) in the 18th and 19th centuries, with the rise of evangelicalism. The personal side of belief was strongly emphasised by the evangelicals, who encouraged close study of the Bible, and were moved by a missionary zeal.

Evangelicalism in America was to feed straight into fundamentalism, which represents a formalisation of evangelical doctrines into a creed strong enough to combat the liberalising trends making themselves felt within American life. There are many interesting links to be established between contemporary American fundamentalism and religious radicalism in 17th-century England. Both are sympathetic to the Jewish cause (the 'conversion of the Jews' being an extremely important principle in their respective theologies, since it's a necessary precondition of the Second Coming of Christ), and both are exceedingly literal-minded when it comes to reading the Bible. Inerrancy is the source of the utter conviction of their rightness. The visionary books of the Bible (Revelation, Daniel, Ezekiel) are an important inspiration in both cases, with their lurid prophecies of the ultimate defeat of the forces of evil by a wrathful God. A Manichean world view pervades both cultures, carrying with it a sense of a universal struggle being fought to the death. It's all very dramatic, endowing the life of each individual believer with a sense of purpose, but it's also very alienating in the way that it simply writes off so much of humanity as being in collusion with the forces of evil – whether we unfortunates are aware of it or not. There's an unforgiving streak in each group of enthusiasts which is impervious to the arguments of the sceptic.

Factionalism is still a feature of religious life in America, although there it seems to be more self-regenerating than self-defeating. Malise Ruthven remarks on how 'religious America has become a divine supermarket where a church can be found, adapted, or invented, to suit almost any taste' (it must have felt much like that in mid-17th-century England too, one suspects, with the qualification that it would be a church for any *Protestant* taste).[24] Sceptics might take heart from the continuing growth of factionalism, but be equally dismayed by the underlying enthusiasm that motivates it. The history of Mormonism provides an instructive case study of factionalism in action. A religion whose roots lie in the evangelical Protestantism of 19th-century eastern America (a hotbed of theological speculation), Mormonism proceeded to split into three groups, still extant today. These are the Church of Jesus Christ of Latter-Day Saints (the main body, whose headquarters are in Salt Lake City, Utah), the much smaller Reorganized Church of Latter Day Saints, and then the tiny splinter group the Church of Christ Temple Lot (the last two based in Independence, Missouri). The doctrinal differences need not concern us here, and to sceptics they would hardly seem all that critical anyway. What is more interesting is how even a relatively small religion can keep on fragmenting further, as its adherents seek an ever purer set of fundamentals by which to guide their conduct. It's that relentless search for doctrinal purity that the sceptic will find worrying; the fact that the divine supermarket seems to be constantly expanding, its product line continuing to diversify to meet buoyant demand. It may not be unified, but fundamentalism is certainly ubiquitous – now opening at a location near you.

## Fundamentalising Politics: Communism and Fascism

Communism and fascism are both prime examples of universal theories – universal theories of decidedly fundamentalist cast. Neither sees its opponents as having any credibility, and each wishes to dominate totally. Not surprisingly, they have generally been sworn enemies – the brief (and more than somewhat cynical on both sides) Nazi–Soviet pact of the late 1930s notwithstanding. Eliminating competitors comes naturally to both, as the many millions of dead they left behind them in the 20th century attest. Fascism carries the Manichean world vision to its logical conclusion, regarding anyone outside the charmed circle as virtually sub-human and therefore disposable. Different rules applied to each group. For the Nazis, there was the master race and then there were those fit enough only to be the slaves of that race. The Jews were eventually graded underneath even that level; disposable in the most literal sense of the 'final solution' of the Holocaust. Communism had a much wider socio-political vision that, in theory, could encompass the whole human race. That was one of its great attractions; the charmed circle was open to all those willing to embrace the cause and its ideals. There was no barrier to entry, and it was irrelevant where you came from on the social scale (many of its leading founding figures were middle- or even upper-class in origin), or, at least in theory, what your nationality or skin colour was. Yet communism could be just as harsh in its way on those who refused to join its ranks. Millions were eliminated in the Soviet Union and China for just that sin, conformity being achieved through the use of brute force and terror tactics (as in the Stalinist purges of the 1930s and Chairman Mao's 'Cultural Revolution' of the 1960s). Tolerance of other viewpoints was never a characteristic of the communist establishment, which could be utterly ruthless in pushing through its socio-political programme. Doctrine took precedence over any human considerations, as it traditionally does in religious fundamentalist circles.

Although fascism has texts it turns to for reinforcement of its political programmes (manifestos like Hitler's *Mein Kampf*, for example, plus various pseudo-scientific works on the subject of race),* it's not as such a text-based movement. There is no work with the authority of the Bible (nor, as Paul Hayes has pointed out, a 'fascist equivalent of *Das Kapital*'),[25] but the ideas behind fascism are taken to be every bit as inerrant. Racial purity is a given that lies beyond negotiation, 'a constituent part of fascist ideology' to be called on to resolve any disputes that may arise over status.[26] Either you meet the criteria or you don't; end of story. As with Christian salvation, there is an arbitrary quality to the division of humankind into an elect and non-elect. Which category you find yourself in is out of your control – no one can choose where, or to whom, they are born, for example – and you simply have to accept your fate as it has been dealt to you. God, and whoever or whatever it is that assigns racial lineage, moves in mysterious ways that human beings will never be able to fathom. This is easier to reconcile yourself to if you're in the category of the elect to whom all the privileges accrue. Life outside the inner

* The Nazis were particularly influenced by the work of thinkers such as the British political philosopher Houston Steward Chamberlain, who propounded controversial theories of race in *Foundations of the Nineteenth Century* (1899). Another important influence on Hitler was Count Arthur de Gobineau's *Essay on the Inequality of the Human Races* (1853–5).

circle is not going to be pleasant in a fascist state, as the Jews were to find out in Nazi Germany.

As an ideology fascism makes no sense. There is little scientific evidence of significant differences between the races (except in the cultural domain), and races are never pure nowadays anyway. Nor can race map unproblematically onto nationality, and nationalities can best be described as mongrel – particularly in Europe, where there has been endless intermixing over the centuries. Despite this – one would think obvious – fact, there is a close connection between fascism and nationalism. The latter may be founded on fairly flimsy pretexts, but it remains capable of inspiring a gut response amongst large sections of the populace. Noting 'the significant contribution made by nationalism to fascist theory', Paul Hayes goes on to observe that nationalism 'generated passions which could be, and were, seized upon by the fascists' in the 1920s and 30s (in Germany and Italy particularly).[27] Those passions can still be exploited by the 21st-century heirs of fascism in Europe, as we'll go on to see in Chapter 7. What the rise of fascism in the period between the First and Second World Wars shows, is how large a market there can be for fundamentalising ideas in politics. In troubled times – and when are we *not* in troubled times – going back to basics (in this case, to racial or nationalist basics) can pay political dividends. A fundamentalist world makes life so much simpler – as long as you're covered by the fundamentals. When it comes to fascism, with its potent blend of race and nationalism, take care to be born in the right place, and to the right parents.

Communism has its very own sacred texts in the works of Marx and Engels; most notably *The Communist Manifesto* and the several volumes of *Capital*. These provide the communist movement with its main doctrinal principles, and the point of communism is to put these principles into political practice with all due haste. In the Soviet Union after the 1917 Revolution this meant reorganising the country into a workers' state, where the means of production were publicly owned and, at least officially, there was no private sector. A certain amount of black market activity notwithstanding, the authorities were largely successful in eliminating the entrepreneurial drive within the population, and, like the fascists after them, had no scruples about resorting to gangster-style tactics of intimidation to enforce their ideological will. When put into practice, communism's idealism became only too worldly. The Russian experience was taken to be the model for the rest of humanity, and used as the basis for the creation of the Soviet empire in Eastern Europe after the Second World War. The Communist Party set itself up as the sole guardian of the working class's interests, and ruled the Soviet Union and its satellite states on behalf of that group. Conformity to the party line was enforced with a rigour that even the most fundamentalist of religions could admire. Just as one is not permitted to opt out of the Muslim faith (that is apostasy, and is punishable by death), so one could not publicly dissociate oneself from communism in a communist state. Officially at least, there are no Muslim atheists; equally, there were no communist atheists in the Soviet empire either. Anyone rash enough to test this proposition was dealt with like an apostate under an Islamic regime: silenced, imprisoned, often executed.

Marxism was turned into a formula in the Soviet world, and what was initially an extremely impressive critique of unbridled industrial capitalism ossified into a monolithic system of belief to rival any major religion. The Communist Party was the only permitted political grouping, turning elections into a sham; hence the claims of total support for the Party's programme by its leadership. There simply was no other body to vote for. The role of the police and the army was to guarantee the safety and integrity of the workers' state. In effect, this meant keeping the Communist Party in power, since it was the representative of the workers and had this special relationship written into the state's constitution. Official opposition was impossible under these circumstances. The result was an authoritarian, totalitarian state with a belligerent stance towards the rest of the world.

Much argument has been expended as to whether Marxism necessarily has to become authoritarian and fundamentalist when put into political practice, but certain elements in the original theory do seem to encourage such a development. The assumption that there is a dialectic (or conflict of opposing forces) working through history that ultimately will lead to the creation of a utopian society, for example, promotes a strong sense of destiny in the theory's supporters. Being on the side of history is a powerful incentive to adhere to a cause through thick and thin, and offers a sense of psychological security to the believer. Marx saw all history as the history of class struggle, with each class overcoming its oppressors in turn, only to create further opposition to its own domination of society. The bourgeoisie overcame the feudal landowners, and the working class would overcome the bourgeoisie, in the process creating the 'dictatorship of the proletariat' in which the means of production would be held in common for everyone's benefit: Marxist utopia, where there would be no more forces in conflict. Marxism assumes an inevitability about this historical process, although it doesn't set any particular time limit on its achievement. It can be like the Christian millennium – always just that little bit further on into the future from wherever you happen to be (Alex Callinicos regards the anti-globalisation movement as a sign that the process is still on track, however).[28] The notion that one is being carried along by historical necessity can soon take on a fundamentalist character. Those who do question that necessity are an offence to the theory's purity, and stand in need of re-education – which the communist system was only too ready to provide. The process has its own internal dynamic, and debate plays no part in it; the theory just has to be accepted, and the individual has no option but to submit to its greater power.

## To Engineer Souls or Not to Engineer Souls?: Artistic Fundamentalism

Wherever Marxism has taken root as an ideology it has rapidly developed an authoritarian ethos (much as it pains me as a socialist to have to admit this). This has expressed itself not just politically, through the banning of opposition parties and of free movement on the part of the population (in case they were exposed to alien ideologies from the outside world, and lost their ideological purity), but in the realm of the arts as well. The aesthetic theory of socialist realism, for example, was imposed on all creative artists in the Soviet Union from the 1930s onwards, with Stalin's cultural commissar A.A. Zhdanov its most enthusiastic advocate. Citing Stalin as his source (a tactic designed to stop argument dead in its tracks if ever there was one), Zhdanov demanded that creative artists become 'engineers of human souls' in the service of communism, which meant in effect becoming propagandists for the party.[29] Socialist realism was a very conservative aesthetic, largely based on 19th-century models, and it represented a rejection of the modernist aesthetic that had come to dominate artistic production in the West. Modernism encouraged experimentation with form and content, and was obsessed with originality and breaking free from tradition. As a result it was often difficult for the general public to understand (think of Picasso in his cubist phase, James Joyce in *Finnegans Wake*, or Arnold Schoenberg's twelve-tone compositions), and it could be very elitist in its attitudes. If the public didn't like a modernist work, that was assumed to be the public's fault and not the artist's, whose personal vision was not to be called into question. Socialist realism, on the other hand, was designed to be as accessible as possible, to appeal to the wider public that modernism disdained. This meant writing, painting and composing music in the style of previous generations rather than inventing new forms and themes that challenged the audience's preconceptions.

Laudable though such objectives might have been initially, being designed to make the arts politically relevant, their manner of implementation was much more questionable. Creative artists were forced to adopt the socialist realist manner, and punished if they did not. There was no negotiation with the Stalinist authorities, whose word on artistic matters, as on all others, was law. Artists in the Soviet Union were treated like political dissidents if they failed to follow the approved official style, and subjected to censure and even imprisonment on occasion. The composer Dmitri Shostakovich was forced to apologise publicly to the Soviet people for writing an opera, *Lady Macbeth of the Mtsensk District* (1934), which the authorities found too modern for their tastes, and was in and out of favour with those authorities throughout his life. The writer Alexander Solzhenitsyn was sentenced to several years in the labour camps of Siberia, an experience which he drew on for his harrowing novel *A Day in the Life of Ivan Denisovich* (1962). Then there was the case of the theatre director Vsevolod Meyerhold, who disappeared into prison in 1939 never to be heard of again (he is thought to have been executed in 1940).

Socialist realism was held to express the fundamentals of communism (glorification of the working class and condemnation of the capitalist West, for example), and those fundamentals could not be deviated from by rogue individuals, whose motives could only be suspect. Marxist artists outside the Soviet Union might refuse to adopt the socialist realist style, Bertolt Brecht being a notable abstainer, but only at the cost of attack by critics, both inside and outside Russia, diligently following the Party line. Brecht was vilified by the influential Hungarian critic and philosopher Georg Lukács for his experimental style of play-writing called 'epic theatre'. This certainly did challenge the audience's preconceptions about drama, by discouraging emotional identification with the characters on stage and insisting that the play's artifice be emphasised at all times. We were not to confuse the theatre and real life. Brecht thought realism was old-fashioned, whereas Lukács considered any artist who moved away from realism to be a mere dilettante who was turning his back on politics. The two figures and their supporters were involved in heated exchanges during the 1930s (when Lukács was mainly resident in Moscow), but it was the realists who prevailed in terms of official policy. Aesthetic fundamentalism replaced artistic freedom, and it would not be until the fall of communism that such ideas fully lost their power and influence. (Brecht's subsequent rehabilitation as an honoured Marxist artist in communist East Germany after the Second World War, founder of the Berliner Ensemble theatre company where his plays became staples of the repertoire, is one of the more amusing ironies of modern Marxist history.)

Strangely enough, one can say similar things about modernism, which became as authoritarian in its turn over the course of the 20th century. Modernism was pushed hard by both artists and critics, and anyone who continued to use older forms or styles tended to be ostracised or derided by his or her peers, dismissed as being out of touch and lacking imagination. To be a *serious* creative artist was to be a modernist. Training within art colleges eventually was geared towards reproducing the modernist style, and it became something like a Party line under communism with the artistic community in the West. Nor was this a development the public at large could just ignore by boycotting galleries and concert halls, refusing to read modernist novels, etc. Arguably the area in which modernism became most entrenched was architecture. The 'new brutalism' as it came to be called – straight lines, concrete and glass, and no ornamentation being its hallmarks – was soon to be the preferred, almost obligatory, style in cities around the globe, thus impinging on the daily lives of the general public whether they liked it or not. And most of them didn't like the new brutalism very much, finding it cold and soulless. The style's tower blocks are still very much part of our urban landscape. Modernism turned into a fundamentalism; an aesthetic which was not to be questioned, with its priesthood absolutely convinced of its rightness. Ultimately it *was* to be questioned by postmodernists, but looking back on aesthetics in the 20th century it does suggest a clash of fundamentalisms, with socialist realism on the one side and modernism on the other struggling for supremacy. It's striking how often in history we find systems of belief adopting a fundamentalist stance, in which rivals are denied any credibility. Even in the arts, antagonistic attitudes are almost a reflex reaction it would seem, with the desire to eliminate competition a compelling motivation for practitioners. When we turn to the world of contemporary religion, as we are about to do, that desire becomes even more compelling.

## CHAPTER FOUR

# Religious Fundamentalism: Time Warp Zones and the Search for Security

Religious fundamentalism's great selling point is that it provides a sense of security for believers in what has become an ever more disorienting world, but it does so at the expense of cultivating an intolerance of others which can have devastating effects on global politics. Antagonism becomes the watchword. Islamic fundamentalism is a potent political force in the Middle East, Africa and Asia, and has inspired terrorist actions such as the 9/11 attacks on America. Christian fundamentalism is an increasingly important player in American right-wing politics, and its pro-Israeli outlook informs American foreign policy, much to the dismay of the Arab world. Jewish fundamentalism is one of the main stumbling blocks to the peace process in the Middle East, and Hindu fundamentalism is once again a sinister factor in Indian politics, openly canvassing anti-Muslim sentiments throughout the country. The more militant religious fundamentalism becomes, the more likely it is to create clashes between rival belief systems. Monotheism does not speak unto monotheism, never mind to polytheism. In the current world order, for example, Islam is in conflict with Judaism and Hinduism, and, at least indirectly, with Christianity (in the sense that the West in general is perceived by most of Islam as a Christian, or at worst post-Christian, culture). Security for believers within individual religions is purchased at the cost of global peace, although no individual religion will consider itself responsible for this state of affairs. Non-believers will always be held to blame instead, and the search for security will continue unabated.

## Why Do People Hate Islam?

In a recent book, *Why Do People Hate America?*, the authors set out to explore why it has come to pass that America can inspire such negative feelings around the globe – in Europe as much as in the Third World.[1] We might pose a similar question: why do people hate Islam? By 'people' here is meant essentially people in the West, although Islam has its internal critics, too (more on this later). In the West, Islam remains more than something of an enigma, an alien cultural force to be treated with considerable suspicion. Increasingly, the popular tendency is to associate it with terrorism, no matter how much scholars may deny that this is sanctioned by Islamic doctrine or representative of the faith in general. Malise Ruthven, for example, has complained of the 'image of Islam conveyed by the media, its almost exclusive association with "terrorism" and "fanaticism", to the detriment of its more humanistic, more rational traditions', but 9/11 has simply intensified this trend.[2] Fairly or not, Islam is widely perceived as a threat to the Western way of life, and the media finds a ready audience for its scare stories about potential Al-Qaeda targets (hardly a week goes by without these at the moment; Kenya's airports have been closed down as I write because of just such a threat). Islamophobia is a recognisable feature of our society, and as the Runnymede Trust Report on the phenomenon makes clear, this makes it very difficult to have meaningful dialogue with Islam: 'How, then, can one tell the difference between legitimate criticism and disagreement on the one hand, or unfounded prejudice and hostility on the other?'[3] And, by the way, any comments made by those of us lacking the religion gene are likely to be filed under the 'hostile' heading.

It's even more difficult to criticise Islamic fundamentalism from within Islam itself, since that is to risk being accused of apostasy (one of the gravest sins in the Islamic canon, as we shall see). Yet some brave voices have been raised about the way Islam has been developing in our era. There is the example of Muhammad Sa'id Al-Ashmawi, a distinguished Egyptian judge, who castigates the fundamentalists for having created a situation in which 'Mercy has been replaced by terrorism, moderation by extremism, scholarship by ignorance, refinement by primitivism, cosmopolitanism by provincialism, renewal by stagnation'.[4] Al-Ashmawi was exercising the tradition of *ijtihad*, independent reasoning in legal judgements. *Ijtihad* was encouraged by a 'revivalist Islam' from the 18th century onwards, until it was overtaken by a Western-oriented reformist movement, eclipsed in its turn by the rise of fundamentalism. Similar sentiments to Al-Ashmawi's have been expressed in the British press in recent years by Ibn Warraq, for whom Islam has turned into a force for repression. 'Islamic correctness' means

> that academics can no longer do their work honestly. A scholar working on recently discovered Koranic manuscripts showed some of his startling conclusions to a distinguished colleague, a world expert on the Koran. The latter did not ask, 'What is the evidence, what are your arguments, is it true?' The colleague simply warned him that his thesis was unacceptable because it would upset Muslims.[5]

There's not much evidence of a humanistic or rational

tradition at work here, not much *ijtihad*, and it's such dogmatic attitudes which fuel the distrust, and even outright hatred, felt for Islam in the West. *Ijtihad*, 'to exert the utmost effort, to struggle, to do one's best to know something', as the Islamic scholar Ziauddin Sardar has defined it, is in conflict with *taqlid*, 'blind and unquestioning following and obedience', in Islamic history.[6] Sardar claims that *ijtihad* is closer to the spirit of the Koran than *taqlid* is, but, sadly, the latter seems to be the attitude currently in the ascendancy in Islamic culture. (It would be difficult to prove Sardar's point anyway, since, like most founding works of religion, the Koran is well capable of supporting conflicting interpretations as to its inner meaning, depending on which passages one chooses to emphasise.)

Similar responses to learning and scientific enquiry can, it's true, be found in Western history. One has only to consider the case of Galileo, whose theories about the nature of the Universe were suppressed by the Catholic Church because they clashed with the theologically derived picture sanctioned by the Church authorities. But such responses are less common since the Enlightenment, and few contemporary scientists or scholars would fear religious disapproval of their work. It's a point often made about Islam that it has never experienced an Enlightenment of its own to bring it into a more modern world. The closest it came was with Islamic Reformism, the Arabic world's response to European domination in the 19th and early 20th centuries, but that subsequently fell foul of fundamentalism. Islam's critics argue that an Enlightenment movement is precisely what is now needed if there is to be any real accommodation between Islam and the secular West.

Tariq Ali goes even further back in European history for a model, arguing the positive effects of the Protestant Reformation and Catholic Counter Reformation on European culture:

We are in desperate need of an Islamic Reformation that sweeps away the crazed conservatism and backwardness of the fundamentalists but, more than that, opens the world of Islam to new ideas which are seen to be more advanced than what is currently on offer from the West.[7]

Islam must be subjected to, and learn to live with, scepticism. The concept of *ijtihad* might even provide a basis for such a development, linking back as it does to a respected tradition of independent thought within Islamic culture. Warraq's disgusted tone indicates that there are at least some within the Islamic world who would concur with this assessment. Equally, there are some within the Western world who reject it, on the grounds that we cannot expect exactly the same pattern of cultural development in the Islamic world as the West: a case of Western 'monoculturalism' rearing its head again, by regarding itself as the natural historical archetype. Yet it's hard to see how debate can be encouraged within Islam, holding out the hope of reform and reinterpretation of doctrine according to cultural change, without a dose of scepticism. If the faith can't withstand any scepticism at all, if it can survive only by means of dogmatism, then it can't be very strong – but that's an atheist speaking, of course.

Islamic fundamentalism's key demand is the implementation of Shari'a law. This system involves some very harsh penalties, such as amputation of the hand for stealing, stoning to death for adultery, and flagellation for assorted other crimes. To the West these are barbaric practices, which should have no place in our own time; but to the fundamentalist mind they are the cornerstone of the Islamic state. A proper Islamic state is one based on Shari'a law, and it's here that religion becomes politics. One of the recommendations of the Runnymede Trust Report on Islamophobia is that we should learn to separate 'political Islam' from 'religious Islam'; yet that is precisely what Shari'a, with its commitment to the establishment of a theocratic state in which Islamic doctrine is put into practice, is designed to prevent. Under Shari'a, politics is simply religion by other means. The political world is little more than a framework for religion to operate within. As Youssef M. Choueiri has observed, there is little basis for accommodation here with rival belief systems: 'Islamic radicalism is a politico-cultural movement that postulates a qualitative contradiction between Western civilization and the religion of Islam.'[8] Another commentator, Johannes J.G. Jansen, speaks of Islamic fundamentalism as having 'a dual nature', in which it is 'both politics and religion' simultaneously.[9] To some extent that is true of all religions, but the separation of religion and politics is a distinguishing feature of Western culture from the Enlightenment onwards (religion being little better than superstition to the more radical Enlightenment thinkers), and majority opinion in the West is very unsympathetic to the idea of theocracy nowadays. It may have existed before in European history, but it's deemed to be anachronistic in a modern or postmodern society. The theocratic state is an alien concept to most of us in the West, although there are those within the Christian Right in America who are attracted by it, and might well move to introduce it if they ever came to power as a political party in their own right (that may well be a long shot, but it has been estimated that as many as a fifth of America's population could be defined as 'Christian Right fundamentalist' in political terms, so it's by no means inconceivable).*

---

* See Didi Herman, *The Antigay Agenda: Orthodox Vision and the Christian Right*, University of Chicago Press, 1997, p. 12. Herman also quotes research which claims that 'over 60% of Americans have no doubt that Christ will return', so Christian Right fundamentalism has a substantial constituency on which to go to work (p. 19).

# Al-Qaeda

Islamic fundamentalism has found its most powerful expression in the activities of the Al-Qaeda movement. Small and mysterious this movement may be, and, as so many commentators keep insisting, unrepresentative of Islam and its ideals, but it has had a dramatic impact on global politics in the past decade or so. It has been the catalyst for a war in Afghanistan which resulted in the Taliban regime being overthrown, and its mere existence has exacerbated political conflicts in the Middle East and Asia – even when it can't be proved that it has had any direct involvement. Al-Qaeda has become a Western obsession, as has its leading figure Osama bin Laden (whereabouts, and even existence, unknown at the present time, as if to point up the West's limitations). Its hand tends to be seen in almost every terrorist action, and there's no doubt that it has provided a focal point for anti-Western feeling in the Islamic world. Difficult though it may be for most of us in the West to comprehend, the 'Bin Laden Brotherhood', as it has been called,[10] stands as a symbol of hope for disaffected Muslims worldwide, for demonstrating that it's possible to cause significant damage to the West (and particularly to America, the 'Great Satan') despite its far superior technological and military resources. Just as hard for us to grasp is that Osama bin Laden is now one of the great heroes of the Islamic world and well on the way to attaining mythic status in Islamic history: post 9/11, as Rohan Gunaratna reports, 'tens of thousands of children born to Muslim parents worldwide have been named Osama'.[11] Whatever happens, or has happened to bin Laden, that myth will continue to grow.

The gulf between Al-Qaeda's world view and that of the West is enormous. Even if dialogue were possible with the movement's leading figures, it's unlikely that it would achieve anything very much. Compromise, particularly compromise

with the West, is not an item on the Al-Qaeda agenda. Negotiation hardly figures there either. We are faced with true
believers, utterly assured of the rightness of their cause and
their religion. The rest of us collectively constitute the forces of
Satan, and are a legitimate subject for *jihad*. Islamic commentators are careful to point out that *jihad* means no more than
'struggle', personal as much as public, and that its use should
not be regarded as threatening by the West. There is, as Ahmed
Rashid points out, a 'greater *jihad*' and a 'lesser *jihad*' to be
extracted from the Prophet Mohammed's writings. The first is
'inward-seeking ... the effort of each Muslim to become a
better human being'; whereas the second 'sanctions rebellion
against an unjust ruler, whether Muslim or not, and ... can
become the means to mobilize ... political and social
struggle'.[12] While no one in the West could object to the first
type of *jihad*, which sounds wholly admirable even to sceptics,
there seems little doubt that Al-Qaeda is engaged in the lesser
variety. For the Bin Laden Brotherhood, struggle means
violent struggle, and in its own eyes it's in a more or less
permanent state of war with Western culture. Bin Laden
himself formally declared *jihad* on the West in 1996,
announcing, in fairly unambiguous fashion, that '[t]he walls
of oppression and humiliation can be torn down only by a hail
of bullets'.[13] That doesn't sound much like a negotiating tactic
– or a statement of greater *jihad* either.

As to what that *jihad* is designed to achieve: John Gray has
insisted that Al-Qaeda is a product of modernity, its 'peculiar
hybrid of theocracy and anarchy ... a by-product of western
radical thought'.[14] Gray also draws attention to Al-Qaeda's
enthusiastic use of modern technology (weaponry, satellite
communications systems, etc.), and thinks it's wrong-headed
to treat the movement 'as a throwback to medieval times'.[15]
Persuasive though Gray can be, and his *Al Qaeda and What it
Means to be Modern* is a very thought-provoking book,

Islamic fundamentalism still suggests that it's motivated by a desire to turn the clock back before modernity to an idealised past. It may use modern methods ('a hail of bullets'), but it does so in the service of a pre-modern value system. Even granting Gray's point that 'there is more than one way of being modern',[16] Al-Qaeda strikes me as being, at best, parasitic on modernity.

## Life in a Time Warp Zone: The Muslim Brotherhood

Modern Islamic fundamentalism dates from the establishment of the Muslim Brotherhood in Egypt in 1928. Some of the greatest theoreticians of fundamentalism have come from the ranks of the Brotherhood (notably Sayyid Qutb), and over the years it has provided the inspiration for the foundation of similar movements in many other Islamic countries. The creation of the Muslim Brotherhood represented a reaction against reforming trends within the Islamic world, which had sought to modernise Islamic societies in order to close the huge technological gap that had opened up with the West. It was this gap which had enabled the West to establish colonial rule over most of the Middle East and the Arabian people. The introduction of Western modes of dress and behaviour was designed to encourage the development of a more Western mentality, in the hope that social and technological progress would follow in its wake. To the Muslim Brotherhood, however, modernisation was a betrayal of their cultural heritage. For such thinkers, as Youssef M. Choueiri has noted, secularisation was equivalent 'to a state of ignorance (*jahiliyyi*) not unlike that which flourished before the rise of Islam in Arabia'.[17]

As we shall go on to see, there are parallels to be found here with American Protestant fundamentalism, which was similarly concerned to resist reforming trends within its own culture. There is a humorous episode in Annie Proulx's novel *That Old Ace in the Hole*, a tale of life in the contemporary Texas Panhandle region, where the hero, an agent for a hog farm corporation located in Denver, is explaining to a relative in a letter the difficulties he's experiencing in trying to blend in with the local community:

> These are real suspicious people. I been reported to the sheriff five or six times for running on the road. It's like nobody does that down here. It's like if they didn't do it in the old days they don't do it now. I'm in a time warp zone.[18]

Something of that 'time warp' mentality can be found in any religious fundamentalist movement, and Islamic fundamentalism is no less imbued with the spirit of 'if they didn't do it in the old days they don't do it now' than the Protestants of Proulx's Texas. In political terms of reference, this soon translates into what Richard Hofstadter has dubbed 'the paranoid style in American politics'.[19]

The Muslim Brotherhood was uncompromisingly anti-modern and anti-Western from the beginning, drawing its inspiration from Islam in its heroic days as an expansionist movement. Its anti-colonialist stance has made it a magnet for the disaffected, 'the only available outlet for those whose religious and cultural sensibilities have been outraged by the impact of Westernization upon their society, in which both the secularizing reformers and the official *'ulama* [professional theologians] had collaborated'.[20] It has been alternately courted and persecuted by successive Egyptian governments (Qutb was executed in 1965 for alleged plotting against the Nasser government, for example), revealing the tension between reformists and traditionalists in the Islamic world.

What is crucial is that the conditions which inspired the development of Islamic fundamentalism persist, even if the countries where it flourishes are no longer formally Western colonies. Western influence is more marked than ever, especially given the enthusiasm of the West's power brokers for globalisation, and fundamentalism remains a reflex response to that perceived cultural threat. The clash of civilisations continues, with universal theory confronting universal theory in an atmosphere of mutual distrust and bitterness: no sign of the end of history in sight here.

## The Suicide and the Martyr

One of the most difficult aspects of Islamic fundamentalism for the West to comprehend is its enthusiastic embrace of martyrdom, so graphically illustrated in the 9/11 attacks. This hardly seems to announce the end of history either. Whatever else we may say of those who hijacked the planes on 9/11, we cannot doubt their sincerity (and the same goes for Palestinian suicide-bombers in the conflict with Israel). To die for one's cause, at one's own hand, is the ultimate proof of one's commitment to that cause. Universal theories can ask no more of one. The recourse to martyrdom is what the West finds most frightening about Islamic fundamentalism, because it's almost impossible to take precautions against. No amount of security is likely to deter the true, lone fanatic from his or her objective, and this is a problem the West may well be wrestling with indefinitely. It's only too easy to see incommensurable cultural differences when we consider the Islamic attitude to martyrdom: the West sees suicide, Islamic true believers an act of *jihad* which is justified by the Koran. Even some Islamic commentators have agreed with the suicide interpretation, and have argued that Islamic theology proscribes this action. Their reading of the Koran is that the suicide will be forced to repeat the action of his or her death for all eternity. Fundamentalists have not been deterred, but as Malise Ruthven reminds us, Christianity has been known to have the same effect on its own believers: 'Christianity was once a cult ... [that] ... urged its adherents to make martyrs of themselves under circumstances that made martyrdom virtually indistinguishable from suicide.'[21] What is crucial is that the individual feels theologically justified in his action, and fundamentalist theology provides just such support. It might even be possible to claim that greater and lesser *jihad* merge in such actions.

The theological niceties of such a debate will be of little interest to the non-fundamentalist, however, whose main concern will be the possibility of more events such as 9/11 being planned and executed. Terrorist attacks are admittedly relatively rare, and we do need to keep our sense of perspective in this regard, but they occur often enough to add a significant layer of threat to our journey through the wilderness. Nor are the conditions that go to the making of suicide bombers likely to disappear in the near future, as the journalist Chris Arnot notes:

> Opportunities for economic advancement are not immediately evident when you happen to be young and reasonably well educated in a Palestinian camp, or what remains of a heavily bombed Iraqi city. There is no careers officer to suggest a training scheme with a firm of chartered accountants or computer analysts. More likely a representative from your local branch of Hamas, Hizbullah or al-Qaida will whisper in your ear: 'Have you considered being a warrior martyr?'[22]

Arnot was interviewing Mark Harrison, Professor of Economics at Warwick University, who has argued that becoming a suicide terrorist provides a solution to the identity crises of young men trapped in the situation outlined. To 'invest in the identity of a warrior martyr' gives their life a meaning it manifestly lacks, as well as guaranteeing them a place in the communal memory of their people.[23] Nor is there a particular personality type who is drawn to this role: 'From a psychological point of view, they have very little in common', Harrison deduces from a study he has conducted of 34 such warrior martyrs.[24]

Religion is only part of the problem for Harrison, who argues for an economic solution to the situation, but that depends on the character of the economic solution being offered by the West. The current models of market fundamentalism and globalisation are at least as much a part of the problem as a solution to Third World economic misery. A robust economy doesn't necessarily undermine religious fundamentalism, which would long since have disappeared from America were that the case; but it might just remove its more extreme manifestations. Warrior martyrs are not a feature of the American Protestant experience,* and anything that would lessen their attractiveness to the Islamic world would be a step in the right direction. That would require some significant re-thinking of Western economic policy and practice, in particular of the market fundamentalist ethic. Sadly, as we'll go on to discuss in Chapter 5, the current ideological climate hardly encourages any such radical questioning of priorities.

## Islam and the 'People of the Book'

Apologists for Islam argue that it can claim a history of tolerance for other religions, comparing it very favourably

---

* Although it's just possible to discern something of the warrior martyr complex in Timothy McVeigh, the Oklahoma City bomber, who felt similarly driven to extreme measures by a sense of political impotence.

with Christianity in this regard. The Ottoman empire is often cited as a classic example of this trait, with Christians – both Catholic and Orthodox varieties – allowed to retain their faith and to worship freely over a period of centuries of Muslim overlordship in the Balkans and Greece, as well as in other scattered outposts throughout the Middle East. It's also pointed out that the Jews fared better under Muslim rule in the Moorish empire than under the Catholic regime that drove the Moors out of Spain in the 15th century. When the entire Jewish community was expelled from Spain in 1492 (except for those who agreed to convert to Christianity), they relocated throughout Europe and the Mediterranean region; but it was under Muslim rule, yet again, that they discovered the greatest freedom. As Frances Yates has observed: '[b]y far the greater number of Jewish exiles went to the east and found a refuge in the Ottoman empire. The Crescent was infinitely more tolerant of Jews than the Cross; within the Turkish domains, they were allowed to profess their religion openly.'[25]

The reasons for this favourable treatment over a period of centuries can be traced back into Muslim theology. Just as Christianity draws on Judaism, Islam draws on both Judaism and Christianity in the construction of its theology. It's rather ironic, but very postmodern, to find that monotheism can be so intertextual. Jews and Christians are accorded respect by Muslims for being 'people of the Book', since figures such as Abraham and Jesus feature in the Koran (Jesus is particularly revered by certain Sufi sects, for example). Zoroastrians – a very small group in today's world – are also 'people of the Book', but religions that are not, such as Hinduism, are effectively treated as forms of paganism by Islam. As one might expect, this is hardly conducive to cultural harmony in nation states like India, with a Hindu majority and, despite the creation of Muslim Pakistan out of India in 1947, a very substantial Muslim minority (12%). Over the history of Islam, being classified as 'people of the Book' has enabled both Jewish and Christian communities to survive within Islamic polities, and largely on that basis tolerance can be claimed as an integral part of the Islamic ethos.

One can, however, overstate this tolerance. Other religions could never claim equality with Islam, and would be allowed to operate only if they acknowledged their inferior status. The relationship between Islam and both Christianity and Judaism was almost colonialist in nature: Islam provided protection for those religions, but at a price. Forcible conversion was not in general an Islamic tactic (Christianity having fewer scruples in this regard),* but to continue worshipping as a Christian or a Jew – or a Zoroastrian – after Islam assumed political power in one's territory, was to accept second-class status from then onwards. There was tolerance only when Jews and Christians 'took their [Muslims'] superiority for granted and had no political ambitions or aspirations of their own':[26] in other words, cultivate your own little garden. Islam could be more generous towards the conquered than other religions, therefore, but we are not dealing with true religious pluralism in such instances (if such an ideal state is ever really possible).

It is because of the sacred nature of 'the Book' that a measure of accommodation is possible with some other religions. There is what amounts to an Islamic version of fundamentalist Christianity's tenet of scriptural inerrancy: 'in Islam the divine is believed to have manifested itself primarily in the form of a text, so that any scientific or linguistic analysis which casts doubt on that text's integrity must threaten the central citadel of faith.'[27] At the very least, this rules out

---

* There is some disagreement amongst commentators on Islamic forced conversion, with Tariq Ali, for example, referring to certain instances of this in Indian history after the Muslim conquest of the country: 'The bulk of Indian Muslims were nonetheless converts: some forced and others voluntary.' (*The Clash of Fundamentalisms*, p. 227.)

debate; other religions must keep their counsel when it comes to the relative merits of their book and Islam's book.

## The Problem of Apostasy

One of the greatest barriers to change in Islamic society is the concept of apostasy. This is taken very seriously indeed by the Islamic authorities, whose interpretation of it is that anyone born to a family of believers cannot renounce their faith. In a modern Christian society you can decide to become an atheist, but there is no equivalent within Islam. The official line is that once a Muslim, always a Muslim; the condition is truly fundamental to your being. To fail to practise Islam is to become an enemy of Islam, and then a potential subject of a *fatwa* decree against your life. There is no opt-out clause in the Muslim religion. Since apostasy is seen everywhere by the more militant fundamentalists (as, to be fair, sin is also by Christian fundamentalists), this makes any kind of reforming impulse very difficult to sustain within the Islamic world.

The case of Salman Rushdie stands as a warning to any Muslim who might think of saying anything at all unorthodox about Islam or its revered figures. You stay in the approved time warp zone or else. Rushdie challenged this by publishing his novel *The Satanic Verses*, in which both Islam and its prophet were treated in satirical – and to the devout, sacrilegious – fashion; to the extent of doubt being cast on his prophet's mission.[28] In consequence, Rushdie was deemed by the Ayatollah Khomeini, then the head cleric of the Iranian state, to be a legitimate target for assassination by any of the Islamic faithful, who stood to become instant heroes for performing such an act. To the true believer, Rushdie was an apostate and therefore could expect no mercy; a state of affairs which drove him into hiding and long-term, round-the-clock police protection. The book itself was publicly burnt by British

Muslims as a warning to the author. It should be recorded that many intellectuals in the Islamic world did speak out on behalf of Rushdie, with one Saudi Arabian sociologist asserting angrily that: 'He is not even an Iranian citizen. ... the *fatwa* of Khomeini reveals to us the planetary tyranny that sets aside the laws and customs of other states.'[29] It seems likely, however, that Rushdie's treatment at the hands of the fundamentalist establishment gave other potential critics lurking within Islam considerable pause for thought. Scepticism and Islam clearly didn't mix very well; best to keep one's doubts to oneself and the new planetary tyranny at bay.

The charge of apostasy effectively turns you into an outlaw, which can have very unfortunate side effects for those who know you, even down to the level of the family. To aid the apostate is to share in his crime, since the apostate is an enemy of Islam. Apostates are written out of the record, and can claim none of the rights or privileges of the faithful. The wife of an apostate who continued to live with him would, for example, be laying herself open to a charge of adultery, which under Shari'a law is punishable by stoning to death. Islam can be particularly unforgiving on the issue.

## Taliban Days

The Taliban regime in Afghanistan constituted one of the purest expressions of Islamic fundamentalism in political action ever seen: a movement, in Roland Jacquard's description, '[b]olstered by a simple ideology, an iron discipline, and the rigorous moral values imposed by its leader'.[30] Nowhere else has fundamentalism been applied with quite such rigour, or managed to exert such tight control over the populace. This was despite the fact that, in Muslim terms of reference, Afghanistan was a relatively open-minded society. The majority of the population were adherents of the Hanafi sect, regarded as the least strict of the four branches of Sunni Islam, and this carried over into their behaviour towards others. As Ahmed Rashid has pointed out, 'no Afghan can insist that the fellow Muslim standing next to him prays also. Traditionally Islam in Afghanistan has been immensely tolerant – to other Muslim sects, other religions and modern lifestyles.'[31] In the chaos that followed the successful war of liberation against the Russians, all this was to change dramatically. The Taliban emerged victorious from civil war and proceeded to impose their uncompromising vision of Islam on the country.

Afghanistan under the Taliban was the fundamentalist dream come true; to the rest of the world, however, the effect was something altogether more nightmarish. Western political commentators were quick to condemn the regime's excessive zeal: 'the Taliban regard Western lifestyles with anathema, equate Western dress with moral laxity, and denounce freedom for women as antithetical to Islamic morality.'[32] It was like watching an entire society being returned forcibly to medieval times, or even earlier. Other than their obsession with modern weaponry, the Taliban more or less banished or prohibited all the trappings of the modern world: 'Western technical progress was outlawed, and bearded madrasa students built public bonfires of video cassettes, VCRs, and televisions. Cassettes of Western music, confiscated from trucks or in public places, were crushed underfoot. Pleasure was prohibited in almost every form' (a prohibition that even extended to pigeon-keeping and kite-flying).[33] Strict dress and behaviour codes were implemented for both men and women, and vigorously enforced by Taliban militants and the Religious Police. Women, as usual in these contexts, came off much the worse in the exercise, effectively being removed from public life: 'Women you should not step outside your residence', as one of the regime's earliest decrees sternly began.[34] With the exception of a few contested areas, Afghanistan was sealed off from Western influence, and an Islamic theocracy established. For several years this truly was a fundamentalist world, and what they didn't do in the old days, they scrupulously didn't do now either.

Such policies were in keeping with the Taliban's intellectual roots in the Deobandi school of Islamic thought, which grew out of a theological college (or *madrasa*) founded in Deoband, near Delhi, in 1867. The Deobandis' original intention was to provide moral leadership for Indian Muslims, who had seen their cultural status threatened by their key role in the 1857 Mutiny against British rule. Although a reform-minded institution in the first place (with a clear anti-colonialist bias), the Deoband *madrasa* soon turned conservative in terms of its teaching, with a strong emphasis on Shari'a law and the subordinate status of women. As Roland Jacquard has noted: 'Deobandi philosophy stresses *taqlid*, or acceptance of old interpretations, rather than reinterpretation of religion according to the times.'[35] In other words, it actively seeks out the time warp zone, where Islam is reduced, in Ahmed Rashid's mocking words, 'to the length of one's beard and the question of whether burka-clad women are allowed to expose their ankles'.[36] The dual nature of Islam – religion and politics simultaneously, as Johannes J.G. Jansen emphasises – is clearly evident in Deobandi philosophy, which wants religion to be the basis for all aspects of human existence: a purist religion for a purist society. Deobandi *madrasas* soon multiplied throughout the Muslim world, proving to be particularly popular in Pakistan, where in the late 1980s there were reckoned to be around 8,000 officially registered and 25,000 unregistered ones in operation, with over half a million students attending.

The protection that was offered Al-Qaeda and its leader Osama bin Laden (hailed as heroes in Afghanistan for their prominent part in the war against the Russians) indicated where the regime's sympathies lay, and they rejected all Western requests to withdraw this support when the West began its crackdown on terrorism. Ultimately, as we know, this was to prove their undoing, but the Taliban managed to hold sway over the nation for several years before the West moved against them, unleashing a chain of events which is still working its complicated way out in global politics. The Taliban have left their mark, and Taliban-like fundamentalist movements are emerging elsewhere in Central Asia, promising future problems in this politically sensitive area only recently freed from Soviet domination. We need to face up to the fact that for a significant section of the Islamic world, the Taliban constitute a role model. Like Osama bin Laden and his Brotherhood, they are well on their way to mythic status within Islamic history.

## 'Forget about Islam'

The essence of Christian fundamentalism has been memorably caught in the words of the contemporary Texan churchgoer we encountered in Chapter 1: 'Either we're going to be in heaven, or we're going to be in hell. Forget about Islam, forget about Buddhism, forget about religion. Jesus Christ says there's only one way to heaven, and that's through Him, OK?'[37] If nothing else, such a statement has the virtue of clarity: you know precisely where you are with this believer; there can be no ambiguity, no grey areas. The phrase 'forget about religion' is particularly revealing. It's as if Christianity has passed beyond the category of religion itself for this particular Protestant. Christianity is not a religion in the sense that other religions are, Christianity is simply 'the truth': accept no substitutes. There will be no ecumenical gesture made here; this is the antagonistic mentality in character-istically combative and unforgiving mode. What the *Oxford*

*Encyclopaedia of the Modern Islamic World* calls fundamentalism's 'absolutist and literalist manner' is clearly alive and well and living in Texas.[38] We might reflect also on the words of yet another Texan Protestant, this time the Rev. Dr Criswell, a Baptist preacher in Dallas: 'What God does with the Jew, the Muslim, the Hindu lies in God's prerogative, not mine.'[39] No need even to *think* about other religions if you're a Texan fundamentalist, it would seem. Non-Christians are practically non-persons. They're certainly outside your time warp zone – and by divine sanction they will stay there.

Fundamentalism in America was a response to liberalising trends in modern life. Its creed, as we have seen, was formulated in the twelve volumes of *The Fundamentals* (1910–15), and consisted of five key tenets: (1) scriptural inerrancy; (2) the Virgin Birth of Christ; (3) Christ's substitutionary atonement; (4) Christ's bodily resurrection; (5) the authenticity of Christ's miracles. These were taken to be absolutely fundamental to Christian belief. None of them was to be questioned or made the subject of theological speculation. In 1923, J. Gresham Machen was to add 'premillennialism' to the list of fundamentals (we'll have reason to come back to premillennialism in more detail soon).

*The Fundamentals* were the culmination of decades of debate amongst American Protestant theologians about how best to preserve their faith in a rapidly changing world, where humanism was beginning to chip away at the religious ethos. Their answer, after much wrangling at conferences, in bible colleges, university theology departments (Princeton being to the fore), and the pages of religious newspapers and journals, was to go 'back to basics'. Humanism was to be confronted by fundamental religious truths that it could not contest; truths that believers would be prepared to defend to the very last. Believers willing to do that have been coming forward with great regularity ever since, and *The Fundamentals* have left an enduring legacy in American culture. What one historian has called the project's 'rock-hard certainties' retain their hold on the public imagination.[40] Fundamentalism is a force of considerable significance in contemporary America, one that politicians ignore at their peril: certainly, few willingly incur its displeasure. As another believer has put it, 'If you're not working for God, you're working for Satan', and no politician wants to be identified with that latter category.[41] That Manichean world view can be very effective in keeping the political class conservative in its actions. As Martin Amis has acidly remarked: 'All US presidents – and all US presidential candidates – have to be religious or have to pretend to be religious. More specifically, they have to subscribe to "born again" Christianity.'[42] Pretend or not, what is proved in such instances is the efficacy of constant pressure from what has been called 'the invisible fundamentalist church authority'.[43]

## Dispensationalism

Biblical inerrancy forms the bedrock of Christian fundamentalist belief. Without that sacred text to refer back to there would be no objective proof, as the fundamentalist sees it anyway, of the rightness of one's actions. Inerrancy simply means that the Bible cannot be wrong, but as Clyde Wilcox amongst others has pointed out, 'Most [fundamentalists] accepted an even stronger view – that the Bible was literally true':[44] literally true, as in 'absolute transcript' of God's mind. We could say that biblical inerrancy is the necessary precondition of fundamentalist belief: take it away and none of the other fundamentals would stand up for very long. In a recent controversy over inerrancy in America, it was said of one such inerrantist that he 'has a gas-balloon theory of theology. One leak and the whole Bible comes down. As a result he spends all his time patching.'[45] It's the doctrine of dispensationalism, however, which arguably has the greatest effect on the behaviour of the contemporary fundamentalist, and this does depend very heavily on the literal truth of the Bible, hence the willingness to patch away if the need arises. Dispensationalism provides the time-scale and the sequence of events for the Second Coming, and for the fundamentalist this is *the* critical event for humankind, the true end of history when God's purposes will be revealed unequivocally for all to see. And not all of us will discover it to be a pleasurable experience either, as our sins are judged and we are found sadly wanting. Some fundamentalists can sound quite gleeful about this prospect, but then Manicheans would.

Fundamentalists believe that human history is divided up into seven eras, or 'dispensations', whose character is determined in advance by God. The last dispensation will consist of the Second Coming of Christ, and his subsequent thousand-year-long reign over humanity, and that is what all fundamentalists are eagerly awaiting. The theory was developed by evangelical thinkers in 19th-century America (most notably John Nelson Darby), who were to lay the groundwork for fundamentalism. As George M. Marsden has concluded, 'the intellectual predispositions associated with dispensationalism gave fundamentalism its characteristic hue'.[46] Dispensationalism gave rise to two main interpretations amongst evangelicals: postmillennial or premillennial. Postmillennialists believed a state of perfection like the millennium would be reached before Christ returned, whereas premillennialists believed that Christ's Second Coming would signal the actual start of the millennium. The former placed more faith in humankind than the latter, who took a more pessimistic view of human nature in which perfection was beyond us without Christ's personal intervention. It's the premillennial interpretation that has dominated in fundamentalist thought, hence its dramatic, apocalyptic quality.

(That quality seems to have passed over into the American militia movement, incidentally, one of whose main arguments for a gun-owning culture is to be prepared for the social and political apocalypse that they claim is imminent. Access to guns equals survival for this constituency. Religious fundamentalist beliefs often lie behind militia ideology – a case of 'praise the lord and pass the ammunition'.)

Dispensationalism has become big business in the publishing industry in America, reinforcing the link between Christian fundamentalism and commerce. Works of scriptural prophecy have had quite phenomenal success in this market. Arguably the greatest practitioner of this genre is Hal Lindsey, whose *The Late Great Planet Earth* shifted 28 million copies between 1970 and 1990. Lindsey has no doubt at all what's in store for true believers: 'It will happen! Someday, a day that only God knows, Jesus Christ is coming to take away all those who believe in Him. ... It will be the living end. The ultimate trip.'[47] We can even speak of the dispensationalist novel, and again there are fortunes to be made for those willing to propagate the premillennialist ethic. Writers such as Salem Kirban, Tim LaHaye and Jerry B. Jenkins have achieved massive sales with their tales of post-Rapture existence. LaHaye and Jenkins' *Left Behind* cycle of novels – eleven to date, starting with the volume of that name in 1995[48] – has now passed the 50 million mark. The novels themselves tend to be looked down on by literary critics, but their literary merit or otherwise is fairly irrelevant to their cultural role. These books are produced to meet a specific need in American society. They help to flesh out the myth of dispensationalism for the general public – the majority of whom really do believe in the imminence of the Second Coming (60% being one estimate of the reach of the belief). For much of their reading public, these books have an educational purpose, preparing them for what's in store; guidebooks on how to comport yourself in apocalyptic times.

We might compare them in that respect to *The Pilgrim's Progress*, which functioned in a similar way for a 17th-century audience, giving theology a narrative cloak that made its message easier to assimilate. Whether the dispensationalist novelists' efforts will last as long as Bunyan's tale seems more doubtful, but that probably depends on fundamentalism's resilience. If it's still around in a century or two, such works might well have taken on an aura of historical significance for believers. The prospect of fundamentalism rolling on into the future is not one that a sceptic will relish, but, for such a person, fundamentalism's persistence into the current age is mystery enough. You would think the patching would be visible to everyone by now, but it appears not.

## Women and Fundamentalism

Women always seem to pose problems to fundamentalist movements, which generally have a very masculine, control-oriented ethos, with deeply traditional ideas about gender roles and sexual politics. Christian fundamentalism is no different in this respect. This is hardly surprising given that, as one commentator has pointed out, 'Fundamentalism was born in an era of anxiety over gender roles'.[49] That anxiety, stemming from the emergence of the 'modern woman' (a phenomenon more marked in American than European society), led to a reassertion of masculine values within Protestant fundamentalism in the late 19th and early 20th centuries in America, that still marks out the movement today. Another impetus for this turn to the masculine was the fact that women made up the majority of churchgoers by the later 19th century, and were beginning to dominate in church organisations, particularly the missionary movement. Bible education was also increasingly in the hands of women. Caught between the modern woman on one hand, and the growing power of women within the Church itself on the other, Protestant leaders set about transforming their church into a much more aggressive organisation that would appeal to men. The new attitude of militancy is well captured in the remarks of the general editor of *The Fundamentals*, A.C. Dixon: 'Above all things I love peace, but next to peace I love a fight, and I believe the next best thing to peace is a theological fight.'[50] Although there's no reason to believe that some women wouldn't agree with such sentiments, in practice they haven't tended to be so aggressive in defence of their religion as men, nor as power-hungry nor status-conscious. Men were concerned to maintain their control over the church, and that involved establishing a strict division of labour between the sexes, with men claiming the main positions of authority in the church hierarchy as their own. Woman's role was henceforth to be centred mainly on the home and family: subordinate, but integral to the new fundamentalist ethos all the same. The fundamentalist movement, as Margaret Lamberts Bendroth has noted, 'had always placed a high priority on the family'.[51] Women had their place, but they had to be kept there. Fundamentalism based itself heavily on the notion of male supremacy.

In practice there was probably more room for negotiation about roles and relationships than the new conservatism might have appeared to offer, and some women did still manage to rise to positions of power and authority (and to assert themselves within the supposedly male-led family unit as well). But there's no denying the essentially masculine cast to Christian fundamentalism; a characteristic it bequeaths to most other forms of fundamentalism that have developed since. Market fundamentalism is a classic example. To quote Bendroth again: 'Businessmen injected the language of capitalism into fundamentalist piety, as unsaved individuals were urged to "do business with God".'[52] In America particularly, there's still a close relationship between religious and market fundamentalism, which share an aggressive, almost messianic quality in the way they present themselves to the world. They have the answer and they want you to know it – and believe it too. We have only to observe the phenomenon of tele-vangelism, with the 'Gospel ... being marketed like soap powders', to recognise how congenial religion finds the commercial ethic.[53] Fundamentalism is, in fact, big business in America, and as big business it's an entirely welcome part of the national scene. (One could speculate on why there are such close correspondences, and many attempts have been made to link capitalism and Protestantism.* These often founder on the lack of really hard evidence, but the American connection might have a simpler explanation. There is a large market for fundamentalism in America, and American capitalism has never been slow to exploit a market. America just likes business.)

In Islam, women's existence is even more circumscribed – unless you are willing to accept the contention of some apologists that wearing the veil liberates women because it frees them from the unwanted attention of men. The most extreme versions of the Islamic dress code require almost total coverage of the woman's body, with only the eyes and mouth visible. Combine this with confinement to the home, polygamy, and divorce as a male prerogative, and one can understand the reluctance of even some Muslim-born commentators to regard Islam as pro-women. For one such, the Iranian Haideh Moghissi (now settled in Canada), Islamic fundamentalism is 'anti-modernity, anti-democracy, and anti-feminism'.[54] Moghissi is a particularly harsh critic of Islamic feminism, arguing against its 'extravagant affirmations of

---

* The most famous being Max Weber, *The Protestant Ethic and the Spirit of Capitalism* (1920), trans. Talcott Parsons, George Allen and Unwin, 1930.

Muslim women's "agency", gender awareness, empowerment and security within a protected space'.[55] The reality, she asserts, is very different, and she can see no future for women under 'the social conservatism that is everywhere the marker of fundamentalist movements'.[56] Women will always suffer more than men under such social regimes, and for postmodernist thinkers to claim otherwise, as many have done, is wishful thinking betraying their naïveté on such matters. Fundamentalism is a case of putting the clock back for Moghissi, for whom the 're-Islamisation' of societies in the Middle East and Asia can only be bad news for the women involved.[57] As an example of what women have to face when re-Islamisation takes hold, we might consider the infamous Hudood Ordinances (1979) in Pakistan, which rule that women's evidence in court cases counts for only half of men's. The Ordinances also take a very severe line on adultery, the recommended punishment for which is death by stoning, and it has been reported that most of the women in the country's jails are convicted adulterers.*

The postmodern commitment to multiculturalism collapses into cultural romanticism in Moghissi's view. She wants real equality on the Western model – problematical though this may still be in practice – instead of the separate spheres of existence for each sex found in Islamic fundamentalist societies, which simply entrench gender stereotypes. Pretending that this isn't inequality makes her angry. Again, we're faced with the problem of universal versus relative values, although it becomes harder to argue the demerits of the former when confronted by a critic with Moghissi's cultural background. We recognise that she can say what she is saying

---

* See Rory McCarthy, 'Destiny and Devotion', *The Guardian,* Weekend, 17 May 2003, pp. 46–55. McCarthy notes that being a rape victim can sometimes lead to a charge of adultery.

only because she is no longer resident in an Islamic state, where her voice almost undoubtedly would be silenced by the male authorities. Islamic feminism is a largely passive phenomenon compared with its far more demanding, and vocal, Western counterpart.

Nevertheless, traditional dress has been claimed as liberating by some Islamic feminists (even if to thinkers like Moghissi the notion of Islamic feminism is a contradiction in terms), because women who embrace it become in a sense invisible. Having kept their part of the bargain by wearing the veil, they can then move around with greater freedom than they could do in Western clothing – at least in theory anyway, since social convention in Islamic societies still favours them remaining in the family home (as the Taliban decree quoted earlier made quite clear). The sad part of the whole exercise is that it depends on a very fundamentalist interpretation of male nature. This is taken to be unchanging, and exactly the way it was pictured by Islam's founders (it's worth observing in passing that separatist feminists can be just as uncompromising on this issue, a phenomenon we'll return to in Chapter 8). As so often in fundamentalist thought, the possibility of development is denied: 'The value system of Islam is immutable, and does not accept change with time because the nature of man does not change. Whatever change time may bring, the values of Islam operate within the same given framework, regardless.'[58] Change can only be associated with a move away from the 'rock-hard certainties' of one's belief, and hence firmly resisted by the true believer. Change becomes a form of apostasy, a wilful refusal to acknowledge the truth and to behave accordingly. Any apparent liberation within this constricting framework hardly counts as such to a Western feminist. It's the framework itself which is the problem. What to Islamic feminists is a 'protected space' for women to operate within, is to most of their Western sisters little better than a prison which simply announces the extent of male dominance: a prison in the wilderness. Women aren't setting the ground rules, male fundamentalists are. It's striking how little input women have to any religious fundamentalist cause; they are invariably the acted upon, rather than the initiators of policy.*

## Fundamentalism and Sexuality

As its treatment of women would indicate, religious fundamentalism has very strict ideas about sexuality. Nowhere is this more evident, however, than when it comes to homosexuality. This is actively persecuted by fundamentalists, for whom it's a sinful and even satanic practice: 'A religious, antigay perspective is shared by many conservative believers of the major American faiths – Christianity, Judaism, and Islam.'[59] Historical prejudice has long since been transformed into doctrine on this issue, and no true fundamentalist is willing to consider the possibility of amending doctrine to fit changing cultural circumstances, never mind directly contravening it. Once doctrine, always doctrine, is the immutable fundamentalist law; the script must be followed regardless of who suffers (it's their fault anyway). Gay theory in our own day emphasises difference, but that's never going to find much of an audience among fundamentalists who are intrinsically conformist in nature. As far back as the now innocent-seeming 1950s, the Christian Right has been warning us against the supposed perils of anything other than marital heterosexuality; the journal *Christianity Today* declaiming in 1958 that 'American society is becoming mentally, morally and emotionally ill with an unrestrained sex mania'.[60] To the baby-

---

* Although it should be recorded that one Islamic fundamentalist terrorist group, Indonesia's Jemaah Ismaliyyah, does recruit women.

boomers who came of age in the 1960s, this will no doubt seem an unrecognisable picture of their parents' generation.

Gay activists have fought back against such discrimination, but in America this has been an uphill struggle requiring considerable commitment against implacable opponents. The Christian Right (CR) has been very active in local and state politics, and has strenuously opposed all campaigns for the liberalisation of public attitudes towards homosexuality. What it wants instead is 'compulsory heterosexuality'. Didi Herman has chronicled the tireless efforts of the Colorado for Family Values movement (CFV) against gay rights legislation in the state in the 1990s, showing how this opposition was 'largely inseparable' from the Christian Right's 'wider, antiliberal agenda'.[61] The CFV set out to overturn gay rights legislation passed by several cities in the state as part of a general campaign against discrimination. A statewide anti-discrimination bill including a sexual orientation clause was proposed, but later withdrawn; an event which spurred the CFV to put forward an amendment (Amendment 2) to the state constitution to prevent any such legislation ever being introduced again in future. Amendment 2's objective left no room for ambiguity: 'No Protected Status Based on Homosexual, Lesbian or Bisexual Orientation' (a similar amendment was put forward in Oregon around the same time by the CR-backed Oregon Citizens' Alliance).[62] The amendment was passed in 1992, but a counter-campaign managed to block it by way of injunction. A lengthy court case ensued, involving various appeals to the Colorado Supreme Court and then the US Supreme Court in Washington. Despite dissenting opinions expressed by several judges, for whom there was a 'moral right of the citizen to disapprove of homosexuality', the injunction was upheld; but not until after three years of intense legal wrangling. Nor did this setback deter the Christian Right from continuing to pursue their original objectives. As Herman records, they simply changed their tactics: 'Antigay politics continues to play out in legislative arenas, as the CR focuses its energies on seizing control of state institutions.'[63] It will take more than a Supreme Court ruling to change the CR's mind about homosexuality – one suspects it would take nothing less than a direct pronouncement from God. Until then, heterosexuality will remain compulsory for the faithful.

## 'Till the Conversion of the Jews'

The conversion of the Jews is one of the most important signs identified with the Christian millennium. For 17th-century poet Andrew Marvell the notion provided a subtle and witty element to his seduction argument in the poem 'To His Coy Mistress':

> Had we but World enough, and Time,
> This coyness Lady were no crime.
> We would sit down, and think which way
> To walk, and pass our long Loves Day.
> Thou by the *Indian Ganges* side
> Should'st Rubies find: I by the Tide
> Of *Humber* would complain. I would
> Love you ten years before the Flood:
> And you should if you please refuse
> Till the Conversion of the *Jews*.[64]

The argument is double-edged, given that this was a period in which millenarian expectations had been running very high. The 'conversion of the Jews' was an event that many thought was imminent, disposing the more radical Protestants of the time (popularly referred to as 'Puritans') to take a sympathetic attitude towards the Jewish cause. Oliver Cromwell even opened negotiations with the Jewish community in Amsterdam in the 1650s, with a view to encouraging them to establish a colony in London (the Jews had been expelled from England in 1290, and were no longer officially resident). The reasoning behind this move on the part of Cromwell and his supporters was that, as Frances Yates has put it:

> a Christianity such as theirs, absolutely purified from Papist abuses, would be congenial to the Jews and would bring about their conversion, an event which would be the signal for the arrival of the millennium. In order to effect their conversion it was necessary to bring them to England so that they could see for themselves the workings of the pure religion.[65]

The project fell through in the wake of anti-Semitic protests, but was resurrected, and then successfully implemented, under the restored monarchy of Charles II (1660–85), with the same hopes in mind. Thanks to millenarian theory, the Jews enjoyed something like protected status within English culture at this time, their conversion keenly awaited by the Christian faithful.

For the American Christian Right of our own day, nothing much has changed in this regard, despite what is now a very long period of waiting. Relations are actively fostered with the Jews, particularly with the Jewish state of Israel, for the same reason – and all this despite a residual anti-Semitism in American life which it doesn't take much to stir up. There is the same Old Testament bias in the American Christian Right outlook that led the Puritans and Cromwell to adopt a pro-Jewish attitude in the mid-17th century. Nor is this to be considered some harmless eccentricity on the part of Christian fundamentalism, since it has come to influence American foreign policy towards the Middle East. Given the political volatility of that region, and its capacity to polarise opinion around the globe, that is a phenomenon which has to be of interest to us all. The Middle East is where various fundamentalisms collide, and none of us can expect to escape the resulting political fall-out.

Christian fundamentalism dictates that Israel deserves protected status in the current world political order because of its critical place in the millenarian scheme. In America, for example, the politically very significant pressure group the Christian Coalition is among the most enthusiastic, if on the face of it unlikely, champions of the Israeli cause. The *Guardian* reporter Matthew Engel has pointedly drawn attention to the underlying irony of the 'unholy alliance' generated by dispensationalist theory:

> Central to the theory ... is the Rapture, the second coming of Christ, which will presage the end of the world. A happy ending depends on the conversion of the Jews. And that, to cut a long story very short, can only happen if the Jews are in possession of all the lands given to them by God. In other words, these Christians are supporting the Jews in order to abolish them.[66]

Israel is almost totally dependent for its survival on American political support, so is likely to cultivate this 'unholy alliance' (in reality only *too* holy, we might say) for as long as it can, all ironies notwithstanding. Both parties are happy with the situation as it now stands, since it serves both their interests, no matter how diverse these may be. There was a similar accommodation reached in the 17th century, in that there was a Jewish belief that their Messiah would not come until they had spread themselves around the world. Logically, settling in England would bring that day closer (one more territory covered, as it were), hence the positive response of Amsterdam Jewry to Cromwell's overtures.*

One does wonder, however, what will happen if the millennium continues to be unduly delayed. At what point will disillusion set in on the Christian Coalition side, and with it, one would guess, the return of an anti-Semitism that is deeply engrained within the Christian, and particularly Christian fundamentalist, tradition? In the meantime, however, the Christian Coalition is firmly behind the Israeli state; as Matthew Engel has reported: 'When the president demanded that Israel withdraw its tanks from the West Bank in Israel, the White House allegedly received 100,000 angry emails from Christian conservatives.'[67] Given the well-attested influence of the Christian Right within the Republican Party, it's unlikely that any Republican president will fail to take heed of the pro-Israeli lobby's views. President Bush has been notably circumspect in this regard. As Engel goes on to report, the 2002 Christian Coalition national conference in Washington DC 'began with a videotaped benediction straight from the Oval office'.[68] When it comes to US–Israeli relations, politics and religion are seemingly inextricably intertwined, and for the foreseeable future – at least up until the actual Second Coming – that's not likely to change.

Everything that happens to Israel is read through dispensationalist doctrine by the fundamentalist movement, eager to discern hints from God as to the imminence of the Second Coming. In his fine book on American fundamentalism, Philip Melling has remarked how the Six Day War between Israel and the Arab states in 1967, when Israel wrested control of the

---

* Ironically enough, when a would-be Jewish Messiah, Sabbatai Zevi, turned up just a few years later in the Ottoman empire, he subsequently became a convert to Islam. We can only conclude that God does indeed move in extremely mysterious ways.

Old City of Jerusalem from the Jordanian authorities, 'had a profound effect on American evangelicals, whose concern for Israel bordered on the rabbinical. For pro-Zionists like [Hal] Lindsey, it was proof positive that Israel had a role in God's plan for humanity, and that the messianic age was near'.[69] The emphasis is very much on the premillennial period which envisages a pivotal role for the Jewish nation:

> It stresses the obligatory salvation of the Jews and their return to Israel as a precondition for the establishment of the Kingdom of God on the Davidic throne of Jerusalem. These events, foretold by the prophets Daniel and Ezekiel and the last book of the Christian Scriptures, Revelation, create a rigorous framework within which all funda-mentalists can understand past and future history, not as a purposeless record, but as a statement of divine will and a preparation for His eventual triumph over the forces of the Antichrist in the coming conflict known as the Tribulation.[70]

Melling's choice of words indicates just why we sceptics have a problem with such theories: 'obligatory', 'precondition', 'foretold' – this is a world where human free will has vanished.

For the more militant orthodox Jewish movements in Israel, this is a state of affairs which can justify their colonisation of the Occupied Territories of the West Bank, on the grounds that it goes against God's will for these to be settled by anyone other than his 'Chosen People'. That latter concept can be interpreted in the most fundamentalist of senses: the charmed circle in this instance is exclusively Judaic. To Zionist funda-mentalists, Palestinians are usurpers preventing the Jewish race from re-establishing Israel as it was geographically in biblical times. This is taken to be a necessary preliminary to the appearance of the Messiah. The Gush Emunim group, for example, led an aggressive campaign both to settle Jews in, and to drive Palestinians out of, the West Bank and Sinai areas in the aftermath of the Arab–Israeli 'October War' of 1973. Gush Emunim translates as 'Community of Believers' or 'Bloc of the Faithful', and they had considerable support within the Israeli political establishment for their endeavours, one commentator identifying 'a close link between the policies of annexation and religion' in this period.[71] It's a link that continues into our own day.

The dispensationalist scheme overrides all human actions and all politics – including, crucially from our point of view, the politics of difference and dissent. All of us are assumed to be playing out parts written in advance, mere pawns moved around by a greater power. There's nothing left to do but let the dispensation run its predetermined course, and if we want to refresh our memory as to what this will involve, we have only to consult the sacred text. For us assorted sceptics, socialists, post-Marxists, libertarians, and supporters of difference and dissent, this is indeed a wilderness in which to be trapped.

## Hare Krishna, Hare Fundamentalism

Fundamentalism is a feature of all 'people of the Book', but it's not confined to this grouping. Hindu fundamentalism is a case in point, and it can be found in some unexpected places. The roaming bands of Hare Krishna followers who have livened up the streets of Western Europe in the last few decades, with their chanting and bright clothing, turn out to be an expression of Hindu fundamentalism. Hare Krishna is the more popular name for the International Society for Krishna Consciousness (ISKCON), which has its roots in the 16th century and a particular form of Vaisnavism – worship of the God Visnu, or Krishna in his human form – as interpreted by the sage Caitanya. According to the scholar of Hinduism, John Brockington, Hare Krishna is 'impeccably orthodox' in terms of the Vaisnava tradition, and this has been a positive factor in its missionary activities: 'its conservative and even reactionary character ... seems to have appealed to a number who were disenchanted with various aspects of the modern West, for the anti-scientific, anti-intellectual and fundamentalist elements in its message seem in some ways a return to the past.'[72] It's yet another constituency seeking 'rock-hard certainties' and the sense of security that these can bring to believers' lives. Another scholar in this area, A.L. Herman, emphasises parallels to the Christian tradition in what he dubs 'Fundamentalist Krishnaism'. The fundamentals here are as follows: (1) 'Lord Krsna is the *only* supreme yet personal Lord of the universe'; (2) 'the *Vedas*, *Upanisads*, and the *Bhagavad Gita* [Hindu sacred texts] are all *literally* true'; (3) 'only devotional ecstasy directed to Lord Krsna leads to liberation and destroys all past wickedness and ignorance'; (4) 'the way of devotionalism is difficult but attainable by everyone'.[73]

Few of us will find Hare Krishna a particularly worrying manifestation, but there's a more sinister side to fundamentalism in contemporary Indian life. Hindu extremist political parties have taken advantage of the growing popularity of fundamentalism in the country openly to persecute India's Muslims. In Bombay in the mid-1990s, for example, the Shiv Sena party won control over local politics, and set in motion what the journalist Shyam Bhatia described as a 'McCarthyite anti-Muslim campaign'.[74] Muslims were treated as illegal immigrants unless they could prove otherwise, and Shiv Sena (Lord Shiva's Army) went to considerable lengths to deny them access to their voting rights. Cases were reported of Indian-born Muslims being kidnapped and deposited in Islamic Bangladesh, which did little to inspire Muslim confidence in the city's ruling authorities. For Shiv Sena's founder,

Bal Thackeray, Muslims were akin to an enemy within the state, and were under an obligation 'to prove their credibility' to other Indians.[75] The only Indian whose loyalty one could be certain of was a Hindu: a truly fundamentalist position to adopt, with religion and politics combining in exemplary fashion.

Flashpoints between the communities have become more common in recent years, as Hindu nationalists have asserted themselves. The 16th-century Muslim mosque in Ayodhya was destroyed by a Hindu mob in 1992, and devotees have campaigned since for it to be replaced by a Hindu temple. When a train full of unruly Hindu activists was returning home from Ayodhya in February 2002, it was attacked by a Muslim crowd in the town of Godhra, enraged at the activists' mistreatment of a local Muslim woman. After 58 of the activists died in the subsequent fire, reprisals were exacted against the Muslim community which left over 700 dead. Animosity on this scale suggests that fundamentalism will continue to be a major factor in Indian political life for the foreseeable future. In Salman Rushdie's scathing assessment of the event: 'What happened in India has happened in God's name. The problem is God.'[76]

## 'Rock-hard Certainties'

So that's what we in the post-Marxist socialist or post-modernist sceptic camp are up against: 'rock-hard certainties'. One of the few things one can say with certainty about postmodern thought is that it doesn't believe in certainty. There are always shades of meaning. Words, texts, and concepts are perpetually open to new, but by definition never definitive, interpretation. There's a genuinely liberating quality to meaning having a degree of imprecision – the only argument amongst postmodernists is just how big that degree is. It's how new situations are created and new correspondences established: the very basis of change. Interpretation, the ability to see things in different ways and to discover new patterns in the phenomena around us, is surely the key to cultural change: no wonder fundamentalists, cultural conservatives to the last man (and they usually are men), fight shy of the activity.

There can be no certainties in a postmodern world, because it's always in a process of change, a process of becoming. Granted, this condition can also be bewildering, especially the older one gets and the less adaptable, but the alternative would appear to be turning into an automaton carrying out someone – or something – else's wishes. Rock-hard certainties are not deemed to come from the realm of the human; they are the product of whatever divinity created your own particular sacred text. Such certainties are devised *for* the human, not *by* the human, a crucial distinction. For that reason alone, non-fundamentalists have to keep pressing the case for difference as hard as they can. We have no choice but to keep pushing on through that wilderness. If we need any other inspiration to do so, we can reflect on the words of another American true believer (from the North East for a change, just to show that we're not prejudiced against Texas) as reported in a sociological study: 'I'm glad I serve a living God that is absolute. He has all the answers. I don't have responsibility. He gives us all the answers. He makes the decisions for me, and that is great!'[77] Which only goes to show that one person's sense of security is another person's nightmare.

When all the answers are given, there's no need to engage in interpretation. Time warp logic applies. The sacred text, or the word, is held to say it all; to be self-sufficient and self-evident. Whereas I was instructed by dialectical materialist zealots to 'go and read some fucking Marx' to resolve my own particular doubts, other fundamentalists would simply substitute the name of their own sacred text or prophet and make the same request (although they might put it more politely). Terry Eagleton has suggested that this is the real error of fundamentalism – that it's so besotted with the word, and with the purity of the word: 'Fundamentalism means sticking strictly to the script, which in turn means being deeply fearful of the improvised, ambiguous or indeterminate.'[78] As Eagleton goes on to point out, meaning is always contaminated in some way because of the public nature of words and writing: 'Since writing is meaning that can be handled by anybody, any time, it is always profane and promiscuous. Meaning that has been written down is bound to be unhygienic.'[79] Purity becomes an unrealisable dream, the sacred text a confidence trick played by power-seekers on the gullible.

Not that this will be a very persuasive argument to those who believe that human beings are mere channels for God's word, and who are as a result all but constitutionally incapable of *not* sticking to the script. For them, the time warp zone is the only sensible place to be, especially if the millennium is just around the corner (as it always seems to be). The problem isn't just that fundamentalists like 'sticking strictly to the script' (whatever turns you on), but that they demand all the rest of us do so too – and to their script, not ours. Given that there are several scripts out there, all totally convinced of their own superiority and completely dismissive of the rival claims of others, that can lead only to conflict. And as we know from recent experience, such conflict isn't always confined to the merely verbal. In a fundamentalist world, the word and text, turned into a holy war, can kill – and not just believers but innocent bystanders too. Scepticism may not be the answer to this, but it's a step in the right direction, a step away from the dreaded time warp zone. Increasing the amount of improvisation, ambiguity and indeterminateness in the realm of ideas can be a positive political act: an antidote to holy war.

## Forget Fundamentalism

Perhaps some of us are missing the religion gene? I would want to say 'spirituality yes, religion no'; but that won't satisfy the fundamentalist temperament with its categorical view that there can be no spirituality without religion (fill in the particular religion as appropriate). The Runnymede Trust asked us to separate religious Islam from political Islam; perhaps we need to make a similar call for the separation of spirituality from religion? Viewed from the sceptic's perspective, religious fundamentalism seems to be more to do with power than spiritual matters (hence its refusal to countenance dissenting views); and power is a political rather than a spiritual issue. What is most striking to the sceptic is how religious fundamentalism, of pretty well all persuasions, seeks to exert control over our thought and behaviour. Individual believers manage to internalise this to a large extent, but the fundamentalist authorities in general still keep a very close watch on adherents; a level of control they want to extend to humanity at large, regardless of our feelings on the matter. These are *real* suspicious people, and it's you they suspect. Monitoring is second nature to the fundamentalist cause, since the purity of belief is always deemed to be in danger of being compromised; apostasy is a live possibility at any time. When apostasy comes onto the scene, control starts to unravel – and we have to remember that the fundamentalist mantra is 'control, control, control'.

It's one of the major paradoxes of fundamentalism, however, that its desire for total control goes hand in hand with an apparent inability ever to achieve this desired condition. Hence the beleaguered stance of so many fundamentalist movements: a threatened 'us' confronting an intransigent 'them' who can never quite be brought to submit to the fundamentalist 'truth' ('them' also including other fundamentalist movements). The sceptic can take some hope from this state of affairs, which seems to confirm recent scientific theory about the nature of systems. According to physicists, the more a system is brought under control the more unstable it becomes – counter-intuitive though this observation may seem to be.* Nevertheless, we must not underestimate the extreme lengths to which the beleaguered fundamentalist will go in the pursuit of control – generally through political channels. The various manoeuvres engaged in by the American anti-gay movement (CFV, for example) tell us what to expect: if at first you don't succeed, try taking over school boards, local councils, even state legislatures. The struggle against religious fundamentalism is a political struggle, since nearly all fundamentalisms aspire to the condition of theocracy. Those of us without the religion gene won't want to move even the tiniest fraction in that direction. 'Forget fundamentalism' could be our battle-cry, even though we know it will never be quite that easy. Moving on to consider market fundamentalism will show us why this is so: our adversary proves to be a many-headed beast, able to draw on very considerable resources in the pursuit of its aims. Another long stretch of wilderness looms ahead of us, I'm afraid.

---

* 'Quantum theory and microphysics require a far more radical revision of the idea of a continuous and predictable path. The quest for precision is not limited by its cost, but by the very nature of matter. It is not true that uncertainty (lack of control) decreases as accuracy goes up: it goes up as well.' (Jean-François Lyotard, *The Postmodern Condition*, p. 56.)

## CHAPTER FIVE

# Market Fundamentalism: The Search for Control and Self-Fulfilment

Market fundamentalism can be considered the current economic paradigm. Even when it's not being applied in its pure form of a totally unregulated market, it still constitutes the ideal against which most Western governments construct their economic policy, and it's certainly the model employed by the International Monetary Fund (IMF) and the World Bank in their dealings with the world's nation states. Its impact on current global politics is immense, and, many would argue, largely negative. The Islamic scholar Akbar S. Ahmed used the term, coined by the international financier George Soros, to describe the ethic behind IMF and World Bank policies towards the Third World; policies which are still being implemented in much the same fashion now as they were when Ahmed was making his critical observations in the early 1990s. (Even Soros, a hugely successful player on the global market scene, is no fan of market fundamentalism, arguing in 1998 that it 'has rendered the global capitalist system unsound and unsustainable'.[1]) Ahmed contended that market fundamentalism was analogous to the religious variety in terms of the code of behaviour demanded of recipients: for example, sobriety and sacrifice for the common good, with the promise that our efforts would bring lasting rewards in the future. Market fundamentalism was, in effect, the Protestant work ethic writ large. The

links between Christian fundamentalism and market funda-
mentalism in America are very tantalising, with the Christian
Right combining the two into a politically very powerful
ideology that has exerted considerable mass appeal throughout the nation. As many commentators have noted, the
Christian Right has come to have effective right of veto over
Republican Party policy, and no aspiring politician in the
party can run the risk of clashing with that constituency.
Given America's dominance in world affairs, that means the
Christian Right is a matter of concern to all of us, no matter
what country we may live in. When a Republican president is
in office, the point applies doubly.

Market fundamentalism, from Ahmed's perspective, had
the form of a new secular religion, the purity of its principles
taking precedence over its social impact. Indeed, social impact
was generally treated as an irrelevance by the champions of the
market and globalisation, if not ignored altogether. The work
of Joseph E. Stiglitz provides a catalogue of reinforcing
evidence for this view, with a succession of African, Asian,
South American and Eastern European countries all seen to
suffer severe social disruption in the name of fiscal purity. As
Stiglitz reveals, IMF and World Bank policies were often little
short of disastrous as far as the majority of their client
countries went. In Argentina's case, they helped to tip the
country into bankruptcy, with both its banking system and its
currency collapsing. The spectre of such a developed country
as Argentina reduced to barter for its internal economic
transactions ('reverse development' as it has been called)[2] is
one that can give all of us pause for thought. Post-communist
Russia didn't fare all that much better, either, at the hands of
the economic fundamentalists. What's most depressing is that
none of the various crises that have come in the wake of IMF
or World Bank intervention has seemed to shake those institutions' faith in market fundamentalism. While some small

adjustments have been made to policy, the show essentially goes on as before. Yet again, the fault is assumed to lie in humanity, not the ideas. As Stiglitz has pointed out, the IMF/ World Bank prescription for post-collapse Argentina is, incredibly enough, more of the same. Plan B is simply Plan A all over again. If Argentina overcomes its current plight, it's more likely to be in spite of, than because of, the efforts of the IMF and World Bank.

The West has had some experience of market fundamentalism in action too, with the popularity, in government circles anyway, of monetarist economic policies in the 1980s and 90s. The misery these caused many European countries – large-scale unemployment, destruction of traditional industries, dramatic increase in homelessness and of those living below the poverty line, the reappearance of supposedly eradicated poverty-related diseases such as tuberculosis and rickets, etc. – was felt by monetarists to be a small price to pay for the assumed benefits of an unrestrained market economy. We were assured that such an economy would transform our lives in the long term (although we should always bear in mind the observation of the economic guru of a previous generation, John Maynard Keynes, that in the long term we are all dead). As someone once said of monetarists, paraphrasing Oscar Wilde, they knew the price of everything but the value of nothing. Britain has learned painfully of late what the market economy can do to the public transport system, with the rail network having been brought to the brink of collapse in just a few years of private operation. Despite the fact that journey times on many inter-city trips are now longer than they were in the Victorian era, market fundamentalists continue to claim that privatisation works (taxed with its failings, including its poor safety record, apologists have been known to draw attention to improvements in train staff uniforms). Evidence to the contrary fails to dent the faith of the true market fundamentalist, any more than it does the committed religious fundamentalist. Economic meltdown, riots, political vacuums that encourage the growth of fascism, none of these will deflect the market fundamentalist from the straight and narrow path of his or her creed. There's only one way to economic heaven, and that's through the market, OK? Meanwhile, the rest of us are marooned in the economic wilderness.

Market fundamentalist policies have generated militant opposition in the West as well as in the Third World, as witness the growth of the anti-globalisation movement in the last decade or so (some of us would seem to lack the capitalist gene as well as the religious). For that movement, market fundamentalism is an anti-libertarian force which represses individuals – although paradoxically enough, there are libertarian trends within market fundamentalism itself which help to complicate matters. My libertarianism and your libertarianism may be incompatible, if mine is social and political and yours is economic: dropping all controls on the economic front, as right-wing libertarians campaign enthusiastically to do, can create severe problems on the social and political fronts. When market fundamentalism joins forces with Christian fundamentalism – the Christian Capitalist Right, as I have dubbed it – then the project becomes ever more sinister. Each fundamentalism shares a desire to control individual behaviour, but each strives to present itself as the path to self-fulfilment. It is self-fulfilment only within fundamentalist terms of reference, however, and these are geared towards the preservation of their systems – and the power that emanates from them.

## Fundamentalism Begets Fundamentalism

Ahmed's remarks about the quasi-religious nature of market fundamentalism are delivered within the context of a study of

Islam and postmodern thought. His book, *Islam and Post-modernism: Predicament and Promise*, forms a companion piece to Ernest Gellner's *Postmodernism, Reason and Religion*. Gellner proves to have more favourable things to say of Islamic fundamentalism than does Ahmed:

> Muslim fundamentalism is an enormously simple, powerful, earthy, sometimes cruel, absorbing, socially fortifying movement, which gives a sense of direction and orientation to millions of men and women, many of whom live lives of bitter poverty and are subject to harsh oppression. It enables them to adjust to a new anonymous mass society by identifying with the old, long-established High Culture of their own faith, and explaining their own deprivation and humiliation as a punishment for having strayed from the true path, rather than a consequence of never having found it.[3]

As Mark Harrison has observed, severe socio-economic deprivation can lead to a crisis of personal identity in such societies, and Islamic fundamentalism, in particular the cult of the warrior martyr that it promotes, can help to alleviate this.[4] In contrast to Gellner, Ahmed's argument is that Islam needs to engage in dialogue with postmodern thought in order to renew itself. 'The old methods and the old certainties will not hold the forces swirling and eddying around Muslim societies', he insists, calling for a more outward-looking Islam, an Islam minus fundamentalism.[5]

The situation is not being helped, however, by the imposition of market fundamentalist principles on politically, and economically, often very fragile Islamic nation states. Ahmed's argument is that such fundamentalism begets funda-mentalism in return: the more zeal there is for the market on the part of the IMF and World Bank, the more zeal will be created in the cause of Islam as a defence mechanism. A beleaguered society tends to close ranks and go back to basics; to favour *taqlid* rather than *ijtihad*. As another commentator has remarked, the net effect of IMF and World Bank policies in the Third World is to 'make the poor even poorer', thus all the more receptive to political extremism directed against the West.[6] In many such cases the poor quite literally have nothing left to lose by signing up to an extremist cause, and we ought to be very concerned by that – on humanitarian no less than self-interested political grounds. Harrison sees an economic solution as the only viable one long term, but, as we said before, that does very much depend on the character of the solution being offered. Let's move on to consider what that currently is.

## This Little Country Went to Market

Joseph E. Stiglitz has been in the vanguard of Western critics of the IMF and the World Bank, and his book *Globalization and its Discontents* makes for depressing reading if one is a postmodern socialist. It ought to make for depressing reading if one is a market fundamentalist as well, given the list of disasters it proceeds to unfold. The author himself shows that it's possible to become a sceptic from within the market fundamentalist establishment (Stiglitz was chief economist and senior vice-president of the World Bank, 1997–2000), but without suggesting that this establishment is undergoing any significant crisis of faith in the wake of recent setbacks. Market fundamentalism itself has proved to be highly resistant to doubt and scepticism, as Stiglitz's book reveals in crushing detail. When it comes to true believers, market fundamentalism can rival any religion in its zeal.

One of the main sources for market fundamentalism is to be found in the theory of 'rational expectations', whereby individuals are deemed to act rationally in a market situation where their personal interests are involved. Stiglitz notes that for some time now economists have been 'enthralled' by this theory, avidly constructing models based on its key assumptions: 'that all participants have the same (if not perfect) information and act perfectly rationally, that markets are perfectly efficient, that unemployment never exists (except when caused by greedy unions or government minimum wages), and where there is never any credit rationing.'[7] Stiglitz is scathing of these assumptions, which he refers to as 'a triumph of ideology over science' (a fundamentalist characteristic of the first order), and even more of the fact that they became the paradigm for American business school graduate work, with dire results for the rest of us: 'Unfortunately, students of these graduate programmes now act as policy-makers in many countries, and are trying to implement programmes based on the ideas.'[8] What the stock market shows instead, Stiglitz claims (drawing on the work of the recent Nobel Prize winners in economics, Daniel Kahneman and Vernon Smith), is that individuals often act very irrationally indeed, and that markets are not – surprise, surprise – all that efficient. The recent 'dotcom bubble' of the 1990s would be proof enough of those contentions: bubbles being by no means uncommon events in economic history.* As all advertising for investment broking in Britain is careful to remind us, stocks can go up as well as down, and you may not recover all your initial investment – but that's no deterrent to the average investor. To play the stock market is to gamble, and that certainly involves elements of irrational behaviour (quite a large amount actually – investors can be very gullible). No economic policy-maker, however, is going to acknowledge that

---

* Going right back through the Wall Street Crash of 1929 to the original source of the term, the South Sea Bubble of 1720.

fact publicly; especially not when they are working at the level of government adviser, or on the staff of the IMF or World Bank. As Stiglitz puts it, at such levels ideology invariably wins out over science – and common-sense as well, it would seem. Which is to say that fundamentalism rears its ugly head.

Stiglitz's complaint sounds much like the one made by Zygmunt Bauman in his book *Intimations of Postmodernity*: in the economic domain, as in the political, we appear to be living without an alternative at present. For neither thinker is this a healthy situation: some kind of opposition is necessary if systems are not to become tyrannical and thus stifle the search for self-fulfilment. With Marxism no longer a credible alternative, economically or politically, the IMF and World Bank have a free hand to do as they wish on the global stage, and the consequences, in Stiglitz's view, have been almost uniformly dire. If ever there was an advertisement for the benefits of difference and dissent it's the current IMF/World Bank monopoly over global economic conduct. To challenge this is to risk being frozen out of the world economic order (the IMF imprimatur really means something to both global investors and other national governments), although there has been the odd brave attempt to do this. Botswana is one such example. After gaining independence from South Africa in 1966, Botswana did work in partnership with the IMF on some projects, but it also made a point of building up a much wider circle of advisers on economic matters, including the Ford Foundation. These advisers helped the government to gain consensus within the nation for its economic policies, such that when a downturn did come it was able to implement austerity measures on its own without provoking a social breakdown. With one brief exception in 1981, Botswana has since steered clear of the IMF, preferring to stay in control of its own economic destiny.

Another example was Malaysia in the South-East Asian

economic crisis of the late 1990s (triggered by the collapse of Thailand's currency, the baht, in 1997). Again, this seemed to call into question the rigour of IMF policies that took no account at all of short-term social costs. As the economies of countries around them went into free fall after adopting IMF prescriptions, the Malaysian government chose instead to intervene directly into the market. It imposed controls on the movement of capital in and out of the country, declared a fixed rate on its currency (the ringgit) against the dollar, and cut interest rates. This was in open opposition to the IMF's free market policies, which recommended cutbacks in government spending, allowing the market to determine the relative value of currencies, and increases (often quite steep) in interest rates. Having backed away from the IMF model of fiscal purity, Malaysia subsequently suffered less economic hardship than its Asian neighbours and recovered far more quickly after the crisis had subsided. China had already decided to go its own way, and, contrary to IMF policy, had embarked on a policy of economic expansion through public works programmes as its method of countering global economic uncertainty (as America did in the 1930s under Roosevelt, with notable success). Stiglitz drew anti-IMF conclusions from the South-East Asian economic crisis as a whole: 'I think it is no accident that the only major East Asian country, China, to avert the crisis took a course directly opposite that advocated by the IMF, and that the country with the shortest downturn, Malaysia, also explicitly rejected an IMF strategy.'[9] You might think the entire experience would give the IMF and World Bank pause for thought, but as their later treatment of Argentina shows, this hasn't been the case. Their belief in free market principles is undimmed.

It's also noticeable that most Western countries aren't as purist in the application of market fundamentalist principles as the IMF and World Bank insist their Third World clients must be. Two examples will serve to illustrate the point. The American government, the world's greatest advocate of market fundamentalism, protects its own steel industry by imposing import duties on foreign steel. Whereas in Europe, the Common Agricultural Policy (CAP) subsidises farmers throughout the European Union in flagrant disregard of the free market ethos. All attempts to reform the CAP are met with hostility, most often led by the French, with their large, and by Western European standards relatively inefficient, agricultural sector. There's more than a certain irony involved in such a situation, given that the economies of Western countries are manifestly those best equipped to cope with the IMF's ideal of a regulation-free market. That most of them pragmatically back away from complete purity, fearing the social consequences (blockades by French farmers, lost votes in blue-collar American steel towns), is an interesting comment on market fundamentalism, although they still acknowledge it as the prevailing paradigm. More to the point, however, they don't prevent the IMF from pursuing purity fairly relentlessly in the under-developed world, despite the economies there lacking the robustness of their counterparts in the West. We aren't talking about real difference and dissent here, nor the emergence of an alternative paradigm, just the success of some special interest political lobbies.

Despite such minor acts of resistance, market fundamentalism still forms the inescapable backdrop to world economic activity. All that the countries mentioned above have done is to cushion the impact of market fundamentalist policies on the local economy, not to challenge the overall ethos itself. The IMF seal of approval is still eagerly sought, by Western no less than Third World nations, developed as well as under-developed economies. Collectively, the IMF and World Bank are the gatekeepers to the world economic order, and, like all gatekeepers, they guard their power jealously.

## Don't Cry to Us, Argentina

The most spectacular casualty of IMF and World Bank policy to date has to be Argentina. After being required to follow IMF/World Bank prescriptions as a price for being bailed out of trouble, first in the 1980s and then again in the 1990s, Argentina eventually found that these merely seemed to compound the original problems. The economy went into free fall, the banking system collapsed, and Argentina was plunged into the worst crisis in its admittedly chequered history. The rest of the world saw a relatively developed economy, rich in natural resources, reduced to the pre-modern condition of barter (as had happened in parts of post-Soviet Russia earlier, after receipt of IMF 'help'). One commentator has described the situation as 'the Argentine Riddle', even allowing for the country's long-term political instability:

> The country once had one of the most vibrant economies in the world. In the 1920s, Argentines compared themselves favourably to France in terms of economic wealth and individual well-being. ... Now Argentines count themselves among the underdeveloped nations of the world. ... Argentines themselves are deeply disappointed about the supposed gap between the country's possibilities and its intractable problems, such as economic stagnation, chronic unemployment, political violence, and sharp class antagonisms. This is the Argentine Riddle.[10]

For the Argentinian nation, the collapse of 2001 was public humiliation of the first order. There had been several close shaves in the IMF and World Bank's dealings with ailing economies over the previous few decades, but with Argentina it was a case of 'the operation was a success, but the patient has died'. The IMF/World Bank response to the situation has been less than sympathetic: as I put it in the heading above, 'Don't Cry to Us, Argentina'. As the historian Jonathan C. Brown has noted:

> the indifference of the IMF and the United States stung many Argentines. While the United States had bailed out Mexico in its 1995 monetary crisis, the US secretary of the treasury, Paul O'Neill, refused to help Argentina, saying that the Argentines themselves had to solve the problems they had created.[11]

O'Neill's response was pure market fundamentalism: the client will always be at fault in such cases; there can't be anything wrong with the policies or the principles behind them. Market fundamentalism is simply the economic 'truth' whose dictates must be obeyed. Argentina can't be allowed to operate counter to this truth just to serve its own interests.

True, it was protecting its own interests, regardless of the economic cost, that had dragged Argentina into difficulties in the first place. There has traditionally been a large bureaucracy and public sector in the country, neither very efficient, with state companies often running at a considerable loss. The IMF became involved during the financial crisis of the 1980s, when inflation was rampant and Argentina was struggling to repay its foreign debts. Although the government of President Raul Alfonsin adopted some of the measures recommended by the IMF, it failed to reduce the country's public sector significantly and the economic situation worsened. By the summer of 1989 the inflation rate was over 1,000%, and the public turned against the government in what was dubbed 'the IMF riots'. The new President, Carlos Menem, pushed forward with the neo-liberal economic policies so beloved of the IMF, and although his government was successful in bringing inflation down to manageable levels in the early

1990s (at one point it had topped the 3,000% mark), its privatisation policies led to major job losses and a marked increase in the unemployment rate. Nevertheless, Argentina was soon being hailed as an economic success story by such luminaries as President Clinton.

It was to be a very short-lived success story, as international debts continued to mount (foreign loans being needed to finance government spending on such necessities as civil service salaries), and the pegging of the Argentine currency, the peso, to the dollar led to deflation as the dollar strengthened against other currencies as the 1990s progressed. Imports became cheaper, and exports dearer, with predictably adverse effects on the economy. One of the government's responses was to freeze bank accounts, which led to considerable suffering for the people. By the end of 2001 there were more riots, including the middle-class led, and memorably named, 'Night of the Saucepans' protest, when demonstrators banged on saucepans to show their contempt of government policies. In the words of one protestor: 'Take your saucepan in hand. And when you again see incompetent politicians, bad administrators, corrupt deputies and senators, traitorous union bosses, and avaricious entrepreneurs, do not allow them to activate a new bomb.'[12] Over a turbulent two-week period, Argentina went through no fewer than four presidents. The final one, Eduardo Duhalde, unpegged the peso from the dollar, the immediate effect of which was to reduce the worth of bank accounts by 40% (not that holders could access these anyway, as they remained frozen). Argentina had certainly been complicit in its own economic crisis, but IMF prescriptions had made a bad situation worse. Argentine culture and IMF policy clashed, with disastrous consequences for the Argentine people.

The Argentine Riddle remains with us to the present day (Carlos Menem has even re-emerged as a presidential candidate, incredibly enough). So does the 'IMF Riddle': how many crises will it take before market fundamentalism is called into question by the world's fiscal police?

## Globalisation and Market Fundamentalism

Despite his criticisms of the IMF and the World Bank, Stiglitz is still in favour of globalisation – if it's handled with sensitivity to local cultural circumstances and flexibility as to its methods: 'I believe that globalization can be reshaped to realize its potential for good.'[13] It's the excesses of market fundamentalism that he's attacking, rather than the capitalist system itself. (Stiglitz has an ally in this respect in the prominent British politician Stephen Byers, who has recently recanted from his position as an advocate of globalisation within Britain's New Labour government, for which he was trade and industry secretary, announcing that he was simply 'wrong' in the pro-free-market views he held while in office: 'The way forward is through a regime of managed trade in which markets are slowly opened up and trade policy levers like subsidies and tariffs are used to help achieve development goals.'[14] Stiglitz is also in favour of such a gradualist approach, as his support for Malaysian and Chinese government econ-omic policy during the South-East Asia crisis of the 1990s reveals. Rather predictably, aid organisations welcomed Byers's 'conversion', coming as it did from someone on the inside of a major Western government, while right-wing economists rejected its premises.*) Globalisation is for Stiglitz

---

* Byers's admission being 'incredibly significant' to Andrew Pendleton of Christian Aid; 'remarkable' to Oxfam; but 'ill-informed', according to Professor David Henderson, formerly in charge of the economics and statistics section of the Organisation for Economic Co-operation and Development (all quoted in Felicity Lawrence, 'Labour's Free Trade Policy Harms Millions, Says Byers', *The Guardian*, 19 May 2003, p. 6).

the most effective, possibly the only, way to improve the living conditions of the world's poorest countries, and for a liberal Western thinker that's a highly desirable objective. Stiglitz, too, wants to see some kind of convergence take place, where the Third World is brought closer to the economic standards of the West.

The other side of the pro-globalisation argument has been trenchantly put by Naomi Klein in her best-selling book *No Logo*, where she concentrates on the human cost of unfettered Western market fundamentalism in action in vulnerable Third World economies:

> Usually, reports about this global web of logos and products are couched in the euphoric marketing rhetoric of the global village, an incredible place where tribes-people in remotest rain forests tap away on laptop computers, Sicilian grandmothers conduct E-business, and 'global teens' share, to borrow a phrase from a Levi's Web site, 'a world-wide style culture'. ... It hasn't taken long for the excitement inspired by these manic renditions of globalization to wear thin, revealing the cracks and fissures beneath its high-gloss facade. More and more over the past four years, we in the West have been catching glimpses of another kind of global village, where the economic divide is widening and cultural choices narrowing. This is a village where some multinationals, far from leveling the global playing field with jobs and technology for all, are in the process of mining the planet's poorest back country for unimaginable profits.[15]

The potential is clearly not being realised here, and Klein seems to be questioning whether it ever could be under the current dispensation. It's a system stacked against the vulnerable – countries no less than individuals.

Globalisation can be regarded as another form of funda-mentalism in its own right. It's sold to the general public, as Klein notes, with quasi-religious zeal, as if it were the answer to all the planet's social and political problems: the only possible way to reach economic salvation. She's a true sceptic on this issue, advocating a very different kind of globalisation instead; the globalisation of an 'anticorporate activism ... that is sowing the seeds of a genuine alternative to corporate rule'.[16] Market fundamentalist corporate culture, like Zygmunt Bauman, sees itself as operating in a world without an alternative; unlike Bauman, it's entirely happy with that situation and wants it to continue indefinitely. Klein's concern is to mobilise the dissent and difference that any fundamentalist movement invariably wants to eliminate. Globalisation, like religious fundamentalism, recognises no competitors; what each wants is a captive audience to work its message on without any hindrance. For 'no logo' substitute 'no questions'.

We might also speak of corporate fundamentalism: the assumption of the world's largest corporations (multi-nationals or transnationals as they are usually referred to) that they have the right to monopolise the global economy, even to the extent of dictating terms to national governments. Some theorists have argued that this is a process that may well make the nation state as we know it redundant, with supporters of 'hyperglobalisation', so called, regarding this as an entirely positive development which they want to see speeded up. Kenichi Ohmae, for example, sings the praises of a 'borderless world' with a 'borderless economy'.[17] To the 'end of history' we can add the 'end of the nation state'. In the current economic climate, Third World countries have little choice but to provide the conditions the multinationals demand for doing business with them; even if it means having to turn a blind eye to their own employment and safety legislation to enable deadlines to be met (thus the creation of 'special economic zones' where production can be carried out). Klein complains '[t]hat corporations have grown so big they have superseded government. That unlike governments, they are accountable only to their shareholders; that we lack the mechanisms to make them answer to a broader public.'[18] Similar points were made by Stiglitz about the IMF and World Bank; that they aren't accountable to the general public, and don't have to suffer close scrutiny of their affairs in any public arena. No one has to stand for election to these bodies, which encourages the preservation of the *status quo*. When even governments cease to be able to check the activities of the multinationals, then we really do have another kind of fundamentalism on our hands. The IMF and the World Bank may be there behind the scenes globally, but multinationals impinge directly on people's everyday lives – and no country is immune from their reach. What we eat and drink, how we clothe ourselves, and how we entertain ourselves, all are controlled to a greater or lesser extent by the big corporations. Hence the support offered by Klein for the new 'generation of troublemakers and shit-disturbers' taking on the corporate fundamentalist machine.[19] (Whether such activity presages a Marxist revival, as some on the left like Alex Callinicos have been arguing, is altogether more problematical.[20] True believers never stop trying.)

## Globalisation's Gray Areas

Globalisation and the market fundamentalist creed have also been attacked with some venom by John Gray, for whom they form yet another example of totalitarianism in action:

> A global free market is a project that was destined to fail. In this, as in much else, it resembles that other twentieth century experiment in utopian social engineering, Marxian socialism. Each was convinced that human progress must

have a single civilization as its goal. Each denied that a modern economy can come in many varieties. Each was ready to exact a large price in suffering from humanity in order to impose its single vision on the world. Each has run aground on vital human needs.[21]

This sweeps away not just the market fundamentalists but their political apologists, such as Francis Fukuyama with his 'incorrigibly Americocentric' views. Gray thinks that globalisation 'will shortly belong to an irrecoverable past', but one has to wonder.[22] Capitalism has proved its resilience over and over again, despite critics from Marx onwards in the mid-19th century prophesying its imminent doom. Gray's ideas are nevertheless worth considering in more detail, since he manages to convey so successfully the anger that anti-globalisation thinkers feel as they watch the sharp practices taking place around them. His book, *False Dawn: The Delusions of Global Capitalism*, is a scathing indictment of the hypocrisy that lies behind market fundamentalism's promises of good times for all if we simply move to a deregulated market on a global scale. There may be good times for shareholders, but the rest of us face a much more uncertain future.

Gray proves to be a true sceptic on the issue of deregulation, arguing that it's more likely to force living standards down than up. The more free the market, the worse the consequences for the population at large: 'In the monetary theory, Gresham's Law tells us that bad money drives out good. In a global free market there is a variation on Gresham's Law: bad capitalism tends to drive out good.'[23] Economic self-fulfilment is simply a chimera under this scheme, which brings instability and insecurity trailing in its wake. It's the increasingly aggressive American model of capitalism that's the culprit, making it impossible for any of the social democratic models favoured in Europe since the post-war period to compete. The former has steadily encroached on the latter in recent years, most European governments – left-wing as well as right – embracing a programme of deregulation of their previously tightly controlled economic systems. In many respects Britain has led the way, with successive governments, both Conservative and Labour, showing an almost boundless faith in the virtues of privatisation. Nationalised industries have been systematically sold off since the Conservative election victory in 1979 (Margaret Thatcher's first term), and what remains in public hands has been forced to privatise at least some aspects of its operation. Under the 'Private Finance Initiative' (PFI), many services in the National Health Service, for example, now go out to private tender after which they are administered on a contract basis. This typically applies to cleaning and portering staff, who often find themselves doing the same job for an outside agency for lower wages than they were paid as NHS staff. Similar things have happened in the civil service, the prison service, and the education system, in all of which PFI is now well entrenched. Despite the chequered record of the process, and widespread public discontent about its impact on essential services (most notably, public transport), further privatisations are in the pipeline.

In purely economic terms, capitalism has won out, and what competition there is lies between different kinds of capitalism rather than between capitalism and socialism. With the Soviet Union gone, there is no economic alternative. You can have all the economic self-fulfilment you want, as long as it's capitalist – and it's more likely to be found as an executive or shareholder than as a contract worker. European and Asian capitalism have traditionally favoured some variant or other of the social democratic model (even China can be included under that heading nowadays), with at least some safeguards provided for workers, but this is being undermined by the current American system. With their outsourcing of production to Third World countries, American companies are undercutting all their competitors in the global market. As Klein has pointed out in *No Logo*, the major American multinationals have simply shed all notions of social responsibility when it comes to wages and working conditions, and European and Asian capitalisms are being forced down the same road if they want to survive. This is the world of what Will Hutton has called 'permanently renegotiable contract relationships no matter who you are, be you a firm and its suppliers, or a GP and a hospital'.[24] Once you contract out in this manner, then it becomes a purely commercial transaction. Goods are supplied, goods are paid for; the welfare of the workers is someone else's problem. If the market fundamentalists had their way, this would be everyone's fate; whatever their occupation, wherever their location.

The environment is also someone else's problem, and, in effect, the West is now exporting its industrial pollution to the Third World, along with its production. In the short term this may be of benefit to the West, but in the long term we shall all suffer:

> More and more of the earth will, as a result, become less and less habitable. At the same time the price will rise for the few societies rich enough to be able to keep their local environments livable, and if, despite this, they persist in imposing the costs of pollution and other environmental social costs on businesses, profits will fall and capital will migrate.[25]

It's a gloomy prognosis, and one that doesn't promise either economic or political stability. Klein records how the migration of capital has led to lower and lower wages in the Third World, as multinationals seek ever keener tenders for the production of their goods. This is the Gresham's Law that

Gray is talking about, and the current system positively encourages it: 'When capital is mobile it will seek its absolute advantage by migrating to countries where the environmental and social costs of enterprises are lowest and profits are highest.'[26] The catchphrase becomes: renegotiation, renegotiation, renegotiation.

Gray's thesis is that American free market capitalism is a very bad capitalism that serves the interests of an élite only, and that it will almost inevitably lead to widespread social disruption when applied elsewhere in the world. Even in America itself it has resulted in a dramatic widening of the gap between rich and poor in the last couple of decades; a situation that's being kept in check largely by an aggressive penal policy which sees more than a million Americans behind bars: what Gray refers to as the 'great incarceration'.[27] (The French cultural theorist Michel Foucault had already argued for such a policy of social control as one of the major identifying features of modern culture, from the 17th century onwards.[28]) The same fate, Gray argues, awaits any country that adopts the American model wholeheartedly, citing the increasing prison population in Britain as thought-provoking evidence for his claim. Gray criticises the New Right ideology that lies behind free market capitalism as based on a very spurious reading of economic history. *Laissez faire* economics was the product of a particular set of circumstances at a particular time (mid-19th-century Britain), and those circumstances are not replicable anywhere else. The notion that the free market is rooted in our psychology is dismissed out of hand by Gray, for whom it's a historical accident which, unfortunately for the mass of humankind, economists now treat as the model for all economic activity. For economists, market fundamentalism is in our genes; for Gray, it goes against the natural human need for security – the very basis of political organisation.

Gray is confident that the need for personal security will

reassert itself and that nation states will not, as hyper-globalisation apologists confidently predict, wither away in the face of aggressive corporate advance of the kind documented by Klein in *No Logo*. But the nation state has clearly suffered from the unchecked spread of free market capitalism, and is no longer the entity it was, its capacity to direct the country's economic life much reduced and subject to validation by outside bodies such as the IMF and World Bank. We live in a world of quality audit (those of us who work in public institutions are daily faced with what amounts to audit fundamentalism), and that even extends to the nation state. That might suggest the free marketeers are in control, but Gray argues that they aren't either. The situation is more one of chaos, where, to draw on the oft-quoted phrase about Hollywood, 'nobody knows anything': 'The reality of the late twentieth-century world market is that it is ungovernable by either sovereign states or multinational corporations.'[29] There seems to be neither control *nor* lasting self-fulfilment on offer in the current dispensation.

Gray's is an apocalyptic vision which sees the dominance of free market capitalism as an almost unmitigated disaster, yet one that carries within itself the seeds of its own destruction. It isn't the first time we've heard this kind of argument – Marx was making the same pronouncement in *Capital* in the 19th century. Gray claims that capitalism has mutated so much that it would no longer be recognisable to Marx: that it's on a scale unimaginable to Marx's generation, and thus not subject to his fairly rigid historical scheme. Postmodern free market capitalism is so fluid and flexible, shifting from country to country as opportunities arise and market circumstances dictate, that it cannot be fought by techniques devised by previous generations of thinkers. Trade unions, for example, are largely powerless when a company transfers production to another country, and the knowledge that this is so easily done hardly promotes union militancy while a contract is being carried out either. But then Marx thought much the same of the capitalism of his own time and the inadequacy of the analyses of his predecessors. Free market capitalism may well manage to reinvent itself, as it has so often in the past – depressing prospect though that may be for the left.

Gray regards free market capitalism as a tragedy for the mass of humankind. It may well make millions for CEOs in the bigger corporations (and 'fat cat' pay is becoming more and more of an issue in British political life), but for the vast majority it spells insecurity and lower living standards. What Gray doesn't consider is whether this might appeal even to the disadvantaged; whether the possibility, slim though it is, of winning big in 'casino capitalism' (as Susan Strange has memorably dubbed the current system)* might be preferable to a life of dull, grey conformity with your entire career mapped out in front of you, 'cradle to grave' as the post-war European welfare state seemed to promise. Gray looks back with a certain amount of nostalgia to the halcyon days of social democracy in the mid-20th century, but for many, these times, with their large amount of social control and bureaucratic regulations, were stultifying rather than satisfying when it came to self-fulfilment. Maybe a majority in the West actually welcomes the excitement that comes along with anarchic, disordered, bandit, slash-and-burn or casino capitalism (to list the various terms Gray deploys); maybe they are lured by the sheer unpredictability of it all?

That was a possibility contemplated by Jean-François Lyotard in his anti-Marxist diatribe *Libidinal Economy*. There he attacked the Marxist notion of false consciousness (that we were so indoctrinated we sometimes acted against our

---

* 'The Western financial system is rapidly coming to resemble nothing as much as a vast casino.' (Susan Strange, *Casino Capitalism*, Blackwell, 1986, p. 1.)

best interests) by suggesting, heretically as far as the Marxist establishment was concerned, that the working class in the 19th century was caught up in the sheer excitement of the Industrial Revolution, and even complicit with it:

> [L]ook at the English proletariat, at what capital, that is to say *their labour*, has done to their body. ... the English unemployed did not become workers to survive, they – hang on tight and spit on me – *enjoyed* [*ils ont joui de*] the hysterical, masochistic, whatever exhaustion it was of *hanging on* in the mines, in the foundries, in the factories in hell, enjoyed the mass destruction of their organic body which was indeed imposed upon them, they enjoyed the decomposition of their personal identity, the identity that the peasant tradition had constructed for them, enjoyed the dissolution of their families and villages, and enjoyed the new monstrous *anonymity* of the suburbs and the pubs in the morning and evening.[30]

Lyotard was deliberately trying to provoke his one-time Marxist colleagues (and he succeeded), but he had hit on something interesting nonetheless. Change can appeal – even *disorienting* change can appeal. Security can also mean boredom and being stuck in a rut: the 1950s saw social democracy in full bloom in Britain, but it also saw the rise of the 'Angry Young Men' movement who found the lifestyle of the time claustrophobic and suffocating. These are not necessarily messages the left wishes to hear, but sometimes casino capitalism may be what the people want. Excitement might win out over political rectitude, even over what appears to be one's own best interests. The bookmaking industry worldwide is well aware of just how much people like to gamble, and lotteries tend to thrive. Perhaps there is a 'casino fundamentalism' lurking in the dark side of human nature?

Such ideas fit in with the theories put forward by the post-Marxist theorist Slavoj Žižek, who argues that there is often a willing suspension of disbelief when it comes to the reception of ideological systems. We may well realise that there is a discrepancy between the claims of an ideology and the reality of its operation (as those living under late communism in Žižek's own Yugoslavia manifestly did, for example), but we are more than capable of deceiving ourselves about this and continuing to believe in the ideal rather than the real. People who do this are being 'guided by an illusion', Žižek contends: 'They know very well how things really are, but still they are doing it as if they did not know.'[31] In other words, we are capable of indoctrinating ourselves. Casino capitalism may well owe its continued existence to just that state of mind; as might fundamentalism in general. In which case the contradictions pointed out by Gray may be less significant than he thinks: self-deception kicks in, and we see what we want to see. That's a state of affairs to give the sceptic cause for reflection, and goes some considerable way towards explaining why it is that we live in a fundamentalist world despite the heavyweight critiques of thinkers like Gray and Klein.

Gray thinks that market fundamentalism is doomed to collapse under the weight of its own contradictions: 'Like other twentieth-century utopias, global *laissez faire* – together with its casualties – will be swallowed into the memory hole of history.'[32] But how do we know it won't make a comeback? Even a cursory glance at history will show that utopia has been an endless source of fascination over the ages (in almost all cultures), and there's no reason to believe it won't continue to be so into the future. We might draw on the concept of 'eternal recurrence' here, and suggest that, even if the current crop of utopian ideas withers away (a big 'if' when it comes to religious fundamentalism), they will be reinvented in another guise eventually. Gray's outlook on our culture is pessimistic enough – we can't go back to the cosy world of social democracy and the post-war consensus – but this might be an even more depressing conclusion to reach.

Anthony Giddens has also weighed in with a critique of globalisation, accusing it of creating a 'runaway world' that we find increasingly taxing to cope with as individuals.* Nevertheless, globalisation seems to be our fate, and we shall have to learn how to live with it. Although critical of certain aspects of the globalisation project, Giddens is more sanguine than Gray about its impact in the Third World, arguing, for example, that economic inequality between nations 'has either stabilised or become reduced' since the mid-20th century.[33] Gray, and the anti-globalisation movement in general (Klein et al.), would firmly disagree, finding almost nothing of value in it. Since it's the World Bank that controls the statistics on which such assessments about world poverty are made, they are doubly sceptical; the World Bank obviously having a vested interest in showing that market fundamentalism works for the benefit of all.† Where Gray sees a system out of control, with the merciful qualification that it will ultimately destroy

---

* Giddens points out that the phrase has been used before, by the anthropologist Edmund Leach in his Reith Lectures on the BBC in the 1970s, but that 'he put a question mark after his title. I don't think one is needed any more.' (Anthony Giddens, *Runaway World: How Globalisation is Reshaping Our Lives*, Profile Books, 2002, p. xxxi.)

† For another sceptical assessment of the World Bank figures on world poverty, see Sanjay G. Reddy and Thomas W. Pogge, 'How *Not* to Count the Poor', http://www.columbia.edu/~sr793/ The authors are scathing about World Bank practices in this area: 'The estimates of the extent, distribution and trend of global income poverty provided in the World Bank's World Development Reports for 1990 and 2000/1 are neither meaningful nor reliable. The Bank uses an arbitrary international poverty line unrelated to any clear conception of poverty. … A new methodology of global poverty assessment, focused directly on the ability of the poor to achieve the most elementary income-dependent human capabilities, is feasible and necessary.'

itself, Giddens sees a runaway world that we can nevertheless come to terms with: 'Many of us feel in the grip of forces over which we have no power. Can we reimpose our will upon them? I believe we can.'[34] In what is probably the most comprehensive account of globalisation to date, there is a similarly upbeat assessment which urges us not to give in to any feelings of 'political fatalism' about the future: 'Globalization does not prefigure the "end of politics"', we are reassured, 'so much as its continuation by new means'.[35] Not everyone will be as optimistic as the authors of *Global Transformations* that those 'new means' will be preferable to the old, when nation states held real power over their own economic destiny, or that they will come about without bitter conflict between the various parties concerned.

No doubt this is a debate which will run and run (the statistics being well capable of supporting conflicting interpretations depending on one's position on the political spectrum), but Gray's contribution, with its decidedly apocalyptic vision of current events, is one that demands our close attention. *False Dawn* is one of the most trenchant critiques of capitalism by a non-Marxist that you are likely to encounter. The author's contention that free market capitalism leads less to globalisation than to a return to a Hobbesian state of nature, strikes me as wholly justified. In that condition we find the world's various nation states, and the styles of capitalism they favour, competing with each other in totally ruthless fashion just to ensure their own survival. That's what we are confronted by in our wilderness, and it's a desperate state of affairs inimical to humankind's longer-term prospects; certainly to any doctrine of either political or economic self-fulfilment. Thomas Hobbes saw the state of nature as a condition in which 'every man is Enemy to every man';[36] substitute 'nation state' for 'man' and you have today's global picture in a nutshell. No one can win if this goes on as it is at present. On a much smaller scale, *False Dawn* is a *Capital* for the 21st century. That we *need* a *Capital* for the 21st century tells us just how serious the situation is.

## The Strange Attraction of the Invisible Hand

Where do market fundamentalists get their confidence from? Just what are the fundamentals that shore up their faith in the market and, to their own satisfaction anyway, guarantee the rightness of all their decisions? The concept of the 'invisible (or hidden) hand' is one place to start. We might call it 'the mysterious case of the invisible hand', because trying to locate it has all the difficulties of tracking down the mastermind in a piece of crime fiction. The hidden hand is known only by its effects, and its sheer elusiveness is one of its most attractive characteristics to the market fundamentalist. It cannot be manipulated, at least not very successfully and not for any significant length of time, and what it yields is the truth, independent, so the story goes, of any mere personal considerations. The invisible hand is what directs the market mechanism from within, the 'ghost in the machine' as it were, and it cannot be resisted. It will always get its way in the end, whatever you as an individual investor may want. The invisible hand is very reminiscent of the God of fundamentalism: it has all the answers and makes all the ultimate decisions. We can probably add the invisible hand to our list of authoritarian personalities; it makes those kinds of demands on us and has that degree of power over our lives. Stiglitz may deny its existence, but to market fundamentalists this is the most fundamental principle of all in their belief system; what justifies the globalisation and hyperglobalisation programmes that Klein and Gray so bitterly oppose. The answer to such protestors from the fundamentalist camp would be that the invisible hand will eventually do its job, and that any of the downsides they mention are to be considered temporary only. Just leave the hand to its own devices.

It's a notion derived from the work of Adam Smith, one of the great founders of modern, free market, *laissez faire* economic theory, the basis for market fundamentalism. The invisible hand was deemed to lie behind individual actions, always prompted by self-interest in Smith's view of human nature, such that collectively they tended to the public good. The effect was rather like a self-correcting mechanism within the market itself, so that all benefitted, although all were motivated to act in the first instance by self-interest:

> A revolution of the greatest importance to the public happiness was … brought about by two different orders of people who had not the least intention to serve the public good. To gratify the most childish vanity was the sole motive of the great proprietors. The merchants and artificers, much less ridiculous, acted merely from a view to their own interest, and in pursuit of their own pedlar principle of turning a penny wherever a penny was to be got. Neither of them had either knowledge or foresight of the great revolution which the folly of the one, and the industry of the other, was gradually bringing about.[37]

The presence of that invisible hand in the market is an article of faith to the market fundamentalist movement, and the reason why its followers argue that the market must always be left as free from outside control and regulation as possible. Even the tiniest measure of regulation will be unacceptable, since the purity of the theory is of paramount importance. That gives the market fundamentalist a handy excuse should the market prove to act erratically: obviously, it wasn't free enough at that point to work in its natural way. The blame lies with us for meddling. It's an explanation which can be used quite shamelessly, over and over again, and is. We are asked to trust the invisible hand, totally.

The invisible hand sounds like a metaphysical concept, and it can be criticised on those grounds. All very well in theory, but does it *really* exist? Or is it just some figment of a theorist's imagination, something we could never conclusively prove or disprove? Intellectual theory is littered with such notions (the Marxist dialectic of history being a prime example); why should we take this one any more seriously? Stiglitz is of this sceptical turn of mind, his advice being to forget invisible hands and concentrate more on correcting the information gaps in the market that work to individual disadvantage. In his analysis it is inequality, not invisibility, that is the problem. To believe otherwise is to inhabit yet another time warp zone impervious to experience. In this context we might also ponder the admission of the American columnist and apologist for market fundamentalism, Thomas Friedman, that '[t]he hidden hand of the market will never work without a hidden fist'.[38] No Marxist could put it better.

Before we dismiss the invisible hand entirely, however, it might be interesting to consider a similar, no less apparently metaphysical, concept that has emerged from physics in recent years – the highly intriguing notion of the 'strange attractor' in chaos and complexity theory. Strange attractors are held to be the driving force behind all systems, both natural and humanly created, the weather no less than the stock market. They have been described as 'the trajectory towards which all other trajectories converge', and in the case of arguably their most powerful manifestation, a black hole, this can involve swallowing all the matter in its vicinity such that it can never escape again – even light being unable to do so.[39] As well as being irresistible forces, strange attractors are essentially unpredictable (just think of weather forecasting, never mind the stock market), since their ultimate agenda is unknown to us. We can deal only with their effects, not their causes. The good news for the market fundamentalist is that, according to this theory, there *is* an invisible hand (a.k.a. strange attractor) behind the workings of the market; the bad news is that it's entirely unpredictable, less the collective product of human action than an extra-human force with its own rationale. It may not have the common good in mind, as the invisible hand of Adam Smith's invention is assumed to do. The unknowable hand, as we might rename it, is a far less comforting notion than the one Smith is offering us.

Strange attractors suggest that we aren't really in control of the world around us. The message of chaos and complexity theory is that systems have their own internal dynamic, which is most certainly hidden from us. Systems can develop and become more complex over time, and with complexity comes the ability to self-organise into something qualitatively different from the original. Our universe is assumed to have a finite lifespan, but it's just possible, if the self-organisation principle is correct, that it may evolve in such a way as to counter this process; that is, to resist the pull of the entropy apparently built into all systems (the second law of thermo-dynamics). We are surrounded by systems, and indeed we are part of those systems, subject to our own strange attractors – whatever they may be. The pessimistic interpretation of this would be that we are simply acting out the programmes of a series of strange attractors, which places us in much the same position as the religious fundamentalist whose life is controlled by a God with an authoritarian personality and a master plan to which we have no access. If that's the real state of affairs with the market, then we are slaves to it rather than self-interested participants motivated by rational expecta-tions. Mankind would be made for the market, rather than the market for mankind (one suspects that most market fundamentalists would be quite happy to accept such a fate, even to treat it as a natural law). Market fundamentalism would be as much an enemy of free will as its religious counterpart is.

## Fundamentalists 'R' Us

How do the belief systems of religious and market fundamentalists compare overall? There are certainly many features they have in common. There is a body of doctrine, and there are demands made on believers, demands they are under an obligation to fulfil. The market, like the Bible, is held to be inerrant – if it's allowed to go about its own business unchecked. Just as the Bible needs no interpretation, so the market needs no tinkering in its mechanisms, by governments or others. (Strange that market fundamentalists are so addicted to insider trading, however; surely that counts as a distortion of the market's natural cycle?) Then, too, if humankind was made to carry out the dictates of God's will, it was also made to abide by the will of the market. Humankind is forced to realise its limitations in both cases; it's the servant of a far greater power, and it must never forget this. There's a clear sense of salvation in each form of fundamentalism, and of there being only one true way to reach it: a straight and narrow path from which one must not deviate, no matter what the temptations. All other routes are to be treated with suspicion. Self-fulfilment is a matter of identifying what's required of you by the higher forces, who will then reward you for your devoutness. To recall the Islamic terminology, what's required of the believer is *taqlid*, not *ijtihad*: that is, submissiveness, not an enquiring mind. The sheer act of performing what the belief system requires constitutes self-fulfilment for such fundamentalists. Putting the ritual into practice becomes an expression of their will, and takes on the character of a holy war at the level of the individual. What you do matters in the overall scheme: you are part of God's and/or the market's master plan.

The mental-set is very similar in each case, therefore, with adherents capable of boundless zeal and enthusiasm for the cause (onward market fundamentalist soldiers). For the sceptic, that fervour is the most depressing part of the whole exercise, since it seems impervious to all counter-arguments, all contrary evidence. Conversions such as those experienced by Joseph E. Stiglitz and Stephen Byers are few and far between: 'wrong' is not a concept that market fundamentalist soldiers recognise with regard to their beliefs. The attitude instead is that the market will be our saviour if we only allow it to be so and cease resisting its claims on us. Rather like born again Christians, we are expected to construct a personal relationship with the market, whereby it directs our lives, ultimately leading us to the promised land of self-fulfilment. It's a seductive vision, but, to hark back to Stephen Byers, it's just plain 'wrong'. Neither economic nor political life is ever that simple. Even the qualified faith in globalisation expressed by figures such as Stiglitz and Byers is arguably misplaced, as if we could have globalisation without any of the market fundamentalist side-effects. That may well prove to be an idle dream, especially given the nature of the players involved and the depth of their investment in full-scale, red-blooded global-isation of the slash-and-burn, wilderness-creating variety so loathed by John Gray and Naomi Klein. To use an American expression, these people play hardball, and they are not about to give up because a few countries suffer economic hardship or socio-political disruption. Don't cry to us Argentina, and that goes for anyone else in difficulty too. It really is a fundamentalist economic world out there.

## CHAPTER SIX

# Political Fundamentalism: The Search for Power

Fundamentalism in the political arena is essentially about power. Political fundamentalism is self-consciously anti-libertarian in its objectives, and concerned to keep the world that way by all the means at its disposal. Theocratic states (that is, those based on religious principles), such as can be found throughout the Islamic world, are certainly anti-libertarian in their bias, but we can identify the fundamentalist ethos at work in Western democracies also. Francis Fukuyama's contention that history had ended because Western-style democracy was now triumphant – even if some parts of the world were lamentably slow in recognising this state of affairs – is a notorious recent instance of such Western political fundamentalism. Fukuyama can imagine no viable alternative to the Western system, merely reactionary ideologies of varying degrees of inadequacy trying to staunch the march of progress: and progress equals the West.

Political fundamentalism also announces itself in the reaction of much of the British political establishment to the European Community, which is perceived as a threat to national sovereignty; a debate intensified by the introduction of a common European currency. The fundamentals of 'Britishness' – including sterling currency – are standardly trotted out as an objection to such blurring of national boundaries, although 'Britishness' is at best a contentious concept. (In practice, Britishness often really means 'Englishness'; but I would have to declare a special interest here as a Scot, I suppose.) The conflict between 'Britishness' and 'Irishness' in Northern Ireland, with its assumption of certain fundamental character traits and attitudes, underpinned by religious division, is another apparently irresolvable dispute over political fundamentals.

Marxism provides yet another example of how resilient the fundamentalist temperament can be when confronted by a serious challenge to its authority. Despite having collapsed as a political force of any real note in Europe (indeed, the world at large, China, and at the moment North Korea, notwithstanding), Marxism still has its adherents who stick rigidly to its doctrinal principles – perhaps more rigidly than ever as an assertion of ideological identity in the face of crisis. The rise of a post-Marxist movement (heavily influenced by postmodern thought) has generated a 'back to basics' reaction from classical Marxist thinkers, who have continued to proclaim the rightness of their theory in the face of all evidence as to its systematic political failure throughout the 20th century. For these hard-liners, Marx's works are equivalent to holy writ and require no post-Marxist tinkering to make them 'relevant' to our time – they are *always* relevant.

So let's take a look at a selection of the political fundamentalisms at work in today's world, from the theocracies of Islam through to the West and what Tariq Ali has called 'the mother of all fundamentalisms', American imperialism.[1] We'll consider Britishness in more detail (plus its rather peculiar Northern Irish variant) as a mini case-study in Western democratic political fundamentalism, as well as Marxism and its internal critics, still disputing what its doctrines really mean after all these years. Along the way we'll also be exploring various attempts to counter political fundamentalism that come under the general heading of 'agonism'. Anti-fundamentalism has its supporters, as we shall see, but it would have to be said that they confront a very considerable, and well-organised, enemy.

## Religion as Politics: A Tour Through the Theocratic World

The Islamic world has several examples of theocratic, semi-theocratic, or would-be theocratic states. Now that the Taliban regime has been brought down in Afghanistan, Iran might stand as the most theocratic of the current line-up of Islamic states. The revolution there in 1979 gave an enormous amount of power to the country's religious leaders, the ayatollahs, starting with the Ayatollah Khomeini, who returned from exile to preside over a vigorous programme of re-Islamisation. There was an initial attempt to create a purist Islamic state, although internal opposition has led to a certain degree of liberalisation over the years. Fanatics aside, the Iranian people have been grudging in their acceptance of clerical rule. In consequence, Khomeini's successors have been a bit more pragmatic in their re-Islamisation policies, and there has been some attempt to increase contacts with the West. Nevertheless, as commentators like Haideh Moghissi have insisted, Iran is still a very repressive state by modern Western standards, particularly when it comes to the treatment of women. At the very least, it's deeply imbued with the social conservatism that she claims as a defining feature of re-Islamised societies.

Pakistan is more difficult to place in theocratic terms, given its political links to the West (all the more assiduously cultivated by the latter in the aftermath of the Afghanistan crisis, when Pakistan's cooperation was crucial to the success of the West's invasion). It was a state founded as a homeland for

India's very substantial Muslim population (one-time rulers of the country), which had been locked in increasingly bitter conflict with the Hindu majority in the latter stages of British imperial rule on the sub-continent. Although this suggests a religious basis, many of the leading figures involved in the Muslim League, which campaigned in British India for the creation of a separate Muslim state, were not particularly religious. In many cases they could even be called atheist (with the qualification already noted that to the Muslim authorities this is apostasy). The motivation for the creation of Pakistan was cultural rather than religious. Yet it's worth recording, as Tariq Ali reminds us, that the literal meaning of Pakistan is 'land of the pure', and Pakistani politics has from an early stage after independence become progressively more religiously inspired, with fundamentalist-minded parties much in evidence.[2] If it wasn't the land of the pure in the first instance, the fundamentalists have done their best to make it so in the interim. Fundamentalist parties have often been blocked from power by the army, however, and there's a considerable discrepancy between Pakistan's Westernised ruling élite and the more remote parts of the country, particularly the northern tribal lands adjacent to Afghanistan. These areas, largely beyond government control, are often militantly Muslim in character, and lately have become a haven for Islamic terrorists such as the Al-Qaeda movement. Bin Laden was based just over the border in Afghanistan for several years until the fall of the Taliban, and was widely thought at that time to have taken refuge in northern Pakistan. There is significant support for Islamic fundamentalism in the country, therefore, and possibly even within government and army circles.

Pakistan often gives the impression of being on the verge of becoming an Islamic fundamentalist state, which, given that it's also a nuclear power (locked in an arms race with India), is cause for considerable disquiet in the West. The United Action

Front (an alliance of fundamentalist groups) is now a significant force in both the national parliament and the country's provincial assemblies, and is very hardline in its political objectives – rule by clerics, Shari'a law, the veil, segregated education, and so on. Tariq Ali makes the danger plain when he points out that 'it is no secret that the fundamentalists have comprehensively penetrated the army. What distinguishes them from the old-style religious groups is that they want to seize state power, and for that they need the army.'[3] A terrorist attack with nuclear weapons is a truly frightening prospect: *jihad* under such conditions hardly bears thinking about. Ali also notes that fundamentalist influence is at its strongest amongst the junior officers, from where the army high command of tomorrow will be drawn: another reason for the West to view events in this area with unease. The sympathetic attitude of the Pakistani army towards the Taliban regime doesn't bode well either, with Ali claiming close links between the two groups. In his reading of the situation, Pakistan's rulers felt they had 'gained a new province' in Afghanistan, thanks to the army's work, and were displeased to see the Taliban defeated by the West.[4] The fact that Shari'a law has just been introduced in the north-west frontier provinces bordering Afghanistan is an indication of where Pakistan may be heading politically.

The West has also watched appalled as Shari'a law has been implemented in some of the Muslim states of Nigeria, despite opposition from the central government in this country with a substantial Christian minority (34%). Sentences of death by stoning for being found guilty of adultery have been passed by regional courts, provoking protest campaigns in the West. Then there was the farce of the Miss World contest in 2002, which was driven from the country after riots by Muslims over facetious remarks made by a local journalist. The remarks were to the effect that Mohammed might have been moved to choose one of the contestants as his bride, and they caused immense offence to the Nigerian Muslim community. Light-hearted asides about the Prophet are no more acceptable to Muslims than the same about Jesus would be to funda-mentalist Christians (think of the fuss that's made every time there's a film about Jesus which portrays him as a human rather than divine being, with desires and failings like the rest of us). One can understand and even sympathise with the offence taken, but not with the riots and deaths that ensued. I have no wish to defend the Miss World contest (even as an instance of postmodern irony in action, as has been suggested by some), but the Muslim response was a chilling reminder of just how little margin for tolerance there can be within a fundamentalist framework. Verbal rejoinders are one thing, riots leading to deaths something else again. The remarks merely added to an already tense political situation in the country, where Muslim identity was felt to be in need of assertion, so Miss World was in a sense just a pretext. But one suspects pretexts can always be found where there is fundamentalist fervour enough.

An ironic aspect of the whole episode is that both Islam and the Miss World contest make similar assumptions about masculinity. The difference is that Islam takes steps to protect women from male lust (the veil), hence the claims made for Islam as a pro-women religion. Women are clearly subordi-nate creatures in both cases, defined almost exclusively in terms of men's reaction to them. Islam covers you up, Miss World exposes you to the male gaze. Yet it's much the same conception of masculinity that generates the opposed responses: men are predators, women are potential victims, and that's just the way things are – deal with it. Social conservatism is a common underlying ethos, even if it's expressing itself differ-ently. The assumptions behind Miss World contests may be deeply depressing, but at least so far they don't involve riots and death – nor stoning for adultery. To Islam, however, Miss World contests are a perversion of the natural order, and cannot therefore go unopposed. The fundamentalist world has to be just so, and if women didn't expose themselves to the male gaze when the religion was being formulated, then they mustn't do so now.

The Israeli state has elements of theocracy about it as well, with the orthodox Jewish movement wielding considerable power within the political system (they are particularly strong advocates of settlement in the West Bank area, for example, probably the single most contentious aspect of Israeli government policy in recent years). Despite the fact that, as with Pakistan and the Muslim League, many of those who campaigned for the creation of Israel were technically atheists rather than religious enthusiasts, the whole notion of a Jewish state involves a fundamentalist mind-set, since it's a return of a people to the territory where their traditional belief system originated and flourished in its purest state. This is going back to basics in an ethnic, a political, a religious, and even a geographical sense, as can be seen in the ideas of the Jewish fundamentalist group Gush Emunim and their very literal interpretation of what it means to be God's Chosen People. In Gilles Kepel's analysis of the orthodox-led re-Judaisation campaign in Israel, Gush Emunim play a critical role:

> Gush took part in the politics of Israel, but never formed a party, though it did have some members elected on the ticket of parties whose aims were compatible with its own. It was most active in the Occupied Territories and Sinai, pressing for a thorough colonization so as to align the frontiers of biblical Israel with those of the longed-for kingdom of the Messiah. From this viewpoint, non-Jews had no right to the land that had been promised to the Chosen People.[5]

Israel is an attempt to recreate the past as if the history in between had not happened (and given that history, that's an entirely understandable desire). The fundamentals of Jewish identity are taken to have precedence over all other claims – and as we know, there are many such claims in this hotly disputed geographical area, where Jewish, Muslim and Christian interests collide. Israel is a democracy, and there are dissenting voices within it which oppose its policies towards the Arab world; but as the official state of Judaism it's always likely to inspire fundamentalist sentiments. Israel's electoral system of proportional representation certainly encourages fundamentalist participation in the political process. The fact that its very existence has been under threat since it was founded is a considerable incentive to adopt a fundamentalist position, where enemies are clearly defined and there is no moral ambiguity. A 'them and us' mentality is a natural by-product of Israel's geo-political situation.

If not a theocracy in the strictest sense, it can be argued that Israel is motivated in large part by theocratic ideals, since these are so much a part of Jewish identity. Ethnicity and religion are all but inseparable in this instance. As Gilles Kepel has pointed out, this has had the effect in orthodox circles of reinforcing the culture of the ghetto, with 'closed communities based on the most uncompromising observance of the *mitsvot* (the sacred duties and prohibitions)' keeping the non-Judaic world at bay, both socially and politically.[6] Israel has immense symbolic significance, and, as we have seen, is nearly as important to Christian fundamentalists as to the Jewish community worldwide. Their motives may vary, but the presence of Jews in Israel is what two of the major religious fundamentalist groups require as a matter of policy. Historical necessity demands it for Jewish and Christian fundamentalist thinkers alike; a rare example of religious fundamentalist cooperation across the monotheistic divide – although we know that it's highly pragmatic and involves radically different objectives. It might end in tears eventually, but for the time being there is unity of purpose.

## Fundamentally British

We might expect to find fundamentalist elements in theocracies or semi-theocracies, but what of the Western democracies? Secular though these are, might we detect fundamentalism expressing itself in their political systems as well? What does it mean, for example, to be British? British in the sense of being fundamentally different from any of our continental European neighbours; a feeling that our island status has served only to reinforce over the centuries. There are symbols of 'Britishness' that can be wheeled into play by interested parties, some of them serious, some of them trivial, but all of them capable of generating nationalist sentiment in certain sections of the population. There is the pound (don't be taken in by arguments for the euro!); British beef (how dare the French reject it, boycott their products in return!); even our sausages and chocolate (how dare the EC say they don't qualify as the real thing because of inadequate meat or cocoa content, they were good enough for our forebears!). It's not difficult to work up a campaign about such issues, which to many count as challenges to our sovereignty and national identity. Today the euro, tomorrow rule from Brussels, so the equation goes. In the meantime we are expected to continue munching on those sub-standard sausages and chocolates for the good of the cause, as defined by such defenders of the faith as the *Daily Mail* and *Sun* newspapers.

The first and most obvious problem with Britishness is that it's the product of four countries, each with its own specific sense of historical self-definition. Scottish, Welsh, or Irish Britishness all differ from English Britishness (and from each other, obviously). No less than any other national identity (although the degree can vary depending on geographical remoteness), Britishness has a mongrel quality to it. This is before we consider immigration, recorded or otherwise, over the centuries (a process considerably accelerated by the growth of empire), and intermarriage with the citizens of other nations – again, an activity that has been going on for centuries. Throw in a Norman invasion, popularly thought for a long time afterwards to have tainted true Englishness, and the notion of Britishness loses any sense of precision at all.* When the British National Party campaigns on behalf of Britishness, or Englishness either for that matter, we might well wonder just what it is they are defending. We know what they *think* they are defending – white, Anglo-Saxon, most likely Protestant, existence – but in terms of cultural heritage this is a nonsense. WASP identity is as mongrel as any other. There is no pure racial identity that can be called Britishness.

The politics of Britishness have to do with power, and its advocates need a fundamental national identity as part of their marketing strategy. Such an identity provides a sense of security for those worried about the encroachments of 'foreign' elements in our society: that is, anything from economic and political refugees from Eastern Europe and the Third World to the despised bureaucrats of Brussels. The political campaign waged against the European Community has traded heavily

---

* English political radicals of the 17th century were still complaining bitterly about the 'Norman yoke', and how this had destroyed Saxon society, which they regarded as their proper heritage. Thus we find the radical Gerard Winstanley asserting that 'the last enslaving conquest which the enemy got over Israel was the Norman over England', and using that as a stick with which to beat the current government: '[Y]ou still lift up that Norman yoke and slavish tyranny, and holds the people as much in bondage as the bastard Conqueror himself and his council of war.' (Gerard Winstanley, *The Law of Freedom and Other Writings* (1652), ed. Christopher Hill, Penguin, 1973, pp. 86, 87.)

on the notion of Britishness, mainly because of fears that the more we're integrated into the EC the more our sovereignty will be eroded (not to mention our beloved sausages and chocolate altered). Even if Britishness is widened past WASPishness, it's still held to involve certain cultural attitudes and lifestyles that can be differentiated clearly from those on the continent. The 'continental yoke' is to be resisted, because it disturbs the power relations in British society that interested parties wish to maintain.

## Fundamentally, There is No Alternative

One of the great exponents of political fundamentalism in British life in recent years was Margaret Thatcher, whose 'conviction politics' struck a recognisably fundamental note: a note, moreover, that resonated strongly with the wider British public – enough to keep her party in power for eighteen years. Thatcher was a response to what she saw as the cosy consensus politics of British life, where both main political parties shared a commitment to the post-war settlement with its extensive welfare-state provision (the National Health Service, etc.). In contrast to this, Thatcher and her colleagues offered an anti-consensus programme which more and more came to embrace the principles of market fundamentalism ('monetarism', as its current form was dubbed) in its search for economic 'salvation'. This time around the suspicion was to be directed against the corporate state, with the new right-wing radicalism marked by 'faith in self-help and the power of voluntary association' instead of state-sponsored action.[7] In this counter-revolution the state was to be reined back in order to allow the market to work its magic for the common good. At the root of this new radicalism lay a conception of the fundamentals of human nature that ran counter to the post-war consensus, with its commitment to collectivism and cooperation. In particular, there was the belief, straight out of the work of Adam Smith, that we were motivated above all by selfishness:

> It is not from the benevolence of the butcher, the brewer, or the baker, that we expect our dinner, but from their regard to their own interest. We address ourselves, not to their humanity but to their self-love, and never talk to them of our own necessities but of their advantages.[8]

Politics was to be returned to the basics of human nature, and that meant the encouragement of a politics of selfishness. Thatcherites took to their task with the enthusiasm of those who had seen the doctrinal light.

It was to be through market fundamentalism that we would return to the path of economic virtue, which the post-war consensus had deserted, leading to the country's progressive economic decline ('Labour Isn't Working', as the Conservatives' 1979 advertising slogan had it, with ironies it would take a few years to reveal as unemployment totals soared to record levels in modern British history under the Tories). Market fundamentalism was to be pursued almost regardless of its short-term costs, and these costs were considerable: massive increases in unemployment, the closure of large sections of Britain's traditional manufacturing industries (coal mining, ship building, steel works, etc.), and widespread civil unrest that threatened the social fabric of the nation. Conviction politics, however, was largely unmoved by the response to its policies, and regarded all opposition as dangerously close to treason. There was no alternative, the nation was told over and over again; the costs had to be borne if we were to achieve our market fundamentalist destiny. The policies had to run their course; the fundamentals had to be reasserted. Privatisation became almost a doctrinal necessity to prove one's commitment to that destiny. In Thatcher's Britain, humankind most certainly was deemed to be made for the market and not the other way round, with the market taking on an almost mystical aura in the process. The invisible hand ruled. This was the new consumer society, in which apologists could argue that 'the market is superior to the ballot box as a means of registering consumer preferences'.[9] Politics was merely market fundamentalism by other means. Sceptics could only feel doubly disenfranchised by such a turn of events.

Conviction politics changed the British political landscape, with the incoming New Labour government of 1997 accepting the broad principles of market fundamentalism no less than their Conservative opponents had done. This was taken to be simply the way of the world, with which even socialists had to comply. Even privatisation was allowed to be defensible, reversing some of the movement's deepest-held doctrinal beliefs, and private encroachment into the public sector continued unchecked. The profit motive was no longer necessarily suspect, suggesting that the radical right's back to basics campaign on behalf of selfishness had been largely successful in capturing the public imagination. Peter Mandelson could hardly have been more explicit on this issue, informing a group of American executives during a visit to California's Silicon Valley in 1998 that he and his colleagues in the New Labour government were 'intensely relaxed about people getting filthy rich'.[10] The socially reforming 1945 Labour government had faded away to a distant memory. There is no indication as yet that the politics of selfishness has lost its popular support, recent market instability and dotcom bubbles notwithstanding. We are still living without an alternative.

## Fundamentally No Surrender

Northern Ireland provides a particularly stark example of opposing political fundamentalisms in action. Here we find

Britishness, as espoused by the Ulster Unionist Party, confronting Irishness, as espoused by the Republican movement, with each side convinced that their fundamentalism holds the key to sovereignty. Neither side is willing to concede very much to the other, because to do so would be to endanger the purity of their own position, and, by extension, their very culture. Extremist groups even more protective of the opposing cultures lie in wait to take advantage of any significant move towards compromise by the main political parties; a state of affairs which has helped to stall the peace process initiated some years ago by the British government. Religion is, to put it mildly, a complicating factor in the political set-up. Northern Ireland Protestantism is of a generally antagonistic disposition (best represented, perhaps, in the person of the Reverend Ian Paisley, theologian and rabble-rousing politician simultaneously), and little inclined towards negotiation with opponents, whom it's all too likely to regard as representatives of the Antichrist. The Manicheans, it would seem, are always with us. The old political slogan of 'no surrender' really means something in this context. You cannot surrender what you consider to be fundamental principles: it's like giving up your birthright. And so the 'Northern Ireland problem' drags on, with no particular end in sight, much to the bemusement, and bafflement, of the mainland British population.

The Britishness that's being defended in this struggle is unrecognisable to much of that mainland population, which only goes to point up the spuriousness of the whole concept. We need to push past the concept itself to its underlying objective, which has little to do with nationalism as such. It is to maintain in power a majority group whose identity is heavily based on theology: a theology which leans towards a fundamentalist interpretation. As with other fundamentalisms, this one is exclusion-minded. Pluralism, which in this context means holding other religious beliefs, doesn't apply.

Being Protestant is a fundamental requirement, and carries with it a historical consciousness, and set of historical commitments, stretching back to the 17th century and the Battle of the Boyne. The inerrancy of the Protestant faith is a matter of doctrine. Even a Protestant atheist is preferable to a Catholic for this political establishment, because the chances are that s/he will have a stake in that historical consciousness and those historical commitments as well. All attempts at bridging this divide tend to fall foul of the extremists eventually (it's hard to know at any one point whether the peace process is still in play or not). The fundamentals of this political position are jealously, and zealously, guarded.

One could argue that the Irishness being fought for in Northern Irish politics is just as spurious conceptually as its Britishness, although it's possibly less fundamentalist in character. A religion lies behind it as well, Catholicism, but it's not quite as exclusion-oriented as its Protestant counterpart. Republicanism doesn't depend on religion to the same extent that the Unionist movement does. Having said that, republicanism is fundamentally opposed to Britishness – of any variety, Unionist or otherwise. There is yet another charmed circle in operation, with its own set of fundamentals to be protected against outsiders.

## Fundamentally Western

Britain is simply one Western democracy, but some see the West itself as the most fundamental of political systems. Francis Fukuyama's claim, in his controversial book *The End of History and the Last Man* (1992), that we were witnessing the historic victory of Western liberal democratic ideology in our time, is a high-profile example of this kind of thinking. Fukuyama was writing in the immediate aftermath of the collapse of the Soviet empire, so his triumphalist views are perhaps not too surprising. There *was* a feeling of triumph in Western political circles at the time, and to many observers Fukuyama merely seemed to be stating the obvious: that the West had won hands down. Communism was vanquished, and it hadn't even required a war to achieve this. Russia and its satellite states appeared to be embracing the capitalist system, and, at least on paper, its political structures as well. The IMF and the World Bank were on hand to offer their advice on how best to make the transition from communism to capitalism (a very mixed blessing as it turned out). The future was Western, and Fukuyama was its most ardent advocate. One might think that the rise of Islamic fundamentalism in the interim period, culminating in the 9/11 attacks on America, would have sown some seeds of doubt in Fukuyama's mind as to his earlier conclusions, but, as we'll see, his perspective on global history remains unaltered. Fukuyama clings to his own rock-hard certainties with no less tenacity than a religious fundamentalist.

The supposed triumph of Western liberal democracy marks for Fukuyama the beginning of the political millennium, in which all the contradictions of humankind's history are resolved. There are clear echoes of Christian Right fundamentalism in his historical overview, with its strong sense of destiny. He is dismissive of the claims of all other political systems, which in his analysis have been superseded by Western democracy, the true end of all humankind's strivings. It's worth quoting Fukuyama's somewhat poetic musings on this process at some length, in order to get the full flavour of his Western fundamentalism:

> Rather than a thousand shoots blossoming into as many different flowering plants, mankind will come to seem like a long wagon train strung out along a road. Some wagons will be pulling into town sharply and crisply, while others

will be bivouacked back in the desert, or else, stuck in ruts in the final pass over the mountains. Several wagons, attacked by Indians, will have been set aflame and abandoned along the way. There will be a few wagoneers who, stunned by the battle, will have lost their sense of direction and are temporarily heading in the wrong direction, while one or two wagons will get tired of the journey and decide to set up permanent camps at particular points back along the road. Others will have found alternative routes to the main road, though they will discover that to get through the final mountain range they all must use the same pass. But the great majority of wagons will be making the slow journey into town, and most will eventually arrive there.[11]

So this was the 'end of history', with all ideologies converging on 'the same pass' on their way into the promised land (California, by the sound of it – cue some surfing music). It wasn't just the West that had won; it was the American dream.

Fukuyama has little time for cultural relativism, which he regards as a European invention designed to assuage the guilt left behind by colonialism. Colonialism is glossed over quickly in his account, the assumption being that it's entirely natural for all societies to gravitate towards the Western political model. In true fundamentalist fashion, Fukuyama looks forward to 'the homogenization of mankind'.[12] No religious fundamentalist could put it better: goodbye difference, goodbye dissent, hello conformity. Having said that, socialists will have to admit that somewhere in the background of their political programmes there lurks a similar commitment. Universal values assume homogenisation on issues such as women's rights, and these clash with the notion of cultural relativism. The minute one strays away from scepticism, it would seem, fundamentalism comes into play. For Fukuyama no such problem comes to mind. He has seen the future, and it's Western – and he's delighted with it.

The future being Western means that we have arrived at the end of history, which in this reading means the end of clashing civilisations, the history that our history books regale us with, in which empire fights empire in monotonous succession. Political systems based on hereditary monarchy, fascism, and communism have all failed, leaving liberal democracy holding the field. Fukuyama can imagine no other system challenging liberal democracy, certainly not in the public esteem, and he regards it as the highest expression of humankind's social and political being. The fundamentalist cast to his thought comes through strongly at such points: liberal democracy is our destiny, and only a fool would fail to recognise, and welcome, this state of affairs. For Fukuyama, the millennium has come and salvation is at hand. Humanity at large is invited to become born-again liberal democrats.

Post-9/11, Fukuyama became embroiled in arguments with critics who claimed that the growth of Islamic fundamentalism called his theories into question. 9/11 was proof to critics that history hadn't ended, but was still very much with us. Civilisations patently were clashing, whether Fukuyama wanted to admit so or not: 'the civilization of man against the civilization of God',[13] as one Muslim activist conceived of it.* Fukuyama, however, remained unrepentant, and more than willing to defend the rock-hard certainties of his Western fundamentalism against all comers:

---

* Omar Bakri. Bakri, who to be fair seems far less dangerous in person than his pronouncements and activities would suggest, was also responsible for a poster campaign in London and Birmingham proclaming that 'The Final Hour Will Not Come Until the Muslims Kill the Jews' (quoted in Jon Ronson, *Them: Adventures with Extremists*, Picador, 2002, pp. 286–7). The Jews have a lot to look forward to, come the millennium.

I believe that in the end I remain right: modernity is a very powerful freight train that will not be derailed by recent events. ... We remain at the end of history because there is only one system that will continue to dominate world politics, that of the liberal-democratic west. This does not imply a world free from conflict, nor the disappearance of culture. But the struggle we face is not the clash of several distinct and equal cultures fighting amongst one another like the great powers of 19th-century Europe. The clash consists of a series of rearguard actions from societies whose traditional existence is indeed threatened by modernisation. The strength of the backlash reflects the severity of the threat. But time is on the side of modernity, and I see no lack of US will to prevail.[14]

It's the standard fundamentalist claim: that one's opponents simply haven't seen the light yet. And the standard fundamentalist response: we won't give up, we shall prevail. It's a temperament seemingly impervious to setback.

It might seem that Fukuyama is less in thrall to the past than the average religious fundamentalist, but his commitment to modernity and modernisation already *is* a commitment to the past for those bitten by the postmodern bug. Fukuyama is defending a cultural lifestyle which many feel has already passed its sell-by date. For postmodern thinkers, modernity and modernisation are the problem, not the solution to the world's current woes (think of the green movement's warnings of imminent ecological disaster if the cult of technological progress is allowed to continue unhindered, for example, as in the hole that has appeared in the earth's ozone layer). Fukuyama is in his own little time warp zone, where scepticism is prohibited. This is the blinkered vision of the fundamentalist thinker protecting the purity of his theory: 'I believe that in the end I remain right.'

## Agonising over Alternatives

As I pointed out at the beginning of the chapter, there are anti-fundamentalist voices to take account of as well, and we'll consider some of the most prominent of these in this section. In sharp contrast to Fukuyama's end-of-history notion is the theory of agonism propounded by both William Connolly and Chantal Mouffe. Here, the notion of an inevitable, and desirable, convergence of all parties is rejected in favour of an adversarial politics. In Mouffe's survey of the contemporary Western political scene, this is what is signally missing:

> Nowadays politics operates supposedly on a neutral terrain and solutions are available that could satisfy everybody. Relations of power and their constitutive role in society are obliterated and the conflicts that they entail reduced to a simple competition of interests that can be harmonized through dialogue. This is the typical liberal perspective that envisages democracy as a competition among elites, making adversary forces invisible and reducing politics to an exchange of arguments and the negotiation of compromises.[15]

For Mouffe, on the other hand, there can be no democracy where there is no adversary:

> the specificity of modern democracy lies in the recognition and the legitimation of conflict and the refusal to suppress it through the imposition of an authoritarian order. A well-functioning democracy calls for a confrontation between democratic political positions, and this requires a real debate about possible alternatives.[16]

It's just such a debate that the school of Fukuyama is denying is necessary any more. Adversaries there are simply those benighted souls who haven't yet recognised that history really has ended, whereas for Mouffe they are the difference between democracy and tyranny. In her reading, the more consensus we have, the less democracy: there is effectively a calculus in operation (and for consensus read conformity). When the political system provides no basis for conflict in its agonistic guise, it soon finds antagonistic expression, to the disbenefit of all. Extreme right-wing parties in particular thrive in such contexts, tapping into the antagonism that builds up in the absence of real political debate and exploiting it for their own nefarious ends.

The way forward for Mouffe is the condition of 'agonistic pluralism' (a term she takes over from Connolly),[17] in which dissent is not just tolerated but actively encouraged for the health of society. She sees liberal democracy as made up of two conflicting traditions: those concerned with liberty (human rights) and those with equality (social and economic as well as political). Liberalism is currently in the ascendancy in the Western democracies, and its drive is towards consensus and an eradication of dissent – exactly what Zygmunt Bauman was worried about in the aftermath of communism's collapse. That is what agonistic pluralism is designed to counter. There must always be a tension between these two traditions, Mouffe contends, without one ever being allowed to swamp the other. That's simply a paradox we must live with, that the two cannot be reconciled. All attempts at reconciliation merely dilute democracy and bring fundamentalism ever closer to the mainstream. The other side to liberalism is the authoritarianism of an equality-biased system such as Marxism, which Mouffe, as one of the leading voices of post-Marxism, is just as concerned to avoid any drift towards. Only if there is openly conducted conflict between liberal democracy's two major sources will right-wing populism be kept at bay: 'A well-functioning democracy calls for a vibrant clash of democratic political positions.'[18] Such vibrant clashes are what fundamentalists of all persuasions – religious, market, and political – set out to expunge from their world, where consensus, forced or otherwise, is the target. Fukuyama is little different from Osama bin Laden in this regard; neither wants adversaries, both want unanimity (although I will concede that unanimity is more aggressively sought by bin Laden than Fukuyama). Mouffe also finds disturbing evidence of the anti-adversarial approach in New Labour's commitment to 'Third Way' politics.

The problem in Mouffe's scheme is keeping both sides committed to the paradox, as well as preventing those vibrant clashes from lapsing into open antagonism. The desire to overcome one's opponent is deeply embedded in the political psyche, and it can be quite ruthless in its methods – eliminate the alternative. Agonistic pluralism is something of a balancing act that requires mutual respect – not a commodity in plentiful supply in the fundamentalist camp. The left has been no better at accepting this paradox as a fact of political life than the right, and doesn't regard its most cherished beliefs as mere debating positions for pluralists to work over. There is a defensiveness about Mouffe's pro-democratic outlook, with the democrats she sides with apparently reduced to preventing the liberals from gaining even more of an ascendancy than they have at present. 'Stop things getting even worse' is not the most inspiring of campaign slogans for the idealistic left, and demonstrates how far it has fallen from grace in recent times. To some extent this is because it has lost the authority of Marxism, long since discredited as a fundamentalism itself. It's no longer there to fall back upon for moral justification for one's political programmes, a *real* alternative to market fundamentalism, and the left is very aware of the resulting vacuum in the realm of ideas. What Mouffe is attempting to do is to construct a non-fundamentalist position on the left, and that entails acknowledging the validity of one's adversaries and espousing a notion of democracy far removed from the 'people's democracy' of Marxist political practice, where opposition was treated as treason.

This is a painful transition for the left to make, and requires a considerable readjustment of its traditional socio-political vision – more, perhaps, than it's realistic to expect in the current cultural climate. Old habits die hard on the fundamentalist left, as we'll see, and the spread of market fundamentalism doesn't exactly stimulate a desire for debate. The far left is clearly playing catch-up on the economic front at the moment, and if anything this provokes a reversion to fundamentals. The beleaguered do tend to go back to basics. Marxists are trained to defend their doctrines to the last, and have an almost pathological attachment to their system of belief, which for them has historical necessity on its side. Instead of the drive towards purity, whether of liberty or equality, Mouffe offers 'the never-ending interrogation of the political by the ethical'.[19] This will no doubt sound defeatist to much of the left, since it seems to preclude any ultimate triumph of their ideas, but for Mouffe it's a necessary precondition for democracy to flourish. There has to be conflict of interest to keep each side honest, since the natural inclination of each is to do what it can to put the other out of business. Mouffe is to be congratulated for trying to keep debate going on the nature of democracy, even if it has no more justification behind it for the time being than to curb the excesses of the liberals. As with scepticism, that is at least a starting point from which to deal with the fundamentalist menace.

William Connolly is equally suspicious of consensus politics and the motives lying behind it, as his theory of 'agonistic democracy' makes clear:

Agonistic democracy breaks with the democratic idealism of communitarianism through its refusal to equate concern for human dignity with a quest for rational consensus. It opens political spaces for agonistic relations of adversarial respect. Democratic agonism does not exhaust social space; it leaves room for other modalities of attachment and detachment. But it does disrupt consensual ideals of political engagement and aspiration. It insists that one significant way to support human dignity is to cultivate agonistic respect between interlocking and contending constituencies.[20]

Consensus politics is intrinsically anti-democratic in this reading, with Connolly arguing that we have to both promote and respect difference if we want democracy to thrive. It's wrong either to suppress difference or to treat it as a threat to one's own identity such that we come to consider it as evil. That means we're faced with the 'paradox of difference':[21] difference is at once necessary to politics, and the generator of some of its most undesirable features. All too often we 'convert differences into otherness and otherness into scapegoats created and maintained to secure the appearance of a true identity'.[22] That's certainly how nationalist fundamentalism functions, demonising the 'other' (these days usually in the guise of immigrants from the Third World), as we'll go on to see in Chapter 7.

Jean-François Lyotard is another major theorist committed to the notion of agonism. In *The Postmodern Condition* he argues the case for what he calls 'little narratives'; that is, pressure groups who take on the might of universal political theories (those 'grand narratives' we mentioned at the beginning of the book). Lyotard envisages something like permanent guerilla warfare in order to undermine the authority of universal theories, and he is as wary of consensus as Connolly and Mouffe. He sings the praises of 'dissensus' instead, regarding this as a critical element of an anti-authoritarian postmodern society. Lyotard is as concerned as Mouffe to prevent the resistance movement from turning into a fundamentalism in its own right, and thinks that little narratives should dissolve once they have achieved their particular objective. Lyotard's ideal would be one-off campaigns against specific abuses perpetrated by governments or multinationals; in effect, what Americans call 'issue politics', which can generate 'rainbow coalitions' cutting across existing party lines and social hierarchies. Ecological issues create the right kind of conditions for little narratives to thrive. Lyotard was himself involved in just such political actions during the 1968 *événements* in Paris, when workers and students ganged up on the French government with some success. Little narratives must not become permanent group-ings, but instead be responses to problems as they arise. If they turn into political parties on the old model, with an executive and a set of doctrines to defend, then they assume an authority that all too likely will mutate into authoritarianism (a crucial step towards fundamentalism).

The weak point of all these theories is that they don't tell us what to do when the opponent chooses not to respect the paradoxes. What if those adversaries spurn the 'real debate about possible alternatives' that Mouffe invites them to participate in? If our opponents were all committed to the principles of agonistic pluralism, then we would have had no problem to address in the first place. When it comes to fundamentalism, of any variety, that's clearly not so, and the desire to eliminate the alternative is always to the fore. Rather like Bunyan's Celestial City in *The Pilgrim's Progress*, agonistic pluralism is the destination we would dearly like to reach, the promised land for sceptics, dissenters and supporters of difference alike. For the moment, however, we're still stuck in the wilderness of fundamentalism surrounded by largely unrepentant neo-liberals like Fukuyama, for whom agonistic pluralism is a delusion and consensus the solution to all our political problems. We can only go on resisting, but that means our politics are forced into the antagonistic shape that fundamentalism prefers. Eco-terrorism is one, rather despairing, response to a culture which isn't providing the proper basis for an adversarial politics, or Mouffe's 'never-ending interrogation of the political by the ethical'; but that way, as we'll go on to see in Chapter 8, not just antagonism but fundamentalism lies. When you have to resort to terrorism to make your points, the political battle is half lost already. No matter how worthy your cause, much of your potential support will most likely become alienated, and it will be only the hard-core fundamentalists who rally round. We then end up with yet another clash of fundamentalisms rather than the agonistic pluralism that would guarantee all voices being heard – although whether that idealistic state can ever be achieved for any length of time is highly debatable.

One of the critics to recognise the fundamentalist cast to Fukuyama's theories was the French deconstructionist philosopher Jacques Derrida, who proceeded to castigate the American thinker in his book *Specters of Marx*:

> it must be cried out, at a time when some have the audacity to neo-evangelize in the name of the ideal of a liberal democracy that has finally realized itself as the ideal of human history: never have violence, inequality, exclusion, famine, and thus economic oppression affected as many human beings in the history of the earth and of humanity.[23]

Fukuyama is that neo-evangelist, speaking in language reminiscent of the Christian Right, and pointedly ignoring all evidence that contradicts his theory. Derrida goes on to inform us of the shortcomings of liberal democracy, holding it responsible for most of the ills of the contemporary world. Whatever thinkers like Fukuyama may say, liberal democracy falls far short of its ideals; it is instead in 'a state of dysfunction in what we call the Western democracies', and has no moral right to dictate to the rest of the world.[24] But fundamentalists, as we know, can always blame humanity for such discrepancies between the real and the ideal; the theory itself is assumed to lie beyond fault.

Derrida's book was also an attempt to resurrect Marx for a postmodern age, where the accent would be on developing Marx's thought rather than blindly following it as if it were a fundamentalist creed. Marx was to be reinvented as 'plural'; that is, as a system capable of generating new interpretations that would help us to address the socio-political problems of our own day: 'this will be our hypothesis or rather our bias: *there is more than one of them, there must be more than one of them*'.[25] Marx was no longer to be read as a set body of ideas, but as a source of inspiration for creative social and political thought now. As another thinker put it, it was time to create a 'postmodern Marx' freed from his fundamentalist-minded supporters, since their impact had been 'to discourage any further engagement between the reader and Marx, and to leave the issues that he raised firmly in the past'.[26] *Specters of Marx* was a contribution, therefore, to the growing literature of post-Marxism, and it's to that anti-fundamentalist movement that we turn our attention next.

## Why Do Marxists Hate Post-Marxists?

Although its supporters will vehemently deny it, Marxism is at heart a fundamentalist doctrine. It demands a high level of conformity in its adherents in this respect. To be a Marxist is to be asked to accept certain key principles that are taken to be beyond question – principles such as history being the history of class struggle, and of there being a dialectic at work within it that's leading towards the ultimate victory of the working class and the establishment of the 'dictatorship of the proletariat'. Particularly in the Western Marxist tradition, there has been much debate on the form that class struggle should take and on the nature of the dialectic, as well as what's really meant by the dictatorship of the proletariat, but anyone daring to raise doubts about the validity of the concepts themselves soon finds out just how sacred these are to the true believers. Opponents soon discover, too, just how little room there is for dissent within the Marxist camp. There are such things as party lines, and anyone refusing to follow these courts expulsion from the movement, as well as vilification from the faithful. Writing about infighting in the Communist Party in France in the later 1940s, when the Party was a very significant presence in French political life, Jean-Paul Sartre observed that 'the opponent is never answered; he is discredited':[27] a comment which neatly sums up what happens when a dissident takes on the hierarchy in such an organisation. The 'absolute imperative to eliminate' competitors is not slow to express itself in such situations. Further, as Sartre notes, the opponent is discredited in the service of a Manichean world view which demands slavish adherence to Marxist doctrine: no latitude is allowed for individual scepticism.

It could be any fundamentalist movement at all that Sartre is talking about: much the same reaction can be expected from the dominant group towards dissidents (or even apparent dissidents – fundamentalists take no chances in such matters). Dissent will never be tolerated for long, agonistic pluralism not being a communist ideal, and the movement will do whatever is necessary to protect its power base. Individuals don't count for much in totalitarian systems, and will be sacrificed for the supposed common good – as determined by the keepers of the flame. For fundamentalists, when their belief system is threatened, the political is personal. We might also note too, harking back to Fukuyama, that Marxists assume both the possibility and the desirability of the 'homogenisation of mankind'. Conformity is an ideal here no less than it is in a religious fundamentalist context.

Post-Marxists have set about challenging some of the most basic tenets of Marxist doctrine. The leading theorists of post-Marxism are Ernesto Laclau and Chantal Mouffe, and it was their book *Hegemony and Socialist Strategy* (1985) that put the movement on the map, and ruffled the feathers of the Western Marxist tradition in doing so. Laclau and Mouffe dared to claim that after decades of setbacks in the political domain, Marxist doctrine was in serious need of re-examination and revision:

> Left-wing thought today stands at a crossroads. The 'evident truths' of the past – the classical forms of analysis and political calculation, the nature of the forces in conflict, the very meaning of the Left's struggles and objectives – have been seriously challenged by an avalanche of historical mutations which have riven the ground on which those truths are constituted. Some of these mutations doubtless correspond to failures and disappointments: from Budapest to Prague and the Polish coup d'etat, from Kabul to the sequels of the Communist victory in Vietnam and Cambodia, a question-mark has fallen more and more heavily over a whole way of conceiving both socialism and the roads that should lead to it.[28]

What Laclau and Mouffe suggested as a remedy was that Marxists should align themselves with the various new social movements that had been emerging around the globe; movements which didn't conform to the classical Marxist idea of revolutionary movements, but which, nevertheless, were challenging the entrenched power structures of the day on behalf of the oppressed. By this they meant ethnic, anti-colonialist, ecological, sexual, and gender-based movements: greens, gays, feminists, etc. (the anti-corporatists so glowingly written up in Naomi Klein's *No Logo* are a more recent version of the phenomenon). Their objective was to renew Marxist theory by opening it out to changes in late-20th-century culture, to become, as they styled it, post-Marxist in outlook (Derrida was one of those who took on board Laclau and Mouffe's ideas, in *Specters of Marx*).

The response that Laclau and Mouffe received soon disabused them of the idea that their intended revision of an entire intellectual tradition could be done without bitter controversy.[29] The Marxist establishment in Britain and America was quick to denounce the two as traitors to the cause, and the tone of their criticism was quite vicious:

> And then there is the exact meaning in which they may be said now to be 'beyond' Marxism. At the point in time, thought and politics they have so far reached, the post-Marxist tag no doubt has a nicer ring to Laclau and Mouffe's ears than would the alternative, 'ex-Marxist'. It evokes an idea of forward movement rather than a change of colours, what purports to be an advance or progress[.] ... My contention will be that at the heart of this post-Marxism there is an intellectual vacuum.[30]

The discrediting machine was already moving into high gear. Laclau and Mouffe were made to appear opportunistic, mere slaves to current intellectual fashion without any argument of real substance to their name. The vitriolic exchanges went on for some years.

Laclau and Mouffe were to be treated as apostates: 'exes' who had turned their back on the truth. There may have been setbacks for the Marxist cause, increasingly so as the 20th century drew to a close, but these were not to be ascribed to any shortcomings in Marxist theory itself. It was a case of 'forget Budapest, Prague, Kabul' (and all the others); we simply had to go back to the original texts and study them all the harder to find the right course of action to correct the setbacks. The answers were there if we knew how to look for them. Humanity had failed, not the belief system; there was no need to go back to the drawing board. It was the classic fundamentalist response to dissent: a refusal to concede that there was any real problem to be addressed at all.

After considering the arguments of their critics, Laclau and Mouffe went on to declare that theirs was a 'Post-Marxism Without Apologies', and that they wouldn't be backing down:

> We believe that, by clearly locating ourselves in a post-Marxist terrain, we not only help to clarify the meaning of contemporary social struggles, but also give to Marxism its theoretical dignity, which can only proceed from recognition of its limitations and of its historicality. Only through such recognition will Marx's work remain present in our tradition and our political culture.[31]

Fundamentalists are not, however, very receptive to the notion of limitations, nor to their belief system having to be updated to take account of historical change. Post-Marxism made no more sense to this group than the idea of post-Christianity would to the Christian Right, or post-Islam to the Muslim faithful. How could you ever be 'post' the 'truth'?

What post-Marxism was suggesting was that class struggle had to be reinterpreted in the light of cultural change, and that what made sense in a 19th-century context didn't necessarily do so now. Marxism had to adapt, doctrine had to adapt, paradoxes had to be acknowledged. The notion of class had become much less precise over the years, and had to be re-thought – otherwise we were fighting yesterday's battles (another post-Marxist thinker, even more blasphemously, was proclaiming the imminent death of the working class in this period and attracting the same kind of opprobrium from the Marxist faithful for daring to do so).[32] There was still an 'us' and 'them', but they were much more fluid than classical Marxist theory had claimed, and perhaps they even changed sides depending on the particular cultural battle being fought. It was Manicheanism for a postmodern world: shifting, imprecise, lacking edges. It was also something of a make-work scheme for cultural theorists, who were required to analyse each cultural conflict on its own merits before pro-nouncing on its place in the revolutionary scheme of things (Mouffe's 'never-ending interrogation' in operation). Nothing was clear-cut any more, and it was no longer enough to spout the approved Marxist doctrines like a fundamentalist mantra.

Post-Marxism set out to be local, tactical, open-minded and open-ended: all the things that a universal theory like Marxism felt compromised its integrity. Marxism was being challenged as to whether it could overcome its fundamentalist past and apparent fundamentalist bias, but the challenge was rebuffed by the Marxist establishment, for whom it could only be condemned as the work of ex- or even anti-Marxists. Dialogue was ruled out in favour of invective directed at the would-be reformers, and a restatement of the fundamentals of the creed: all too common a fundamentalist response when the power base is threatened in any way. There is a reflex reaction to antagonistically inclined systems at such points.

# More Fundamentalist Than Thou:
# The Christian Right

We conclude our survey of political fundamentalism with some reflections on America, a state where religion and politics interact in ways that can appear almost theocratic viewed from a Western European perspective. There is the case of the American Christian Right, for example, which has turned to politics as the most effective way of expounding its belief system, and has had considerable success in both local and national terms. While it cannot be said to control the Republican Party, many commentators have argued that it has come to possess something of a veto over its policy-making; there is what Will Hutton calls 'a Faustian pact' between the two.[33] Republican presidents and presidential candidates are very careful not to offend the Christian Right, whose support can be crucial in national elections. We're still somewhat bemused in Britain to hear of such phenomena as prayer breakfasts (even the Democrats do this, as in the case of Bill Clinton trying to atone for the sins of Monicagate), as well as the mawkish and sentimental tone in which American politicians speak of religion or invoke God's help for their endeavours. Although some tentative moves have been made in that direction of late by both of Britain's major political parties, particularly the Conservatives under Iain Duncan Smith, most British politicians do not, as the saying goes, 'do God' (full support from sceptics there, with a watchful eye to be kept on all such reactionary trends). But maintaining an outward appearance of evangelical piety is an essential part of American political existence, and nowhere more so than in the Republican Party. With an estimated 20% of the population subscribing to Christian Right views, this isn't a constituency the Republican Party can afford to ignore, particularly given the disproportionate numbers of the Christian Right who

167

become activists within the Party. No American politician, and especially no Republican politician, can ever take the risk of being thought to be 'working for Satan': not with so many 'real suspicious people' around in his party monitoring his every statement for traces of apostasy. If you're going to err, make sure you err on the side of piety.

Although not all the Christian Right could be described as card-carrying fundamentalists (evangelicals can be much more pragmatic about doctrinal matters), fundamentalism is clearly a huge presence within the movement. Nor is this a recent phenomenon; Richard Hofstadter was expressing disquiet about 'the effects of a resurgent fundamentalism on secular politics' in America as long ago as 1966, arguing that this was a major factor in the development of a 'paranoid style' of political discourse marked by 'the spirit of ascetic Protestantism'.[34] Ascetic Protestantism encourages a very narrow social vision heavily dependent on rock-hard certainties by which to plot one's course through life. Commentators have remarked how this spills over into the political domain, where we find a 'very literal, fundamentalist interpretation' of the American Constitution being favoured by the 'Radical Right'.[35] It's just such an interpretation that has inspired the development of the militia movement, as we shall be investigating in Chapter 7. Suffice to say for the time being that it's in the militia movement that Hofstadter's paranoid style finds its fullest expression and most committed exponents. When it comes to suspicion of others, the militias know few peers in today's world. They consider themselves to be confronted by a vast conspiracy, possibly organised by the United Nations, determined to enslave the American people. Even the American government itself is probably part of this conspiracy, hence the movement's obsession with guns to protect their constitutional rights. More than somewhat paradoxically, the complaint here is of a *lack* of a Western political triumph.

## 'The Mother of All Fundamentalisms'

The Radical Right notwithstanding, most commentators do see the West as by some measure the major power bloc of our time, although not all of them are happy about this state of affairs. Like Zygmunt Bauman, Tariq Ali bemoans the fact that the triumph of the West has left the rest of the world without a real political alternative around which to organise. More specifically, it's the triumph of America that he's worried about. The geo-political and cultural dominance that America exerts constitutes for Ali an 'imperialist fundamentalism', and is the gravest threat facing the world today. It is imperialist fundamentalism that has inspired the resurgence of Islamic fundamentalism in our own time, Ali contends, and that remains its most effective recruiting agent. To those who refuse to accept that America is now the only game left in town, there's nowhere else to turn. Ali is at one with Akbar S. Ahmed in believing that fundamentalism begets fundamentalism. Despite his staunchly professed atheism (he claims the 'unbeliever's gene'),[36] Ali is at pains to insist that Islam need not be a fundamentalist creed, and that for most of its history it has not been. Fundamentalism is for him a distortion of what is best in Islam, and masks its considerable cultural diversity: '[T]he world of Islam has not been monolithic for over a thousand years. The social and cultural differences between Senegalese, Chinese, Indonesian, Arab and South Asian Muslims are far greater than the similarities they share with non-Muslim members of the same community.'[37] For all his fears of the possibility of a fundamentalist regime coming to power in a nuclear-armed Pakistan, Ali is fairly sanguine about the extent of the terrorist threat posed by Islamic fundamentalism, arguing that: 'I think that Osama and his group have reached a political dead-end. It was a grand spectacle, but nothing more. ... It will be a footnote in the history of this century. Nothing more.'[38] (As I write, the headline news is of a terrorist attack in Riyadh, Saudi Arabia, that has left 29 dead and 194 wounded. The attacks were all in Western compounds of the city, and Al-Qaeda is the prime suspect. Ali's assessment seems somewhat premature: Al-Qaeda hasn't accepted that it has reached a political dead-end yet, nor that its actions constitute a mere footnote to the history of our period. Contrast Ali's views, too, with those of the Al-Qaeda expert Rohan Gunaratna, for whom '[t]he global fight against Al Qaeda will be the defining conflict of the early 21st century'.[39]) Far more dangerous, in Ali's opinion, is American imperialist fundamentalism. This 'mother of all fundamentalisms', as he dubs it, infiltrates into almost every corner of the global political scene – and always to deleterious effect as far as local cultural values are concerned. For all his atheism, Ali comes close to the Islamic fundamentalist view of America as the 'Great Satan' from which only evil can be expected.

Ali's vision of imperialist fundamentalism is of a vast conspiracy which is systematically moving towards its goal of world domination, ruthlessly eliminating all competitors as it goes. He also regards it as deeply hypocritical, espousing democracy at home (at least in theory) but not abroad. America's client states in the Third World over the last few decades have had a depressing tendency to be dictatorships, often of a decidedly militaristic character. As long as the regimes in question were anti-communist, America was happy to turn a blind eye to their failings on such matters as human rights and free elections, which meant that states like Pakistan and Saudi Arabia could retain American support despite the endemic corruption of their political élites and their incorrigibly cynical attitude towards democratic principles and institutions. Pakistan has had a series of military dictatorships since independence, with democratic principles and institutions in suspension more often than they have been in operation. It's also worth remembering that Saddam Hussein's regime in Iraq had American backing up until the Gulf War of 1991, and that Islamic fundamentalism was exploited by America to help bring down the communist government in Afghanistan. That the Taliban might never have come to power without the boost provided by imperialist fundamentalism is an irony not lost on thinkers like Ali. Since his book was written we have had the American-led war against Iraq, which has generated a movement amongst Shia clergy there to establish a hard-line Islamic state on the Iranian model as a replacement for Saddam Hussein's regime. Fundamentalism reaps what it sows, and it's by no means clear at the moment how America will be able to keep the lid on this new outbreak of Islamic fundamentalist fervour. It wanted regime change, and now it's being offered just that, with extra added irony.

If there's hypocrisy regarding democracy abroad on the part of imperialist fundamentalists, that doesn't necessarily mean democratic ideals are being upheld at home either. Imperialist fundamentalism has its power élites as well, and can manipulate democratic institutions to its own advantage when so required. George Bush's disputed presidential victory in 2000, with his brother Jeb a key player in helping him win through the appeal process set up against him by his opponents in Florida, where Jeb Bush just happened to be Governor, is evidence enough of that. To much of the outside world this looked no less questionable than Third World election practices which it had traditionally been encouraged to condemn (especially by America, in its moral high ground pose as defender of the democratic ideal). With his Marxist background, Ali is deeply sceptical of the motives of the imperialist fundamentalist establishment in general. It's just that the Third World brings that establishment's hypocrisy out into the open, where its *realpolitik* becomes painfully obvious to friend and foe alike.

Ali's solution to the stranglehold that fundamentalism has come to exert over global Islamic culture is an Islamic Reformation, in which, as in the Christian version, traditional doctrine could be challenged, publicly debated, and even altered. Ahmed, as we have seen in Chapter 5, called for something similar, as did Ziauddin Sardar (see Chapter 4); in other words, for a move from *taqlid* to *ijtihad* so that Islam could move forward. Ali feels that the Reformation was a positive event in Western culture, which opened up the possibility of the Enlightenment. As he argues in a letter to a friend, to pass up this opportunity is to condemn the Islamic world 'to re-living old battles' on into the indefinite future.[40] One wonders whether the Christian Reformation is quite as desirable a phenomenon as Ali thinks, however, since it gave rise to Protestant fundamentalism as well as to the Enlightenment and modernity. It also gave birth to the Counter-Reformation, which has helped Catholicism to survive through to our own time with most of its hierarchical and doctrinal structures still largely intact. Nor has the Catholic Church gone on to embrace scepticism as a result of the emergence of a Protestant adversary: it still regards itself as the only true religion, and harbours hopes of drawing Protestants back into the fold. Protestant fundamentalism learned well from its predecessor in this respect: fundamentalist attitudes are deeply engrained in the Christian tradition.

Ali seems to suggest that the advent of the Enlightenment and modernity resolved the religious issue in the West, yet we need look no further than Northern Ireland, where Protestants and Catholics are still at daggers drawn (rifles drawn might be a more accurate analogy), to see that this isn't necessarily the case. The religious divide is as sharp, and as intensely felt, in that context as it ever has been. An Islamic Reformation might well lead to even more holy wars, or, depressing prospect, even more virulent forms of religious fundamentalism than we are having to face up to at present. As Ali himself concedes, even within present-day Islam there can be extreme intolerance towards co-religionists: 'Some Deobandi factions want the Shias to be declared heretics, and preferably physically exterminated.'[41] (As we have seen, the Deobandi school of Islamic thought is noted as amongst the most traditional, and one of the major intellectual sources of modern Islamic fundamentalism.) How a Reformation would improve this state of affairs is by no means clear, especially when we recall that many Northern Irish Protestants are still persuaded that the Pope is the Antichrist – and not just in the metaphorical sense either: the Reverend Ian Paisley can give you chapter and verse on this issue any time it's required. Some *ijtihad* might be a good idea in Northern Ireland, too.

Imperialist fundamentalism is an interesting addition to our list of fundamentalisms, even if Ali's conspiracy-oriented line on it is rather too neat. There's more than a hint of Marxism about it, yet another fundamentalism which feels it has the answers to all the world's problems. Aside from its historical tendency towards intolerance, Marxism has the added drawback of being a Western theory, dependent on Western intellectual history and cultural values (Enlightenment, modernity), and thus suspect to defenders of difference no less than to the non-Western world. For many non-Westerners, Marxism can look as imperialist as America currently can (John Gray makes just such a point in *False Dawn*, identifying Enlightenment values as the source of the problems we now face with the globalisation project). Ali's desire for an Islamic Reformation might strike some commentators as yet another example of Western notions being imposed on the Islamic world, although his own background – born in what is now

Pakistan before partition from India – does endow him with a credibility that Western-born critics of Islam must lack. Nevertheless, Ali's attempt to do justice to Islam is commendable, since few Marxist-oriented thinkers are willing to see religion as anything other than the 'opium of the masses'. He genuinely tries to see it in a positive light historically, despite his ideological biases.

Perhaps Ali's concern is more to do justice to the Islamic world than Islam itself, and one wonders, as one does with Christianity, whether the religion was in fact largely irrelevant to the cultural advances made in that world (and Islam can boast many such, both intellectual and technological, as Ali emphasises). Would these have happened anyway without a monotheistic religion in place? Perhaps we tend to give too much credit to religion for all the positive developments that occur in a culture: the world before modern monotheism wasn't exactly without its cultural glories, after all. Cultural development can be explained without reference to God (of whatever persuasion). But, again, this is a member of the sceptics' union speaking, and we find it hard to regard religion as anything other than an excuse to exercise control over others; a method of trading on human vulnerability in order to gain power. We feel no need to defend religion's past, and are likely to consider most attempts to do so as special pleading. Even if agonistic pluralism were accepted by the religious community at large, we wouldn't be persuaded of the need for organised religion – especially given its lamentable track record in terms of human relations. Various attempts at ecumenism notwithstanding, that seems an unlikely scenario for us to encounter in the current cultural climate.

CHAPTER SEVEN

# Nationalist Fundamentalism:
# The Search for Self-Definition

Another aspect of fundamentalism to make its mark in the
political arena in recent times has been nationalist fundamentalism. The rise of the political right across Europe has
been very much tied up with a fear of immigrants (whether of
the economic refugee or asylum seeker variety, it makes little
difference), and an allied desire to maintain the supposed
purity of one's national culture against all 'alien' invasion. We
can speak of the growth of a nationalist fundamentalism in
most of the countries of the European Community, and it's a
phenomenon capable of attracting support from both the left
and the right, depending on the particular issue that's being
addressed. What is at stake here is something very basic indeed
– self-definition: Who am I? Where do I belong? It can be
psychologically disorienting for this to be threatened (although
postmodernists claim it as a liberating experience), and it can
promote a very reductive conception of national identity, such
as that espoused by the British National Party. Elsewhere in
Europe, similar reactions are at work in the anti-immigration
movements in Holland and France. In Holland, the assassinated political leader Pim Fortuyn made a considerable impact
on national politics with his call for immigration to be halted,
while also demanding that existing immigrants conform to the
Dutch way of life if they wanted to remain resident. While not

racist in the stricter sense, Fortuyn's policies, an intriguing blend of libertarianism and cultural imperialism, did involve the eradication of cultural differences, which immigrants can find very intimidating. What the West experiences as difference, they experience as their cultural identity, after all.

Jean-Marie Le Pen's National Front Party in France has scored notable electoral gains running on an anti-immigrant platform, and Germany, Austria and Italy all have their anti-immigration movements also. Jörg Haider's Austrian Freedom Party even harbours ambitions to create a pan-European right-wing grouping to assert European identity against outsiders. Perhaps we can speak of European fundamentalism? If we can, then it might seem disturbingly close to fascism for some; with a charmed circle of white Europeans militantly confronting the rest of the world. It's worth noting that Haider is on record as having Nazi sympathies, which hardly encourages confidence in the proposed project.

Movements such as these represent a rejection of the multiculturalist ethos which the left still generally supports across Europe, and which even right-wing governments feel obliged to pay lip-service to (if often no more than that – hypocrisy is rife in this area). Similar fundamentalist attitudes can be found at work in Australia in recent years, with its refusal to admit Afghan refugees (brilliantly satirised in Steve Bell's *Guardian* cartoon strip),* and even in America, supposedly the world's great melting pot, where the militia movement has set itself up to defend a very reductive vision of what it means to be American. Fundamental to the militias, it would seem, is carrying a gun: it also helps to be white.

Contradictions abound in such cases, as they do in the fact

---

\* Culminating in an Australian policeman singing, to the tune of 'Waltzing Matilda', 'don't come a-seeking asylum with me' as the refugees were chased across the Australian outback.

that such societies are all in favour of the free movement of capital across national boundaries (market fundamentalism in action), but not of all the world's citizens – unless they are rich, that is. Libertarianism tends to be very selectively applied by the Western political establishment. When it comes to national self-definition the drawbridge comes down, and this despite nationalist self-definition being one of the woolliest concepts imaginable. Whether such self-definition is possible is highly debatable; whether it is desirable even more so.

## Le Pen and French Fundamentalism

Le Pen has led a strong campaign against immigration and multiculturalism in French life for quite some time now, and with considerable success. His political party, the National Front, polls well at both local and national level, and has run several town and city councils in the south, where its power base seems to be strongest (although it does have significant support in several other regions of the country too). It's fair to say that the National Front has exacerbated racial tensions throughout the nation, and that it has exploited these with some considerable skill. The more racial tension there is, the more Le Pen seems justified in peddling his anti-immigration message: it becomes a self-fulfilling prophecy. It was a persuasive enough message to convince the French electorate that he deserved to come second in the run-off for the final stage of the French presidential elections in 2002. His subsequent heavy defeat in the final ballot, a result achieved only by all other parties throwing their support behind Jacques Chirac (a hated figure on the left, ironically enough), could not disguise the widespread acceptance that Le Pen's ideas had attained amongst the electorate. The fact that the political establishment was forced to gang up on Le Pen merely proved what an important figure he had become.

Le Pen came to prominence in the early 1980s, when the National Front first experienced a measure of electoral success (the party itself having been founded in 1972). Immigration was becoming an issue of some importance in French public life of the time, and Le Pen and his colleagues were quick to capitalise on this phenomenon. As the BBC correspondent Jonathan Marcus has observed, the National Front's extreme stance on immigration went a long way towards setting the agenda for the popular debate on the topic: 'Immigration, in this populist view, was presented as a rising tide of mainly North African and Muslim faces. Immigration was linked to unemployment, to urban crime and delinquency, indeed to all of France's urban ills.'[1] The government of Jacques Chirac even proposed some amendments to the Nationality code, which would have made it more difficult for immigrants to obtain French citizenship, in a bid to attract National Front supporters. Widespread opposition forced the government to withdraw the planned reform, but the immigration issue continued to arouse strong passions. The National Front had proved a point, and in Jonathan Marcus's summarisation of the events of the 1980s, it was becoming clear 'that there was considerable mileage in the immigration issue for a Party that had no scruples and was willing to present an explicitly racist policy'.[2] Since then, the National Front has done its best to be that party.

Le Pen's role in the so-called 'Headscarves Affair' of 1989 brought the racist quality of his nationalist fundamentalism to the fore. The 'Affair' concerned the banning of some girls from school, in the town of Creil, for wearing Muslim headscarves in the classroom. For the school's Principal, the girls' action was an example of 'excessive external display of religious or cultural ties', and therefore inappropriate within a public institution in a country that assumed a separation of church and state.[3] Soon there was a full-scale national debate raging about the issue, with wide support shown for the school's decision. Many took the line that wearing a headscarf clashed with the traditional French policy on immigration, which was to encourage assimilation into French culture. On this reading, the headscarf signalled a blatant refusal to assimilate. Others, primarily on the left, argued the case for multiculturalism and the right to maintain one's own traditions within French life, as long as these harmed no one. Le Pen, in typically provocative fashion, saw the wearing of headscarves as a symbol of incipient Islamic fundamentalism. The government handled the affair ineptly and managed to please no one by the various compromises and contradictory statements they made, whereas Le Pen gained valuable publicity for his cause. The leader of a French anti-racism group, Pierre Aidenbaum, noted sadly that Le Pen's talent in exploiting the immigration issue had led to 'a normalisation of racist rhetoric' in French life.[4] In other words, Le Pen was setting the terms of reference for the debate about national self-definition. The Muslim population of France, for all its moderation, was beginning to be seen by many as a threat to France's very existence: Le Pen's nationalist fundamentalism had gone mainstream.

Le Pen certainly sees France's national identity as being in danger from a range of enemies, with Islam high on the list (communism has been another of his bugbears over the years). Given a falling birth rate amongst France's indigenous population, immigration from Islamic countries constitutes a demographic time-bomb to someone of Le Pen's political outlook: 'The more homogeneous a country, the more it possesses an historic density, the more it develops an energy which is proportional to the size of its population', in Le Pen's own words.[5] National identity is the charmed circle into which outsiders cannot break, and its purity is to be protected at all costs. Just to hammer the point home about the racist cast to Le Pen's thought, he's also on record as saying of his party:

'We believe in the superiority of western civilisation';[6] which is barely disguised code for white supremacism. Couple such views with a suspicion of the humanistic ideals of the French Revolution and a commitment to traditional Christian belief (Le Pen has drawn support from the ultra-traditionalist Catholic movement Chrétienté solidarité), and one has a confirmed back-to-basics campaign, determined to turn the clock back to supposedly simpler times when neither difference nor dissent disturbed the political landscape. It's good old-fashioned cultural nostalgia of the most dubious kind; nostalgia for that elusive organic society, with its unified system of cultural values, that was always just a few generations ago in the nation's past. (Perhaps we could define a fundamentalist as someone for whom the millennium is always just about to come, and the cultural golden age has always just gone?) Immigration becomes the key issue around which opposition to the forces of pluralism and multiculturalism can be organised; the means by which the message of racial purity and superiority can be brought to the attention of a mass audience. We can consider it a matter of doctrine, which no National Front supporter would dare to challenge. Jonathan Marcus has perceptively compared immigration's role in the ideology of the National Front to that of class struggle in classical Marxist thought.

If we need any further proof of the continuing appeal of such ideas we need only refer to Marcus's assessment that '[t]he 1995 Presidential election could well mark Le Pen's political swansong', and that the party might be in need of a new leader to take it into the future.[7] In fact, the National Front did well in the 1995 elections, winning the mayoral elections in the towns of Orange, Marignane and Toulon. As an indication of how the party planned to use its growing influence at local level, we can cite the words of a Front councillor from the south: 'We will take care that a certain immigrant population does not install itself in the market.'[8] One can only wonder what the 'care' involved, but it certainly had the preservation of French identity in mind, so that was alright then. Another commentator suggested in 1999 that Le Pen's star finally was waning (despite the National Front polling 4.5 million votes in the 1997 elections), and that he was leading his party down 'the path of division and possible marginalization'.[9] Yet Le Pen continues to confound his critics, and it took a concerted effort from both the right and left political establishment in France to block him in the last presidential election. Le Pen and the National Front still loom menacingly over the French political scene into the 21st century. Leader and party would seem to be somewhat less 'resistible' than Marcus had thought; the demand for nationalist fundamentalism more deeply rooted than his analysis of the National Front phenomenon had identified.

## Pim Fortuyn and Dutch Fundamentalism

Pim Fortuyn's short but eventful career points up the very complex nature of nationalist fundamentalism in contemporary Western culture. To many, Fortuyn was the acceptable face of nationalist fundamentalism, and he found a ready audience for his views even within liberal Dutch society. He didn't fit the stereotype of what a nationalist fundamentalist was supposed to be like, and at his death was being talked of as a future Prime Minister. Although his words could be turned to racist account, he was not as such a racist, remarking at one point that he could hardly be considered anti-Moroccan, given that he had had so many Moroccans as sexual partners. As a homosexual, he already cut an anomalous figure in a movement with decidedly conformist tendencies (home, family, heterosexuality, conformity, the usual right-wing commitments). If there was such a thing as an anti-identikit nationalist fundamentalist, then Fortuyn was it. Fortuyn's anti-immigration stance was of the 'enough is enough' variety, allowing those immigrants already integrated into Dutch life to remain. The demand for integration was an argument against multiculturalism that challenged the prevailing cultural consensus, but Fortuyn could be difficult to place in terms of conventional political life – hence his ability to appeal across the political spectrum. To quote a *Guardian* editorial, 'Fortuyn broke the mould of traditional Dutch politics' with a brand of 'charismatic populism' that caught the mood of the times.[10] It was a mood of nationalism turning in on itself.

The complexity of Fortuyn's position can be seen in his reaction to Islam. He described it as culturally backward, which sounds right-wing and Le Pen territory; but backward mainly because of its treatment of women and gays, which was a libertarian sentiment that the left would support whole-heartedly. Combatting discrimination against these groups is high up on the left's agenda, after all. Fortuyn's argument was that Dutch society's liberalism was being put at risk by reactionary ideas smuggled in under the banner of multi-culturalism. It was as if he was calling the left's bluff: support multiculturalism or support gay and women's rights – you can't do both. And if you choose gay and women's rights, you certainly cannot continue to support Islam, given its poor record in this respect. His killer went on to claim at his trial that he acted in protest against Fortuyn's anti-Muslim views, which had turned Dutch Muslims into 'scapegoats' for the society's ills: a bizarre case of *jihad* by proxy, as it were, that turned the dead politician into a possible martyr figure for both the right and the left. Fortuyn was nationalism with a liberal twist: a fundamentalism resisting funda-mentalism.

## Fundamentalism versus the Nation State

One of the most striking features of nationalist fundamentalism is how it can create divisions even within apparently well-established, modern nation states. Since the 1980s Yugoslavia has broken up into a collection of smaller states each with its own separate ethnic identity, and even some of these smaller states are proving to be unstable in their turn, with ethnic factions still at loggerheads with each other. Religion yet again is a complicating factor; Muslims, Catholics and Orthodox Christians all having their own agenda to pursue. As a nation state Yugoslavia was always an uneasy federal coalition, the Balkans having a centuries-long tradition of ethnic conflict to draw upon, but communism seemed to keep the lid on its simmering national tensions from the Second World War onwards (in retrospect, a considerable achievement). When communism went into decline, however, the situation changed quite dramatically, civil war breaking out all over the federation as old ethnic hatreds resurfaced with a vengeance. Yugoslavia as an entity failed to provide the necessary sense of self-definition to the country's various ethnic groupings, and the nation that was soon descended into chaos. The region remains unstable to this day. Whereas to outsiders the region's ethnic groupings seemed to have more in common than to divide them, nationalist self-definition decreed otherwise. One suspects that the United Kingdom might appear much the same to many outsiders, too, and that the division between, for example, Scots and English would be just as difficult to understand. Again, there would appear to be more to unite than to divide the respective peoples, yet Scottish nationalism thrives and independence has to be considered a distinct possibility in the not too distant future.

Nor are we dealing with postmodern-style pluralism in the Yugoslavian situation; relations between its former constituent parts are based on an attitude of openly expressed antagonism. The need to assert each particular nationalist self-definition is clearly deeply felt; enough to engage in protracted war with one's erstwhile fellow citizens. Where this will all end is still unclear. The 'Balkan Question' that so exercised late 19th- and early 20th-century European politicians looks as if it will continue to be with us for some time yet.

The fault-lines that opened up in Yugoslavia can also be seen in Italian society. The recently created political party the Northern League (Liga Nord) has campaigned for autonomy for the northern part of the country; that is, for the wealthiest part at the expense of the economically less developed south (it has also suggested that the Italian coastguards should fire on boats carrying illegal immigrants). Since the unification of the country in the 19th century, there has been a marked difference between north and south in Italy. It has been a common view in the north, where almost all the major Italian industries are located, that they are subsidising the south, which is regarded as backward in Western European terms. The 'southern problem' is of long standing. Italy is a country in which regional and city identities are traditionally very strong (a legacy of the system of fiercely independent city-states in medieval and Renaissance times), and national self-definition is probably a looser concept than it is in most other Western European nations. But the situation there does make us aware how easily new fundamentalisms, with their own charmed circles and principles of exclusion, can be created in the area of national self-definition. It is noticeable, too, how rapidly antagonism comes onto the scene; the Northern League is anything but well disposed towards its southern compatriots. Similar problems have arisen in Spain, with Catalan – and particularly Basque – separatists rejecting the notion of Spanish self-definition for their regions. Basque separatism has a history of terrorist activity too, through the political movement ETA, which has been responsible for various outrages over the last few years.

## British Fundamentalism

Britain consists of four distinct nations, so the notion of British fundamentalism is problematical right from the start. This is even more the case now that devolution has occurred, and we have a Scottish Parliament and a Welsh Assembly in place (the Northern Irish equivalent is in suspension at the moment, but is a constituent part of the current political settlement all the same). Nevertheless, we have a British National Party (BNP) fighting on our behalf to protect our assumed common cultural heritage. The BNP has proved to be the most resilient of the various neo-Nazi parties which emerged in Britain in the post-war period. Fascism had a certain vogue in Britain in the 1930s, particularly through the activities of the charismatic politician Oswald Mosley and his Blackshirt movement (the British Union of Fascists). The Second World War put paid to such movements, but several smaller far right parties began to exploit immigration issues in the 1950s and 60s, and the BNP, formed from the union of two such groups in 1960 (the White Defence League and the National Labour Party), soon became amongst the highest profile of these. The philosophy of the BNP unashamedly harked back to fascism's 'glory' days of the 1930s, being 'based on racial nationalism, on the need to preserve the northern European folk, predominantly nordic in race, and to free Britain from Jewish domination'.[11]

Although the BNP is a minor player on the British political scene, it has succeeded in winning some council seats around the country in local elections in recent years, and creating some degree of unease within the political establishment in the process. Small though it is, its reach is increasing and the BNP is doing its best to become, in the words of its new leader, Nick

Griffin, 'acceptable and electable'.[12] Griffin has hopes to attract more graduates like himself into the party, to dispel the working-class thug image that most of the public associate with it. There's no doubt in the BNP's mind about what's fundamental to being British – being white. Its political programme, like that of the National Front in France, revolves around the issue of immigration, and it has long been an advocate of compulsory repatriation of non-whites. Nick Griffin wants to soften that stance, on the pragmatic (or cynical) grounds that it's 'a vote loser', but it's clear where his real sympathies lie: 'Every time a multiracial society has been tried in history, it's ended in horrible bloodshed. All we're doing is trying to motivate people in a political direction.'[13] As the writer Nick Ryan remarks, after interviewing Griffin for his book *Homeland: Into a World of Hate* (a chilling survey of the far right internationally): 'He keeps talking of "our people", as though they were some static, inherent nation';[14] which of course they are to someone like Griffin. Griffin's 'people' are fundamentally British, just as Le Pen's 'people' are fundamentally French. Skin colour makes it easier to establish those fundamentals in the public mind.

The BNP has had markedly less success than Le Pen's National Front, with their several million votes in national elections, although it has become 'acceptable and electable' enough, as we saw above, to win some council seats in local elections (successfully exploiting tensions between the white and Asian populations in northern towns such as Oldham and Burnley, for example). Some commentators have simply written off the BNP as a credible political force, with the historian Richard Thurlow, for example, arguing that the outlook is 'bleak for neo-fascists and racial nationalists' in general in British politics.[15] Thurlow treats the BNP as the tail-end of British fascism, which he dismisses as 'small beer' historically.[16] He may well be right, but one suspects there is probably quite widespread tacit support for the idea of the 'inherent nation', regardless of how much of a myth it is. There is certainly an 'inherent nation' to protect as far as the anti-European lobby in British political life is concerned. It's not fascist to be anti-European, but it's interesting that both groups are accessing that same myth of nationalist fundamentalism in their own particular way – and that it can resonate far wider than the charmed circle of activists in either case.

## 'Gundamentalism': The American Militia Movement

The American militia movement may not be huge in numbers, but it has succeeded nonetheless in having a dramatic impact on American life, with federal agencies such as the FBI and the BATF (the Bureau of Alcohol, Tobacco and Firearms) devoting considerable resources to monitoring its activities in recent years. The wittiest definition of the movement that I have heard dubs it 'gundamentalism'.[17] That very cleverly indeed sums up the kind of self-definition we're dealing with in this instance: the self-definition felt to be enshrined in the constitutional right to bear arms, and to use them in defence of the constitution. For the militia movement, the American constitution is to be read as a set of fundamentals that cannot be altered, the most rock-hard of the rock-hard certainties by which they conduct their lives, and gundamentalism is the logical response to any attempts to interfere with these. The cultural differences between the 18th and 21st centuries, between a society without and a society with a strong central government entrusted to protect the rights of the individual, are simply ignored by these 'patriots'. Gundamentalists act as if they're in a state of nature with nothing to protect themselves but their guns. In many ways they haven't moved past the revolutionary consciousness of the late 18th century, or the frontier consciousness that succeeded this in 19th-century America: the land of 'a man's gotta do what a man's gotta do' (with a gun usually). We are talking about inerrancy again, sticking strictly to the script. What was said then in the constitution still applies now, and will for ever after in this interpretation. As far as gundamentalists are concerned, history is on their side, and that's always enough to justify any fundamentalist cause. The time warp zone beckons, and with it the utter conviction of the true believer.

Jon Ronson gives a scary, though also wryly humorous, account of this milieu in his book *Them: Adventures with Extremists*. He visits an Aryan Nations headquarters in Idaho, where he finds an environment radiating 'rage and psychosis' against an outside world that the militants believe to be largely in the control of the Jews (the old clichés about the banking system, etc., are trotted out yet again, with no sense of irony at all in their use).[18] The conversion of the Jews doesn't figure in this ideology; Ronson notes how the camp leader's office uses an Israeli flag as a doormat to demonstrate the movement's contempt for their perceived enemies. (In fact, many gundamentalists reject the tenets of premillennialist dispensationalism.) This is a belief system with its own roll call of anti-government martyrs who have died for the cause, such as the Oklahoma City bomber Timothy McVeigh, and the victims of sieges at Waco, Texas, and Ruby Ridge, Idaho (broken up by the BATF and FBI respectively, with loss of life in each case).* Gundamentalism is the militiamen's response to a world they believe to be in conspiracy against them, right down to their own government, which the more extreme elements among the movement take to be under the control of the United Nations

---

* The Ruby Ridge siege involved the Christian Identity sect member Randy Weaver and his family (his wife and son were killed); Waco, the Branch Davidian sect under its charismatic leader David Koresh.

(how the rest of us have managed to miss this takeover is something of a mystery). As another of the extremists interviewed by Ronson puts it: 'There's a whole buffet of corruption out there.'[19] The beleaguered mentality so often found in fundamentalism is much in evidence in the movement's supporters, with their conspiracy-oriented view of existence. It's the militia versus the world, and all you can put your faith in to restore the natural order of things is your gun. Attempts to pass laws circumscribing, or even abolishing, gun use in American life can only be seen as the work of the enemy (and the ultra-patriotic National Rifle Association can always be guaranteed to whip up national support against that enemy when the gundamentalist culture is threatened by legislators).

The militia movement is of relatively recent origin, most of the groups forming in the early to mid-1990s, although it sees itself as standing in a long tradition dating back to the militias of colonial and revolutionary America (it also has more modern forerunners such as the Posse Comitatus, founded in 1969, which challenged the legality of any form of government past the local level). The Second Amendment to the Constitution provides its legal basis (although this is contested), and the increasing power of the federal government its justification for reinvoking that Amendment's principles over 200 years later: 'A well-regulated Militia, being necessary to the security of a free State, the right of the people to keep and bear Arms, shall not be infringed.' Add in the belief that a 'New World Order', controlled through the United Nations, has plans underway to enslave the United States as part of its campaign for global domination (UN forces are at this moment hiding out in America's national parks ready for action, apparently) and you have a potent cocktail capable of motivating a significant number of individuals to join, or offer support for, their local militia. And there always is a local militia: every American state has at least one such organisation, many have several. Just to name-check a few, you can choose from: the Militia of Montana, the Oklahoma Constitutional Militia, the Georgia Republic Militia, the Arizona Viper Militia, the Washington State Militia, the West Virginia Mountaineer Militia, the Texas Unified Field Forces, the California High Desert Militia, the Kentucky State Militia, the Ohio Unorganized Militia Assistance and Advisory Committee, and the Michigan Militia (the Anti-Defamation League website, 'Militia Watchdog', will provide all the others for you if you care to consult its 'Extremism by State' map of the United States).[20] The Michigan Militia (now split into two factions) was initially led by one Norm Olson, who neatly demonstrated the links between religious and political fundamentalism by combining the roles of minister and gunshop owner. One is tempted to say 'only in America', until one reflects on the enthusiastic support shown for paramilitary activity by many religious leaders in the Muslim world, not to mention our very own Northern Ireland. Religion and extremist politics can blend together very naturally.

The militia movement grew out of the right-wing response to the sieges at Ruby Ridge and Waco. Many on the right felt these were the actions of a totalitarian government which had lost touch with its citizens, and became convinced that guns were the only way of protecting their rights. As the 'Militia Watchdog' website puts it: 'Many militia members were radical guns-rights advocates, people who believed that, in fact, there could be no such things as illegal firearms and whose anti-government ire was formed in large part because of fear and suspicion of imminent gun confiscation.'[21] Gun confiscation would be a breach of the Second Amendment, and however they may differ over their ultimate political objectives (some militia being more committed to violence than others), that remains the primary militia concern. To quote the leader of the Kentucky State Militia, Charlie

Puckett, militia members see themselves as engaged in 'resecuring for ourselves and our descendants the ideals of liberty ... bequeathed to us as our birthright'.[22] These comments, incidentally, were delivered to his followers in a letter congratulating them on the success of one of their regular machine-gun shoots: all good family entertainment, no doubt. With the lead given by the Montana Militia, founded by John, David and Randy Trochmann (all of whom had links with the white supremacist Aryan Nations sect), and their newsletter, *Taking Aim*, the movement grew rapidly. Its membership may have fluctuated over the decade since then, but it's still a force to be reckoned with in American political life. In the stern words of the 'Militia Watchdog', the militia movement is not 'dismissible as a comic subject'.[23]

To consider the debate over the meaning of the Second Amendment is to enter a hall of mirrors where you're never sure what, or who, to believe. There are militias and then there are 'unorganised militias' (the male population governed by the laws covering militias). You have the right to assemble with other members of the unorganised militia, but not to take the law into your own hands when you do so. There are state laws on the topic, and there are federal laws on the topic, and areas of possible dispute between these. The Amendment allows for the existence of an armed citizen militia, but this can be interpreted in dramatically different ways. For the militia movement, it means that they're justified in organising to protect themselves against any perceived infringement of their sovereign rights. To their opponents, there's no such right to organise outside state control, and paramilitary activity is contrary to the constitution. It's a complex argument which revolves around the question of whether individuals have total sovereignty over themselves, or whether they have ceded at least some of this sovereignty to the state's legislature. The issue becomes even more complex when the relationship between the individual states and the federal government is taken into account. Many militia supporters feel that the federal government has, illegally, taken away powers that rightly belong to the states. Without wishing to go into this issue in any detail, what is clear is that we are entering a lawyers' paradise at this point. There's enough vagueness in the relevant legislation to encourage prolonged legal wrangling, and militia members are certainly prone to indulge in this activity. (Anyone who does wish to pursue this further, however, is directed to the Anti-Defamation League website.)[24]

Militias date back to America's colonial past, when each of the colonies possessed one. During the United States' early years, control of the militia largely passed to the states, until the Constitution of 1789 saw a division of responsibility drawn up between the states and the federal government. Since then the federal government has gradually come to exercise more and more control over the organised militia movement, which now goes under the name of the National Guard. As for the unorganised militia, as Sheldon Seps and Mark Pitcavage point out, they have never been pressed into service since the concept was devised in the 1830s. This isn't surprising, given that 'it was a term invented to allow individuals to escape from compulsory military duty'.[25] There's more than a certain irony involved in the concept being used now to justify putting together a paramilitary group operating outside the mainstream political system – political self-definition in its purest form. All claims by the 'new militia' (as they are somewhat disparagingly referred to by Seps and Pitcavage)[26] to be carrying on the noble public traditions of the old militia tend to collapse when we look more closely at the historical record. New militia fundamentalism has little basis in historical fact, and requires a very partial reading of the Constitution and all the subsequent legislation generated by it at both state and federal level.

As an example of just how literal the fundamentalism can be, the Trochmanns took the line in the early days of the Militia of Montana that only white males could count as American citizens, on the basis that those were the only ones qualified to be so when the country was founded. If they didn't include non-whites, or non-Christians, in the old days, then we couldn't do so now either. Multiculturalism was being declared unconstitutional in the world's great melting pot, with a blind eye turned to over 200 years of history. The Trochmanns have since played down these views (and there are in fact some African American militia movements in other states), but there's a definite white supremacist streak running through militia ideology. Fundamentalism of one kind so easily begets fundamentalism of another.

## Constitutional Holy War: The Montana Freemen

The Montana Freemen are an instructive example of the kind of thinking that goes into what Ted Daniels has called 'Constitutional fundamentalism'.[27] As Daniels points out, the Freemen are part of a wider 'Christian Constitutionalist movement [which] believes that the Bill of Rights and the Constitution are divinely inspired, nearly holy writ on a par with the Bible'.[28] The copious biblical references and allusions in the Freemen's pronouncements let us know how inseparable politics and religion are to this group (thus their 'Lawful Chain of Command' is described as starting with 'Almighty God, pursuant to His Holy Scriptures, creator of all good and evil').[29] One of the group's leading figures, LeRoy Schweizer, has called for the creation of a 'theocratic republic' in the United States, run by property-owning white males.[30] The Freemen refuse to recognise the authority of the current government of the United States, on the grounds of the dubious constitutional status of President Roosevelt's Proclamation of Emergency and War Powers and then the Emergency Banking Act of 1933. As another Christian Constitutionalist document puts it with reference to the Banking Act: 'This act effectively suspended the Constitution and granted dictatorial powers to the President, a situation which continues to this day.'[31] In consequence, the Freemen became embroiled in a long-running dispute with both the federal and state governments, even submitting a 'Citizens Declaration of War' to the authorities. The dispute escalated into an FBI-led siege of the Montana ranch where leading figures in the Freemen movement had set up a command centre in 1994. Unlike Waco and Ruby Ridge, it eventually ended peacefully (the FBI being more sensitive in its handling of the situation this time around, in the hope of keeping the martyr count down), but not before the Freemen had gained considerable publicity, and public sympathy, for their constitutional 'holy war' against the government.

Many in the militia movement were vocal in support of the Freemen (John Trochmann being a high-profile case), although others were more circumspect about taking on the FBI on their behalf. Nevertheless, the Freemen clearly had a constituency for their beliefs, and it wouldn't have required much to turn the Montana siege into another Waco or Ruby Ridge, thus providing yet more ammunition for the conspiracy theorists within the militia movement. Conspiracy can always be relied upon to spur the fundamentalist faithful on to yet greater efforts. Some militia supporters saw the Freemen's cause as providing enough basis for a civil war: constitutional fundamentalism could be taken no further than that. For the truly committed, the pursuit of national self-definition knows no bounds and recognises no other loyalties.

## CHAPTER EIGHT

# Fundamentalism at Large: The Search for Purity of Thought and Deed – Everywhere

There are many other examples of the fundamentalist ethic in everyday life and thought that deserve our attention. We can identify some 'soft' types (political correctness, biological essentialism) and some harder-edged varieties (the environmental, pro-life, and animal rights movements). Behind soft versions of fundamentalism lies a desire for purity of thought that can be just as authoritarian as that found in the larger-scale versions we have been considering throughout the book. Political correctness (PC) started with the best of intentions, to minimise all forms of discrimination in our society, but in many cases it has ossified into a set of rigid rules and procedures that all too often curb individual freedom and encourage petty tyranny. This is particularly the case in America, where PC has become almost a substitute for left-wing politics in the university system; but it has also infiltrated into British life. PC can in fact become a barrier to change, and is only too prone to create a backlash (see almost any edition of the *Daily Mail* newspaper for examples of this in action; it can be a gift to social conservatives of the 'Disgusted of Tunbridge Wells' variety). PC is well worth investigating to reveal fundamentalism at work in our everyday dealings with each other. It is designed to reach inside our very thought processes, the objective of both religious fundamentalism and ideological fundamentalisms such as communism. Fundamentalism can be seen at work also in the more extreme versions of feminist thought where biological fundamentals (biological essentialism, so-called) have on occasion been put forward to justify separatist policies. Again, it is the abuses I will be concerned with; the way that certain scientific data have been manipulated to close off debate and the expression of dissenting viewpoints. The 'hard' versions outlined above demand purity of deed as well as of thought, and in extreme cases are quite capable of resorting to terrorist violence to make their point. Opposition is simply not tolerated, and to such activists almost all of us count as opposition if we do nothing to bring to an end the abuses they see as being perpetrated by our society.

## Feminism and Separatist Feminism

Feminism has been one of the most significant, and positive, developments in Western culture over the last century or so, and the feminist movement has had a dramatic impact on the way we live. Second-wave feminism (that is, the later-20th-century form) has been tireless in its efforts to reduce discrimination against women, whether in public or private life, and it has been highly successful in introducing its values into the cultural mainstream where they now enjoy at least tacit acceptance. Feminism has been an important factor in reducing prejudice in Western society, and it has made some inroads in the Third World, too, where it often finds itself in conflict with the forces of religious fundamentalism: Islamic feminism, as we have seen, being a contested term. Feminism turns into a fundamentalism itself, however, when it embraces biological essentialism. It may not be a case of wishing physically to eliminate competitors (although Valerie Solanis and the SCUM movement did, notoriously enough, put this on their agenda),* but biological essentialism certainly claims the existence of a charmed circle, this time dictated by gender. Biological essentialists believe that male and female nature are fundamentally different, to the point of being irreconcilable. Nature trumps nurture, and biology culture, in this outlook, as memorably set out in the following defence of political lesbianism by the Leeds Revolutionary Feminist Group:

> Men are the enemy. Heterosexual women are collaborators with the enemy. All the good work that our heterosexual feminist sisters do for women is undermined by the counter-revolutionary activity they engage in with men. Being a heterosexual feminist is like being in the resistance in Nazi-occupied Europe where in the daytime you blow up a bridge, in the evening you rush to repair it. ... Every woman who lives with or fucks a man helps to maintain the oppression of her sisters and hinders our struggle.[1]

Granted, this is an extreme view and it attracted opposition from many other feminists, but it does show how easily essentialism could take on a fundamentalist character. This is women addressing other women; men simply don't figure in the equation. Although debate did follow, with many respondents to the Group's manifesto (a selection included in the pamphlet), it didn't shake the separatists' faith in the rightness of their beliefs: 'us' and 'them' were clearly distinguished, and would stay so. For many feminists this was dogmatism and authoritarianism in action; the very traits that underpin fundamentalism.

---

* SCUM stands for 'Society for Cutting Up Men', and Solanis went so far as to attempt to assassinate Andy Warhol as a symbol of male oppression. She was unsuccessful, but Warhol was badly wounded in her attack.

197

As the Leeds Revolutionary Feminist Group pamphlet uncompromisingly establishes, separatist feminism was deeply pessimistic about gender and sexual politics, and advocated separate spheres of existence as the only possible solution. The assumption, as with Islamic theology, was that there was no point in trying to change male nature, and that women would always be at risk from this in a mixed society: 'What part does sexuality play in the oppression of women? Only in the system of oppression that is male supremacy does the oppressor actually invade and colonise the interior of the body of the oppressed.'² Separation, including cessation of sexual contact between men and women, was to be the new regime, and it was to be strictly enforced and policed. Only one way to feminist heaven: expel the enemy completely from your life.

## PC World

It's easy to criticise PC, and anyone who has worked in a public institution such as a university or the civil service knows what a deadening effect it can have on communication, both formal and informal. There are approved phrases and attitudes that are dutifully trotted out in meetings, letters and e-mails, to the extent where they are practically emptied of meaning. They aren't just approved, they are expected, and that creates the conditions in which petty tyranny can thrive. Someone is always more PC than thou, and keen to point this out in order to score points. When they do, you have no possible comeback: PC is a set of rules, not a debating forum. One doesn't need to be an unreconstructed conservative to be sceptical of the apparatus that has come to surround PC, to wonder whether it does any more than just salve the consciences of the WASPs who are arguably its most voci-ferous exponents; as if one only had to say the appropriate words often enough and oppression would melt away. But we need to remind ourselves of the virtues of PC first. PC was a very idealistic attempt to attack prejudice and discrimination at the grass roots, in our everyday language and communication in the public sphere. It was a search for purity of thought with all the best of liberal intentions, and there's no denying that it had significant achievements to its name. It made people address the unthinking prejudice so often present in their conversation, for example, and that can only be regarded as a positive development. Whether it actually eradicated the prejudice from everyone's thought is another matter, but one had to start somewhere.

Along with the realisation that prejudice could be encoded in our conversation came a recognition of the sheer WASPishness of Western culture. What Naomi Klein has dubbed 'the politics of personal representation' came to dominate the left-wing political agenda in the 1980s and 90s, bringing a whole new set of prejudices to the surface.[3] Where were the positive representations of blacks and gays in the media? Why were ethnic minorities in general so often represented in stereotypical ways? Why were women so often represented in stereotypical ways? The images that the media gave us helped to form our world view (ours was a media-saturated culture, after all), and if we saw mainly stereotypes there then the impulse to stereotype was reinforced in turn. The demand for positive role models did have an effect on the media, who found themselves under attack from pressure groups if they failed to take such ideas into account. No doubt some of this response was inspired less by political conviction than by cynicism and self-interest; a desire more to open up new markets than to open up cultural debate. But an important point had been scored nevertheless, and, again, at least *some* thinking about the issue of power relations in our culture had to be done by those concerned, even if the motivation was largely commercial. Cynical or not, this was surely a step in the right direction for a democratic society, and one that has had entirely beneficial effects on the self-esteem of previously discriminated-against sections of the populace. As we noted in Chapter 4, anti-gay legislation can still be put forward in American political life (and in Britain too, as witness the ban on 'promoting' homosexuality within the school system, put forward by the Conservative government in the 1980s), but it meets much tougher opposition than it used to, and the more positive images of gay identity that we find in the media nowadays undoubtedly contribute to this reaction.

The downside is that there's now what amounts to a grammar of PC, which can turn it into a form of dogmatism in its own right. PC closes off debate, demanding adherence to a formula which can be as unthinking in its turn as the prejudices it set out to eradicate in the first place: approved words, approved images, approved attitudes. PC is essentially a leftish initiative and it inherits some of the less attractive qualities of hard-left politics, such as its tendency towards sanctimoniousness and dogmatic insistence on its rightness. Much of the energy that has been poured into PC is a sign of powerlessness on the left; a recognition that they are having little impact in the wider public arena, and are being forced to work in the more symbolic areas of our culture instead. This is most pronounced in America, where the absence of any national left-wing politics of note has meant that PC has become one of the few outlets for progressive thought – hence its popularity on campus, its real stronghold. It's far easier to have an effect on people's language than their voting habits, but this can be a hollow victory which leaves the real power structures in one's society essentially untouched – and that would seem to be the case in America. We have to remember that America is a country where 'liberal' is widely considered to be an insult. Using the 'l' word against a political opponent is a sure-fire way of whipping up popular support, as liberals are thought by many to be little better than communists, and thus a threat to the integrity of the state. How this could come to pass in a nation founded on the best principles of Enlightenment thought is one of life's little ironies. The American constitution is surely one of the classic documents of modern liberalism, and yet its most rabid supporters tend to be right-wingers such as the 'gundamentalists' of the militia movement that we met in Chapter 7.

Naomi Klein, a self-confessed devotee of the politics of personal representation in her university days in Canada, has since come to recognise the limitations of identity politics in such an environment:

The slogan 'the personal is political' came to replace the economic as political and, in the end, the Political as political as well. The more importance we placed on representation issues, the more central a role they seemed to elbow for themselves in our lives – perhaps because, in the absence of more tangible political goals, any movement that is about fighting for better social mirrors is going to eventually fall victim to its own narcissism.[4]

The public backlash that such narcissism generated was predictable, with the political right sounding off about this assumed threat to free speech. As Klein points out, however, big business proved more than willing to incorporate such ideas if they helped to sell their products. When it comes to sales, market fundamentalists are nothing if not pragmatic. Advertising for major brands was soon providing positive, non-stereotypical representations of women, gays, and a wide range of ethnic minorities (think of the Benetton ads of recent years, for example), as the corporate sector strove to expand its reach and thus improve its profit margins. For the left, it must have seemed as if PC had been captured by the enemy, their political radicalism reduced to the status of a mere market commodity. Given that many of the brands adopting this imagery were also engaged in using sweatshop labour in Third World countries to manufacture the products in question, this must have been doubly galling. You could argue too, of course, that such a turn of events merely revealed the superficial nature of PC, which had become more concerned with image than substance. In this case, the left's bluff had been called, and as one academic astutely observed, the real problem with PC was that it was 'impersonating political struggle'.[5] That was certainly not what was intended originally; but once the fundamentalists turned it into a formula, PC ceased to pose any real threat to the establishment, who were able to incorporate most of its demands without any great strain on their power base. If PC could improve profits, then PC was fine by the corporate sector.

## 'This is Jihad, Pal': Fundamentally Harder-Edged

When we turn to such topics as environmentalism, abortion, and animal rights, we can be confronted with a much more dogmatic mental-set meriting the label of fundamentalism in its stricter sense. The more extreme elements in movements devoted to these causes are, for example, capable of acts of violent terrorism. Terrorism is a denial of debate, and thus of difference and dissent, those fundamentally fundamentalist characteristics. The case for terrorism in these areas is that the authorities don't always listen to dissenting opinions expressed through the normal channels. Terrorism can therefore be a gesture of sheer frustration as much as anything else; as, admittedly, it often is in the political realm. Further, activists can find themselves up against a market fundamentalism that's oblivious to the environmental effects of its policies.

Oblivious and also uncaring, viewing the world as simply there to be exploited for commercial benefit. (You can generate oil by pulverising large quantities of the right kind of rocks, and some enthusiasts have called for wholesale destruction of the Rocky Mountains in America in order to release their hidden oil riches. Some have even claimed that God placed the oil there for that purpose, and is waiting to see it exploited. One's heart sinks when confronted by such 'logic', which predictably provokes what has been called the 'green rage' of radical environmentalists.[6]) The zeal of the market fundamentalist doesn't accept the need for debate, especially given capitalism's apparently conclusive triumph over the communist economic alternative. Any tampering with the action of the invisible hand is to humanity's ultimate disadvantage and is to be blocked. If the market has an adverse effect on the globe's ecology, then we shall just have to learn to live with that. Or that adverse effect can simply be denied, or treated as a temporary problem only: what matters is progress now – complications can be dealt with later. It's easy to see why market fundamentalism can provoke violent reactions on occasion, when it takes such a cavalier attitude to what to so many others are vitally important ethical issues.

Some non-fundamentalist Muslim thinkers see a positive role for the Islamic world in resisting the abuses of globalisation and the corporate culture that drives it. Ziauddin Sardar, for example, urges Muslim intellectuals to break free of 'the conceptual framework of the Occident' in which they are caught, and to question whether banking, economic development, and technological innovation are all 'really necessary in an Islamic society'.[7] A reinvigorated Islam, drawing on its largely lapsed ideals (Sardar feels its 'recent past' does 'little credit' to Islamic culture),[8] could reintroduce an ethical dimension into world politics, particularly in the area of economic policy, that would be to everyone's benefit.

That's precisely what the anti-globalisation and anti-market fundamentalist supporters want as well, but Sardar argues that Islam is in the best position to arrest the imposition of Western cultural models on the entire world: 'The Muslim civilisation is the only civilisation that still preserves something of its essence, that has the potential to stand up to the dominant civilisation of the Occident, and that can provide the much-needed value structure which can lead mankind to safety.'[9] Islam becomes our hope for the future, although one would have to say that since Sardar's book was written in 1979 there's little evidence that real progress is being made on that front. For the present at any rate, Islamic fundamentalism has taken on the role of chief opponent of Western values, and its political vision signally lacks the generosity of spirit associated with Sardar's. Terrorism and *jihad* send out a very different message to Sardar, and provoke a very different response – from sceptics and market fundamentalists alike. The same goes for terrorism on the part of any of the movements listed above: sympathy declines rapidly at that point.

Radical environmentalists preach an 'ecological consciousness' which they feel most of us have lost, and consider themselves to be engaged in a 'war *for* the environment'.[10] They defend terrorist actions as the only way to prevent severe, and possibly irreparable, damage being done to the Earth's ecological system by big business or government interests: '[e]cological grand larceny', as one apologist has described it.[11] Thus we have the following explanation for an act of 'ecotage' (ecological sabotage) undertaken by the Earth Liberation Front (ELF) in Colorado in 1998:

> On behalf of the lynx, five buildings and four ski lifts at Vail were reduced to ashes on the night of Sunday, October 18th. Vail, Inc. is already the largest ski operation in North America and now wants to expand even

further. The 12 miles of roads and 885 acres of clearcuts will ruin the last, best lynx habitat in the state. Putting profits ahead of Colorado's wildlife will not be tolerated. This action is just a warning. We will be back if this greedy corporation continues to trespass into wild and unroaded areas. For your safety and convenience, we strongly advise skiers to choose other destinations until Vail cancels its inexcusable plans for expansion.[12]

'Green rage' in this instance caused twelve million dollars' worth of damage. Incidents such as this are thought-provoking enough, but it's even more disturbing to learn that ELF members have been arrested on suspicion of planned action against nuclear power facilities in the American southwest. According to the Chief of the Domestic Terrorism Section of the FBI's Counterterrorism Division, the ELF and the Animal Liberation Front (ALF) between them 'have committed more than 600 criminal acts in the United States since 1996, resulting in damages in excess of 43 million dollars'.[13] The full fundamentalist bias of radical environmentalism comes across in the words of the Earth First! group activist Mike Roselle: 'This is Jihad, pal. There are no innocent bystanders, because in these desperate hours, bystanders are not innocent. We'll broaden our theater of conflict.'[14]

Radical environmentalism can be traced back to the 'deep ecology' movement, formulated by the Norwegian philosopher Arne Naess in the early 1970s. The key principles of deep ecology were that non-human life had a value of its own, independent of human considerations, and that the population of the Earth should decrease in order to enable non-human life to flourish in all its diversity and richness.[15] Deep ecologists call for a move from an anthropocentric (human-centred) to an ecocentric (nature-centred) world view, in which human beings see themselves as an integral part of nature. Just *how* integral is revealed in the words of the deep ecology supporter, philosopher Michael E. Zimmerman: 'The other day I saw a TV program about the burning of the Amazon rainforest, and I felt terrible. I became anxious and I felt this tremendous sadness, a sense of irreparable loss.'[16] Once this intimate connection is made between the human and the natural, our actions are supposed to be directed towards conserving our world rather than exploiting it (which is what the Earth Liberation Front feels its terrorist activities will achieve). For radical ecologists, modernity hasn't been in the best interests of the planet, and there are some correspondences with postmodern thought to be noted in this respect. The more extreme proponents of deep ecology advocate turning the clock back to a pre-industrial society to minimise damage to the Earth, and critics have sensed an authoritarian edge to their politics which has led to the use of the term 'eco-fascism'. Deep ecology fanatics are certainly not geared for compromise with their opponents, and their concern for the environment tends to swamp all other considerations. From such a position, dialogue can seem like weakness – or even surrender.

Abortion and animal rights arouse strong feelings which can take on a fundamentalist character; fundamental enough to have led to terrorist activity on several occasions (although it has to be stressed that only a minority within the movements in question are involved). Abortion clinics and animal-testing laboratories have been blown up, doctors and scientists killed and injured, in the name of purity of thought and deed. In one of the most celebrated cases, Paul Hill, a one-time minister, shot dead the doctor John Britton and his bodyguard outside a Pensacola, Florida clinic in 1994. Hill went on to become a hero to anti-abortion extremists, defending his actions in an essay entitled 'I Shot an Abortionist' and showing no remorse at all for his crime, for which he was eventually executed in

September 2003. It has been estimated that 1,750 assaults and 50 murders have been committed by the pro-life movement in America over the last 25 years. This may not be on quite the scale of Islamic terrorism, but it's as hard to counter in its way, and as inimical to the values of a pluralist society. The following sentiments by Randall Terry, founder of the anti-abortion group 'Operation Rescue', let us know what to expect from this sector: 'I want you to just let a wave of intolerance wash over you. ... Our goal is a Christian country. We have a biblical duty, we are called by God, to conquer this country.'[17] Yet again, the rest of us find ourselves confronted by a belief system inspired by a dominating idea, or 'grand narrative', that demands uncritical allegiance on the part of its followers.

In the case of abortion, a direct challenge is being offered to the tradition of liberal thought, as well as to feminism (the opposition often comes from Christian fundamentalist groups). Both liberalism and feminism regard abortion as a largely private matter, given that we are assumed to have control over our own bodies. For feminism this is an article of faith: 'free abortion on demand, a woman's right to choose', as the old campaign slogan had it. Bodies are an emotive issue in our culture: nothing is more central to our notion of autonomy than having control over our own body (an autonomy denied women by heterosexuality, as we have seen separatist feminists angrily arguing). It can be a worrying thought that others could come to usurp that control for their own ends; especially if it were in the service of a fundamentalist system of belief. The question of free will arises again, as it does when faced with religious fundamentalism. Are we simply a channel for other forces, or can we dissent from these and follow our own inclinations? Must there be purity of thought and deed? More importantly, who establishes the criteria for purity of thought and deed, and for what end? Sceptics will see the hand of authoritarianism behind all such searches for purity, and with that a bid for political power that they will wish strongly to resist.

The right-to-life issue is a particularly tricky one for liberals. They are rarely in the business of denying rights to anyone, their objective being to extend them as much as possible, but in this instance they come into conflict with rights claimed by feminism: 'a woman's right to choose', etc. Opposing feminism is not a position a liberal particularly wants to get into, especially if it involves challenging the notion of female autonomy (that's generally a non-negotiable issue for feminists). At the very least we have competing rights here between the foetus and the woman carrying it, and the issue of personal autonomy becomes very clouded in consequence. Opinions vary widely as to the foetus's claim to rights that supersede the woman's with regard to her body. For the philosopher Judith Jarvis Thomson, for example, 'the foetus is not a person from the moment of conception. A newly fertilized ovum, a newly implanted clump of cells, is no more a person than an acorn is an oak tree.'[18] She also argues that there's considerable room for debate as to the extent to which the foetus 'has a right to the use of its mother's body'.[19] Some of the more radical theorists on this topic would deny rights not just to the foetus, but to babies up to several years old, on the basis that they are not independent organisms capable of surviving on their own. The issue of rights hardly exists at all for such thinkers, for whom abortion is problematical only on emotional and not on any moral grounds. Michael Tooley,[20] for example, provocatively argues that neither the foetus nor the infant has a right to life, since neither has a conception of itself as a person; the condition he lays down as necessary for that right to apply.*

---

* Compare that with the US Supreme Court ruling in the Roe vs Wade case (1973), which allowed American states to pass anti-abortion legislation

On the other side of the fence, it's possible to find both liberals and conservatives arguing for a right to life on the grounds that the foetus and the infant possess the potential to become persons. This is a complex debate which is by no means yet resolved, but the critical aspect from our point of view is that it can take a fundamentalist turn. Religious conservatives often interpret 'potential' as 'actual', at which point we are talking about murder if abortion occurs. (Just to confuse the issue further, the pro-life campaign in America opposes a woman's right to choose with a baby's right to choose, in which case abortion is wrong because 'babies don't choose to die'.[21]) Liberals might well want to debate at what stage potential persons become actual ones, and thus when rights come into operation, which would give feminists some scope for reply (although the more fundamentalist feminists might consider that to be too large a concession to make from doctrinal purity). For the more militant elements on the religious side, however, there's no basis for debate. We are instead down to fundamentals which override all such considerations as autonomy over one's body, and there will be no negotiation: the pro-life lobby, like its pro-choice opponent, deals in 'absolutes'.[22] Postmodernists prefer to deal with all such dilemmas on a 'case by case' basis, given that they don't believe in any universal theory which will provide all the right answers.[†] This is anathema to the right-to-life fundamentalists, for whom each case must be dealt with by the same doctrinal principles. The system of belief specifies *in advance* what can and cannot be done; the script has already been written.

covering only the third trimester of pregnancy, on the grounds that the foetus could in theory survive outside the womb by this stage.

[†] 'One works "case by case" even when one is producing a constitution[.] ... And so, when the question of what justice consists in is raised, the answer is: "It remains to be seen in each case."' (Jean-François Lyotard and Jean-Loup Thébaud, *Just Gaming*, trans. Wlad Godzich, Manchester University Press, 1985, pp. 28, 99.)

Animal rights is yet another tricky area for the liberal. By and large, liberals are likely to agree with the principle, rights being one of the cornerstones of the liberal ethos and of the Enlightenment tradition from which the ethos is derived. The point of the Enlightenment tradition was to ensure equality of treatment, and it's equality which is being sought by the animal rights theorists. The difficulty for liberals comes when we move, as for example the ALF does, from polemic to terrorism; or the imposition of an ideology on others. At that point, warning bells start ringing. The philosopher Peter Singer has campaigned eloquently for animal rights, with what sound like impeccable liberal sentiments: 'I am arguing that we extend to other species the basic principle of equality that most of us recognize should be extended to all members of our own species.'[23] Singer is opposed to 'speciesism', in which the believer 'allows the interests of his own species to override the greater interests of members of other species', and he thinks most human beings are guilty of this sin.[24] You could say that this sounds like an argument against human fundamentalism. Meat-eating is the root of the problem for Singer, and he can find no justification for it, arguing for a soy-bean-based diet instead. Meat really is murder for this thinker, who calls on us simply to stop the practice altogether. He also comes out strongly against vivisection, and sees no 'sharp division' between species, 'but rather a continuum along which we move gradually'.[25] The argument is that eventually all sentient beings ought to have the concept of rights extended to them, which would prevent us from acting in a speciesist fashion towards them, as we normally do at present.

Most liberals are likely to find these sentiments at the very least thought-provoking (more likely to persuade on vivisection than meat-eating, probably), but still want to draw the line at extending them into acts of terrorism. Singer has certainly established grounds for debate, and he's not advocating terrorism in the cause of animal rights, but if this argument is ever to be won it will have to be through debate, not violence. The notion that meat is murder has to overcome the entire cultural history not just of humankind, but of the animal kingdom itself, in which all species exist in a food chain with each other. Speciesism is clearly built into the food chain, and it's not just 'pleasures of taste' that drive it, as Singer argues is the case with human beings (as if it were mere thoughtlessness on our part).[26] Whether we need to follow the practice of other species in this matter is, I admit, an interesting question, and certainly well worth debate. What does seem odd, however, is to argue that the difference between human beings and non-humans is more a matter of degree than kind, while asking us to act differently from other species as regards the operation of the food chain. It would also seem that we're the only species capable of theorising and granting rights: surely that qualifies as difference in kind?

Without plunging any further into what is still a very controversial issue (about which, like many others, I have very mixed feelings which can change from day to day), we need to remind ourselves of just what's at stake. Is it really possible to reduce such a complex debate, so deeply entangled in humanity's cultural history, to simple slogans such as 'meat is murder'? In effect, that's what the more militant wing of animal rights has done in order to justify its terrorist actions. That kind of reduction to doctrine and dogmatism is a fundamentalist characteristic ('abortion is murder', 'there's only one way to heaven', and so on), and it signals the end of debate for true believers. Purity of deed demands that we stop eating meat, and purity is a doctrinal obligation we are all deemed to be under. We end up with what amounts to yet another holy war on our hands: 'This is Jihad, pal.' Forget the authoritarian personality: perhaps there's a holy war personality we should be worrying about?

## Fundamentalists to the Right, Fundamentalists to the Left

The search for purity of thought and deed is a fundamentalist characteristic, therefore, and is all around us in daily life: fundamentalists to the right of us, fundamentalists to the left (quite literally, in political terms of reference), all in possession of their very own rock-hard certainties. Purity in this respect means thinking and acting by rote, sticking strictly to the script, because all the matters of substance have been decided a long time ago. All that's required of you as a believer is to act out the necessary rituals and keep the faith. What's depressing to the sceptic is just how readily so many people can fall into these patterns of behaviour, almost as if there were a default mechanism in operation within us when confronted by universalising theories (that behavioural 'strange attractor' we speculated on back in Chapter 5 perhaps?). The desire to adhere to systems of belief promising a simple method of putting the world to rights is deeply encoded in us, it would seem. Just how deep, the sceptic almost fears to find out; maybe sceptics are a vanishingly small minority? The problem doesn't lie in PC, or abortion rights, or animal rights, or any of the other fundamentalisms we have considered over the course of this book, but in that latent desire to conform to an overarching belief system that promises easy, straightforward solutions to highly complex cultural issues. And the wilderness is just full of such solutions.

## CHAPTER NINE

# Conclusion: Saying No to Fundamentalism

I said at the beginning that this book would be a defence of difference and dissent, and that's where our journey through the wilderness of fundamentalism will end. It has also been a defence of a certain kind of postmodern outlook; a low-level one perhaps, less interested in abstruse speculations about identity, meaning or incommensurability, than in promoting scepticism towards authority and resistance to authoritarianism as a standard attitude. But it's no less valuable for that, I would argue, and it has the virtue of combining the best of both the modern and postmodern cultural projects. There is an innate scepticism and suspicion to Enlightenment thought, from where both modernity and postmodernity spring (taking the latter as a somewhat disillusioned version of the former). A different kind of suspicion, I hasten to add, from that espoused by the 'real suspicious people' of the fundamentalist movement; a suspicion directed against authority, not on behalf of authority. At its best, Enlightenment thought aimed to reform authority, to make it publicly accountable rather than a law unto itself. In principle, that remains the basis of the modern nation state, with its regular elections of public officials and auditing of public institutions. Authoritarianism was the enemy for the Enlightenment, as it has remained for postmodernism, which regards it as the inevitable outcome of all attempts to formulate authority, whatever the context. In my days at university, the more anarchistically inclined elements in student politics used to have a slogan that 'no matter who you elect, the executive always wins', and postmoderns would most likely agree with the sentiment. Whether or not one wants to go as far as that in mistrust of authority in general, it's clear from post-Enlightenment history that authority needs very careful monitoring, and that scepticism has an important role to play in the process. The more scepticism the better: a case of Enlightenment plus postmodernism rather than post-modernism versus the Enlightenment.

Opting for 'Enlightenment Plus' might suggest a lapse back into the heresy of Western cultural superiority, where multi-culturalism is replaced by an all too obviously Western monoculturalism. Perhaps that's inevitable when one espouses the kind of commitments I outlined at the beginning of the book: equality of opportunity; an end to cultural oppression and the tyranny of tradition; the eradication of discrimination on the grounds of gender, ethnic group, social position, or sexual preference. I suppose these have to be described as universal values (and largely Enlightenment-derived), although I would rather see them as universal preconditions for normal existence. One could call the right to survive a universal value too, but who would want to argue that this involves any particular ideological position, Western or otherwise? The Islamic world, as Tariq Ali, Akbar Ahmed and Ziauddin Sardar have all argued, needs to engage with values such as the above if it doesn't want to be left behind culturally by the West. Sardar is laudably honest in admitting the gap that already exists: 'Our recent past, that is the last four centuries, and our present, I submit, do little credit to the ideals of Islam; still less do they reflect the civilisation that was once the pace-setter of humanity.'[1] At least in theory, Islam *could* adapt to accommodate these values, but that change will have to come from within Islam itself; it cannot be imposed by the West without drawing the charge of imperialist fundamentalism, and thus adding to the general air of mistrust that characterises relations between these two worlds at present. There is a pressing need for more voices such as the trio just mentioned, and all those from within Islam who bravely spoke up against the *fatwa* placed on Salman Rushdie by the Iranian authorities.

Sadly, current evidence suggests that withdrawal into *taqlid* is the more popular response to Islam's ongoing contest with the West and its Enlightenment-based value system. A tyrannical regime has been removed in Iraq, but that hasn't led to the sudden emergence of a Western-style democratic ethos, as the American and British invaders had hoped would be the case. Instead, the more sinister forces of Islamic fundamentalism (never a very potent movement under the old Ba'ath party regime of Saddam Hussein) have begun to exert themselves. Whatever political settlement is reached, trouble is being stored up for the future. Nor has the considerable pressure applied on Pakistan to keep it within the Western orbit, before, during and after the Afghan war, prevented fundamentalists from implementing Shari'a law in the north-west provinces of the country bordering Afghanistan. For the time being anyway, fundamentalism gives the impression of winning the battle for hearts and minds.

## Why Worry?

How much should we worry at all this evidence of fundamentalist activity and a fundamentalist mind-set? Should we not just allow that there *is* a fundamentalist world out there, but that we can stay apart from it? Could there not be separate spheres that the two sides inhabit? If individuals want to be religious fundamentalists then just leave them to it – that's their right, even if we find it mystifying on our side that anyone would want to commit themselves in this way. That would be the liberal position to take; an acknowledgement that pluralism may include – indeed, almost definitely *will* include – belief systems with which you do not personally agree, or even deeply dislike. The ethics of pluralism demand that such systems be given the same space to express themselves. All well and good, until we realise that the same tolerance is not being extended back. Fundamentalism is neither pluralist-minded nor oriented towards peaceful co-existence with its perceived enemies. In its most virulent forms it seeks to eliminate all competitors: seeks, as in regards it as a non-negotiable duty.

You cannot simply ignore religious fundamentalists; they are in the main control freaks, and you are part of the landscape over which they are determined to exert their control. Islamic fundamentalists have decided they don't want any Westerners to be present in Saudi Arabia, for example, since it's the cradle of their religion. If that means driving Westerners out by terrorist attacks, then that's what will have to be done. Never mind that the Americans have agreed to withdraw their armed forces from the country, which was one of the major demands of the Al-Qaeda leaders; there can never be purity of existence for the committed if there are any infidels around at all. Setbacks merely spur fundamentalists on to greater efforts to obtain political power by which to dictate your lifestyle. Who's to say that Al-Qaeda will not succeed in coming to power in a country like Saudi Arabia? And what if bin Laden is not dead? Such a doomsday scenario has been a source of speculation within the Western political establishment. Theocracy has a powerful hold over the fundamentalist imagination, and theocracy is the last place sceptics want to find themselves: the ultimate wilderness. Think of those Taliban days again, with bans on such subversive activities as kite-flying and pigeon-keeping: there's not much fun in fundamentalism.

In our own day, theocracy only really flourishes in the Islamic world. We have seen that there are sceptics there too, and they are to be commended for speaking out in societies which actively discourage the practice. Those Islamic intellectuals who defended Salman Rushdie in the book *For Rushdie*, even when they disagreed with his ideas, are a sign of hope to the Western sceptic:

> Salman Rushdie, who was raised in a Muslim milieu, knew very well that he was subjecting to ridicule the beliefs and sentiments of hundreds of millions of Muslim believers, and that in their eyes he was committing a sacrilege. Nonetheless, his condemnation to death is no less acceptable for all of that. This condemnation is contrary to the spirit of Islam, in which the individual is ultimately responsible for his acts, *morally speaking*, to God alone. It is also contrary to the spirit of pardon, which is one of the divine attributes on which the Koran insists most strongly and in a constant and absolute fashion.[2]

Sentiments like these are a salutary reminder that Islamic societies are no more homogeneous than their Western counterparts, and that no matter how hard the Islamic authorities might try they cannot eradicate dissent totally (although they are notably successful at keeping it under very close supervision). They are also a reminder that Islam can be interpreted in a more forgiving way than it often is, with mercy rather than justice to the fore (as is also the case with Christianity, of course). Western sceptics would certainly like to see that side of Islam developed much more than it has been of late, and to find common cause with their counterparts in the Islamic world: *ijtihad* without frontiers.

Yet scepticism is rarely evident in the official picture that Islam likes to present of itself these days. This tends to look severe rather than merciful, and to gravitate towards the fundamentalist end of the spectrum. *Jihad* in the most militant sense is threatened too frequently for comfort, even if it's probably just a rhetorical gesture much of the time, born of frustration and political impotence (with which we can certainly sympathise, unless we're card-carrying Western imperialists). Yet the *jihad* reflex is still worrying in terms of what it reveals about cultural difference. Calling for *jihad* is not the way to inspire cross-cultural debate. We can engage in heated exchanges across the cultural divide, but that will hardly improve already strained relations. This is not meant to be an anti-Islamic campaign on my part, just a recognition of current political realities. Christian fundamentalism would move towards theocracy too, one suspects, if it thought there was any chance it could get away with it. There is as much of an obsession there with God's justice as in fundamentalist Islam (yet again, as Rushdie pointed out, '[t]he problem is God'). Consider the dispensationalists and their impatience for the arrival of Judgement Day and God's punishment of the wicked – that is, all non-fundamentalists. It's religion in general, rather than Islam in particular, that I'm sceptical about, since it can all too easily succumb to the pull of fundamentalism. Going back to what I said about recent physics (chaos, complexity), fundamentalism can appear to be the strange attractor at the heart of the religious enterprise; the point it spirals into with a depressing inevitability, as we have seen occur over and over again in recent times. But then, this is a sceptic speaking, who is largely immune to the pull that such ideas can exert on those with the religious gene.

The situation is arguably even worse when it comes to market fundamentalism. As far as the world's most powerful politicians and economists are concerned, this is the economic paradigm to end all economic paradigms, and it's in no need of any alteration whatsoever. (It's probably a good rule of thumb to beware of anyone who announces the end of anything in the political domain; it generally means that they want to protect their own position of privilege. 'End' really means *status quo* in this context, I would suggest, with Francis Fukuyama's pro-American 'end of history' being exemplary in this regard.) In market fundamentalism, humankind is deemed to have reached both its economic and political destiny (the capitalist version of the Marxist utopia), and it will be made to comply with that destiny, with the IMF and the World Bank leading the charge towards global convergence. And for the time being anyway, it's extremely difficult for any country to opt out of the globalisation programme that these bodies are promoting without risking significant damage to its economic prospects. John Gray may well believe that market fundamentalism, like all forms of totalitarianism, will eventually collapse under the weight of its own contradictions; but one suspects (or dreads) that it's more resilient than he thinks, as religious fundamentalism has proved itself to be.

This is not meant to be a counsel of despair (although I confess it can feel that way on occasion; don't these people ever give up?), but a warning against trusting in yet another form of historical inevitability. Waiting for oppressive systems of belief to wither away can be the most fruitless of pastimes for sceptics. We should never underestimate the ability of such systems to both survive and thrive despite flying in the face of reason: lack of logic never deterred a true believer, and it's unlikely to in the future. That religion can continue to be such a potent factor in our lives, after nearly three centuries of Enlightenment thought, has to be a sobering thought to the sceptic: the God hypothesis is holding up remarkably well, considering. Having seen off the communist challenge of the 20th century, market fundamentalism may be well on the way to becoming just as deeply embedded in global culture, its tentacles reaching seemingly everywhere.

Political fundamentalism, too, is all around us; as is nationalist fundamentalism. The search for power and self-definition goes on ceaselessly, no matter how international the world gives the appearance of becoming. Globalisation has very little effect on these forms of fundamentalism, which, if anything, are intensified by events in the economic world. We may have free movement of capital across national boundaries, but we certainly do not have free movement of people. The rich are always welcome everywhere, but not the poor. As transnational corporations restlessly switch their outsourced production from country to country in search of the best deal, dictating terms to national governments in the process, economic refugees are subject to increasingly tough entrance barriers into the developed world, and then strict controls if they are ever lucky enough to make it there. If these are the 'new means' in the conduct of global politics promised by the authors of *Global Transformations*, then they hardly inspire confidence.[3] By any standards this is élitist and discriminatory, and it places the Third World at a considerable disadvantage in its dealings with both Western corporations and governments: the traffic is largely one way, as are the profits. The West is operating contradictory policies in this respect, and the global reach of today's media makes everyone more and more aware of the economic inequalities between the West and the Third World that result. Images of the West transmitted around the globe merely compound the feelings of inferiority of those outside the charmed circle (the majority of the human race, we need to remember), the almost obscene wealth they picture generating both envy and hatred in return. Envy and hatred constitute very effective recruiting agents for Islamic fundamentalism and its cult of the warrior martyr. Again, we would have to say that market fundamentalism reaps what it sows. As globalisation spreads, nationalist fundamentalism becomes more common in the West and religious fundamentalism more common in the Third World, and this is no accident.

## Wilderness Now?

Having described the wilderness around us, and demonstrated the sheer scale of the problem by which we are confronted, what conclusions can we draw as to how to survive in a fundamentalist world, and perhaps even push back its frontiers? Above all, I would like to reiterate the commitment, expressed throughout the book, to scepticism of all efforts that are made to control our social, political and economic destiny. If this sounds simply negative, mere reaction rather than action, we have to remind ourselves of just how little self-criticism there is within fundamentalist movements, the first instinct of which is to eliminate opposition, inside and outside the organisation. The more scepticism there is around in society the better, and it needs to be cultivated enthusiastically. Criticism is the life-blood of a pluralist culture and the bane of a fundamentalist one, and this is true whether we are dealing with the Islamic or imperialist variety: neither likes being scrutinised closely or having its objectives called into question.

It would be nice to sign off on an optimistic note, by saying that surely the legion of sceptics, dissenters, postmoderns, and post-Marxist socialists will overcome the forces of fundamentalism in all walks of life, that difference will prevail. Sadly, I suspect that this isn't on the cards at present, and that what we're in for instead is a protracted cultural struggle against those very same forces. In defiance of the theories of such postmodern thinkers as Jean-François Lyotard, the 'grand narratives' we identified at the beginning of this book have renewed themselves (if they ever really went away), and millions of the world's population seem more than happy to submit to their authority and do 'battle royal' in their service –

even to the extent of offering up their own lives on occasion, as in the practice of suicide terrorism. Warrior martyrs seem to be queuing up for assignments as I write. Whatever Western commentators may say about the law of diminishing returns applying in this market – the more martyrs become commonplace, the less impact each individual one is likely to have – it's currently thriving as never before. The demand for universal theories seems as strong as ever, and various contenders have moved into the vacuum left by the collapse of arguably the 20th century's most successful universal theory (certainly its most aggressive), Marxist communism. It was the decline in authority of such theories that prompted Lyotard in the late 1970s to postulate 'the postmodern condition', in which we were held to have broken free from the spell of the universal. Marxism was redundant for Lyotard, and by implication so most religions should have been too, having at least some of the same pretensions to absolute control of the individual. Cynicism and scepticism were the order of the day, and with the collapse of the Soviet empire over the course of the next decade Lyotard's claims seemed to have been vindicated.

A paradigm shift did indeed appear to have taken place, a move to a world that had largely ceased to worship authority for its own sake and was prepared to reinvent politics on a much more human, local scale without ideological preconceptions. There would be no 'authority mindedness' in operation here. In this new political order, individuals were no longer to be sacrificed to universal theories, but would take more control over their own lives: the 'little narrative', as Lyotard conceived of it, would come into its own, and all would benefit. A mere quarter of a century later, that assessment already looks extremely optimistic, and we find ourselves confronted by the very considerable forces of religious and market fundamentalism, with political and nationalist fundamentalism not far behind in terms of power and influence over world affairs. Postmodern sceptics were clearly premature in declaring that they had won the day, and that institutional authority had lost its hold over us. All too many of the world's population prefer the apparent security of fundamentalist beliefs to the continual revision and critical scrutiny of one's ideas associated with postmodern thought: it's wilderness now, with holy war a perpetual threat on the horizon.

## Just Say No ...

Fundamentalism and libertarianism are locked in conflict in today's world, therefore, and it's a conflict that none of us can avoid – not with Al-Qaeda, the Christian Right, and slash-and-burn capitalism all forging ahead single-mindedly with their respective programmes. This conflict invites us to make critical choices about the way we wish to see our culture developing: towards, or away from, authoritarian control, or even 'authority mindedness'; towards, or away from, a new dark age of dogma. Fundamentalism can be defended to some extent – not all 'progress' is desirable, after all (just think of the 'progress' that has led to a hole in the Earth's ozone layer), and some dialogue must always be maintained with the past if we are to avoid being in a perpetual state of confusion. I hope this book has shown, however, that fundamentalism is nevertheless an inappropriate and misguided response to cultural change. Going 'back to basics' acts as an encouragement to us to retreat into our prejudices – whether these be religious, economic, or political. The evidence is that we are only too disposed to make such retreats, to become 'real suspicious people' viewing the rest of the world from behind the barricades of our beliefs – and once those barricades go up they are notoriously difficult to dismantle.

Recent scientific theory has claimed that the optimum condition for species to be in is at the 'edge of chaos', where control is only just maintained in the face of a constantly changing environment.[4] Species which achieve this delicately poised state thrive; those which refuse to rise to the challenge stagnate – and eventually die away. I am arguing that fundamentalism leads to stagnation, and that it's therefore in our best interests to overcome the temptation to withdraw into it, understandable though that temptation may often be. Fundamentalism simply repeats what went before (or an idealised version of it). And as we have observed, it needs no authoritarian personality to be so attracted. (Interestingly enough in this context, Ziauddin Sardar has argued that 'the Muslim system is characterised by an entropic drift towards a "steady state" – a state of constancy *vis-à-vis* the values and boundaries of the system', yet that is precisely what complexity theorists assert leads to decline and so should be countered.[5]) Fundamentalism denies that there are other valid viewpoints or systems of belief, but that is what libertarianism at its best insists upon – multiple perspectives. We should become as vocal as we can in support of a diversity of perspectives throughout all global cultures.

So we haven't yet reached the end of the era of universal theories, or grand narratives. There are those among us who are striving to make this a new dark age of dogma, in which everyone has to stick to the script and submit to a higher authority. But that's just what has to be resisted. Hence this personal odyssey in discovering how to face up to undesirable cultural trends, without a universal theory on hand to provide instant guidance on how to proceed (the post-Marxist, postmodern dilemma). I want to work towards a position where Lyotard's claim will become true, and we are no longer the prisoners of universal theories: I want us to cultivate an *anti*-authority mindedness. This book has been an examination of those forces which collectively prevent that desirable shift from occurring, and I leave the scene less convinced than ever of the validity of their arguments, less attracted than ever by the spurious sense of psychological security they are offering the individual. Better to be prey to doubts, and to give other viewpoints the benefit of those (with the proviso that it's reciprocal, as part of a mutual 'never-ending interrogation'). The clock must not go back – not to Taliban days, nor dispensationalist days, nor *laissez faire* days, nor dialectic of history days, nor white supremacy days. Fundamentalism needs to be unmasked: it's about power, power over others, and that's what postmodern sceptics reserve their deepest scepticism for. Just say no to fundamentalism, of whatever variety. And keep saying it.

# Bibliography

Adorno, T.W., Frenkel-Brunswik, Else, Levinson, Daniel J., and Sandford, R. Nevitt, *The Authoritarian Personality*, New York, Evanston, IL and London: Harper Row, 1950.

Ahmed, Akbar S., *Postmodernism and Islam: Predicament and Promise*, London and New York: Routledge, 1992.

Ali, Tariq, *The Clash of Fundamentalisms: Crusades, Jihads and Modernity*, London and New York: Verso, 2002.

Amis, Martin, 'The Palace of the End', *The Guardian*, 4 March 2003, p. 23.

Ammerman, Nancy Tatom, *Bible Believers: Fundamentalists in the Modern World*, New Brunswick, NJ and London: Rutgers University Press, 1987.

Anti-Defamation League, 'The Militia Movement – Extremism in America', http://militia-watchdog.org/

Arnot, Chris, 'What Makes a Martyr?', *The Guardian*, Education, 29 April 2003, p. 14.

Atkisson, Alan, and Zimmerman, Michael E., 'Introduction to Deep Ecology: An Interview with Michael E. Zimmerman', http://www.context.org/ICLIB/IC22/Zimmrman.htm

Barber, Benjamin R., *Jihad vs. McWorld: Terrorism's Challenge to Democracy*, 3rd edn, London: Corgi, 2003.

Bauman, Zygmunt, *Intimations of Postmodernity*, London: Routledge, 1992.

Bendroth, Margaret Lamberts, *Fundamentalism and Gender, 1875 to the Present*, New Haven, CT and London: Yale University Press, 1993.

Bhatia, Shyam, 'Bombay's McCarthyite Terror', *The Observer*, 23 April 1995, p. 16.

Brockington, John, *Hinduism and Christianity*, Basingstoke and London: Macmillan, 1992.

Brown, Jonathan C., *A Brief History of Argentina*, New York: Facts on File, 2003.

Bunyan, John, *The Pilgrim's Progress* (1678), ed. Roger Sharrock, Harmondsworth: Penguin, 1965.

— *The Holy War* (1682), eds Roger Sharrock and James F. Forrest, Oxford: Clarendon Press, 1980.

— *Miscellaneous Works*, I, ed. T.L. Underwood and Roger Sharrock, Oxford: Clarendon Press, 1980.

Byers, Stephen, 'I Was Wrong. Free Market Trade Policies Hurt the Poor', *The Guardian*, 19 May 2003, p. 18.

Callinicos, Alex, *An Anti-Capitalist Manifesto*, Cambridge: Polity Press, 2003.

Carver, Terrell, *The Postmodern Marx*, Manchester: Manchester University Press, 1998.

Choueiri, Youssef M., *Islamic Fundamentalism*, London: Pinter, 1990.

Cohn, Norman, *The Pursuit of the Millennium: Revolutionary Millenarians and Mystical Anarchists of the Middle Ages*, London: Secker and Warburg, 1957.

Connolly, William E., *Identity/Difference: Democratic Negotiations of Political Paradox*, Ithaca, NY and London: Cornell University Press, 1991.

— *The Augustinian Imperative: A Reflection on the Politics of Morality*, Newbury Park, CA and London: Sage, 1993.

— *The Ethos of Pluralization*, Minneapolis, MN: University of Minnesota Press, 1995.

Cook, Elizabeth Adell, Jelen, Ted G., and Wilcox, Clyde, *Between Two Absolutes: Public Opinion and the Politics of Abortion*, Boulder, CO and Oxford: Westview Press, 1992.

Daniels, Ted, *A Doomsday Reader: Prophets, Predictors, and Hucksters of Salvation*, New York and London: New York University Press, 1999.

Dawkins, Richard, *Unweaving the Rainbow: Science, Delusion and the Appetite for Wonder*, Harmondsworth: Penguin, 1998.

DeClair, Edward G., *Politics on the Fringe: The People, Policies and Organization of the French National Front*, Durham, NC and London: Duke University Press, 1999.

Derrida, Jacques, *Specters of Marx: The State of the Debt, the Work of Mourning, and the New International*, trans. Peggy Kamuf, New York and London: Routledge, 1994.

Devall, Bill, and Sessions, George, *Deep Ecology: Living as if Nature Mattered*, Salt Lake City, UH: Peregrine Smith, 1985.

Dixon, A.C., ed., *The Fundamentals* (1910–15), New York and London: Garland, 1988.

Eagleton, Terry, 'Pedants and Partisans', *The Guardian*, Review, 27 February 2003, p. 36.

'Ecoterrorism and Ecoterrorists – Acts of Ecoterrorism', http://www.envirotruth.org/ecoterrorism.cfm

'Eco-terrorism in Vail, CO', http://www.econedlink.org/lessons/index.cfm

Elton, G.R., *Reformation Europe, 1517–1559*, London: Fontana, 1963.

Engel, Matthew, 'Meet the New Zionists', *The Guardian*, G2, 28 October 2002, pp. 2–3.

Epstein, Benjamin R., and Forster, Arnold, *The Radical Right: Report on the John Birch Society and its Allies*, New York: Random House, 1966.

Esposito, John, ed., *The Oxford Encyclopaedia of the Modern Islamic World*, I–IV, New York and Oxford: Oxford University Press, 1995.

*For Rushdie: Essays by Arab and Muslim Writers in Defense of Free Speech*, trans. Kevin Anderson and Kenneth Whitehead, New York: George Braziller, 1994.

Foucault, Michel, *Madness and Civilization: A History of Insanity in the Age of Reason*, trans. Richard Howard, London: Tavistock, 1967.

— *Discipline and Punish: The Birth of the Prison*, trans. Alan Sheridan, Harmondsworth: Penguin, 1979.

Fukuyama, Francis, *The End of History and the Last Man*, London: Hamish Hamilton, 1992.

— 'The West Has Won', *The Guardian*, 11 October 2001, p. 21.

Gay, Peter, *The Enlightenment: An Interpretation. The Rise of Modern Paganism*, New York and London: W.W. Norton, 1977.

Gellner, Ernest, *Postmodernism, Reason and Religion*, London and New York: Routledge, 1992.

Geras, Norman, 'Post-Marxism?', *New Left Review*, 163 (1987), pp. 40–82.

Giddens, Anthony, *Runaway World: How Globalisation is Reshaping Our Lives*, 2nd edn, London: Profile Books, 2002.

Gleick, James, *Chaos: Making a New Science*. London: Cardinal, 1988.

Gorki, Maxim, et al., *Soviet Writers' Congress 1934: The Debate on Socialist Realism and Modernism in the Soviet Union* (1935), ed. H.G. Scott, London: Lawrence and Wishart, 1977.

Gorz, André, *Farewell to the Working Class: An Essay on Post-Industrial Socialism*, trans. Mike Sonenescher, London: Pluto Press, 1982.

Gray, John, *False Dawn: The Delusions of Global Capitalism*, 2nd edn, London: Granta, 1999.

— *Al Qaeda and What it Means to be Modern*, London: Faber and Faber, 2003.

Green, David R., *The New Right: The Counterrevolution in Political, Economic and Social Thought*, Brighton: Harvester Wheatsheaf, 1987.

Gunaratna, Rohan, *Inside Al Qaeda: Global Network of Terror*, London: Hurst and Co., 2002.

Haraway, Donna, *Simians, Cyborgs, and Women: The Reinvention of Nature*, London: Free Association Books, 1991.

Harrison, Mark, 'The Logic of Suicide Terrorism', http://makeashorterlink.com/?C4AC12334

Hayes, Paul, *Fascism*, London: George Allen and Unwin, 1973.

Held, David, McGrew, Anthony, Goldblatt, David, and Perraton, Jonathan, *Global Transformations: Politics, Economics and Culture*, Cambridge: Polity Press, 1999.

Herman, A.L., *A Brief Introduction to Hinduism: Religion, Philosophy, and Ways of Liberation*, Boulder, CO and Oxford: Westview Press, 1991.

Herman, Didi, *The Antigay Agenda: Orthodox Vision and the Christian Right*, Chicago and London: University of Chicago Press, 1997.

Hill, Christopher, *The Century of Revolution, 1603–1714*, 2nd edn, Wokingham: Van Nostrand Reinhold, 1980.

Hobbes, Thomas, *Leviathan*, ed. C.B. Macpherson, Harmondsworth: Penguin, 1968.

Hofstadter, Richard, *The Paranoid Style in American Politics, and Other Essays*, London: Jonathan Cape, 1966.

Horgan, John, *The End of Science: Facing the Limits of Knowledge in the Twilight of the Scientific Age*, London: Little, Brown, 1997.

Hughes, Ann, ed., *Seventeenth-Century England: A Changing Culture. Volume I: Primary Sources*, London: Ward Lock Educational, 1980.

Hutton, Will, *The State We're In*, London: Vintage, 1996.

— *The State to Come*, London: Vintage, 1997.

— 'Praise the Lord, Pass the Votes', *The Observer*, 18 May 2003, p. 28.

Jacquard, Roland, *In the Name of Osama Bin Laden: Global Terrorism and the Bin Laden Brotherhood*, trans. George Holoch, Durham, NC and London: Duke University Press, 2002.

Jansen, Johannes J.G., *The Dual Nature of Islamic Fundamentalism*, London: Hurst and Co., 1997.

Jarboe, James F., 'Congressional Statement, FBI: The Threat of Eco-Terrorism', 12 February 2002, http://www.fbi.gov/congress/congress02/jarboe021202.htm

Jelen, Ted, ed., *Religion and American Political Behaviour*, New York: Praeger, 1989.

Kepel, Gilles, *The Revenge of God: The Resurgence of Islam, Christianity and Judaism in the Modern World*, trans. Alan Braley, Cambridge: Polity Press, 1994.

Kilsby, Jill, *Spain: Rise and Decline, 1474–1643*, London: Hodder and Stoughton, 1986.

Klein, Naomi, *No Logo*, London: HarperCollins, 2001.

— 'The Daily War', *The Guardian*, 17 March 2003, p. 20.

Laclau, Ernesto, and Mouffe, Chantal, *Hegemony and Socialist Strategy: Towards a Radical Democratic Politics*, London: Verso, 1985.

— 'Post-Marxism Without Apologies', *New Left Review*, 166 (1987), pp. 79–106.

LaHaye, Tim, and Jenkins, Jerry B., *Left Behind*, Wheaton, IL: Tyndale House, 1995.

Lawrence, Felicity, 'Labour's Free Trade Policy Harms Millions, Says Byers', *The Guardian*, 19 May 2003, p. 6.

Leeds Revolutionary Feminist Group, *Love Your Enemy?: The Debate Between Heterosexual Feminism and Political Lesbianism*, London: Onlywomen Press, 1981.

Lewin, Roger, *Complexity: Life on the Edge of Chaos*, London, Phoenix, 1993.

Lindberg, Carter, *The European Reformations*, Oxford and Malden, MA: Blackwell, 1996.

Lindsey, Hal, with Carlson, C.C., *The Late Great Planet Earth*, Grand Rapids, MI: Zondervan, 1970.

Lipset, Seymour Martin, and Raab, Earl, *The Politics of Unreason: Right-Wing Extremism in America, 1790–1977*, 2nd edn, Chicago and London: University of Chicago Press, 1978.

Lyotard, Jean-François, *The Postmodern Condition: A Report on Knowledge*, trans. Geoff Bennington and Brian Massumi, Manchester: Manchester University Press, 1984.

— *Libidinal Economy*, trans. Iain Hamilton Grant, London: Athlone Press, 1993.

— and Thébaud, Jean-Loup, *Just Gaming*, trans. Wlad Godzich, Manchester: Manchester University Press, 1985.

Maley, William, ed., *Fundamentalism Reborn?: Afghanistan and the Taliban*, London: Hurst and Co., 1998.

Manes, Christopher, *Green Rage: Radical Environmentalism and the Unmaking of Civilization*, London: Little, Brown, 1990.

Marsden, George M., *Fundamentalism and American Culture: The Shaping of Twentieth-Century Evangelism: 1870–1925*, New York and Oxford: Oxford University Press, 1980.

— *Reforming Fundamentalism: Fuller Seminary and the New Evangelicalism*, Grand Rapids, MI: William B. Eerdmans, 1987.

Marvell, Andrew, *Poems of Andrew Marvell*, eds James Reeves and Martin Seymour-Smith, London: Heinemann, 1969.

McCarthy, Rory, 'Destiny and Devotion', *The Guardian*, Weekend, 17 May 2003, pp. 46–55.

Melling, Philip, *Fundamentalism in America: Millennialism, Identity and Militant Religion*, Edinburgh: Edinburgh University Press, 1999.

Milton, John, *Poetical Works*, ed. Douglas Bush, Oxford: Oxford University Press, 1966.

Moghissi, Haideh, *Feminism and Islamic Fundamentalism: The Limits of Postmodern Analysis*, London and New York: Zed Books, 1999.

Mouffe, Chantal, *The Democratic Paradox*, London: Verso, 2000.

Neiwert, David, 'Patriot Spring: Showdown in Big Sky Country', Pacific Rim News Service, http://militia-watchdog.org/contrib. htm/neiwert1.htm

Ohmae, Kenichi, *The End of the Nation State: The Rise of Regional Economies*, London: HarperCollins, 1995.

Outram, Dorinda, *The Enlightenment*, Cambridge: Cambridge University Press, 1995.

Ovendale, Ritchie, *The Origins of the Arab-Israeli Wars*, 2nd edn, London and New York: Longman, 1992.

Plant, Sadie, *Zeros + Ones: Digital Women and the New Techno-culture*, London: Fourth Estate, 1998.

Proulx, Annie, *That Old Ace in the Hole*, London: Fourth Estate, 2002.

Rashid, Ahmed, *Taliban: The Story of the Afghan Warlords*, 2nd edn, London, Basingstoke and Oxford: Macmillan, 2001.

— *Jihad: The Rise of Militant Islam in Central Asia*, New Haven, CT and London: Yale University Press, 2003.

Reddy, Sanjay G., and Pogge, Thomas W., 'How *Not* to Count the Poor', http://www.columbia.edu/~sr793/

Riley-Smith, Jonathan, *The Crusades: A Short History*, London: Athlone Press, 1987.

Ronson, Jon, *Them: Adventures with Extremists*, London, Basingstoke and Oxford: Picador, 2002.

Runnymede Trust, *Islamophobia: A Challenge For Us All: Report of the Runnymede Trust Commission on British Muslims and Islamophobia*, London: The Runnymede Trust, 1997.

Rushdie, Salman, *The Satanic Verses*, London: Vintage, 1988.

— 'Religion, As Ever, Is the Poison in India's Blood', *The Guardian*, Review, 9 March 2002, p. 12.

Ruthven, Malise, *The Divine Supermarket: Travels in Search of the Soul of America*, London: Chatto and Windus, 1989.

— *Islam in the World*, 2nd edn, Harmondsworth: Penguin, 1991.

— *Islam: A Very Short Introduction*, Oxford: Oxford University Press, 1997.

Ryan, Nick, *Homeland: Into a World of Hate*, Edinburgh and London: Mainstream, 2003.

Sardar, Ziauddin, *The Future of Muslim Civilisation*, London: Croom Helm, 1979.

— and Davies, Merryl Wyn, *Why Do People Hate America?*, 2nd edn, Cambridge: Icon Books, 2003.

Sartre, Jean-Paul, *What is Literature?* (1948), trans. Bernard Frechtman, London: Methuen, 1967.

Scarce, Rik, *Eco-Warriors: Understanding the Radical Environmental Movement*, Chicago: Noble Press, 1990.

Seps, Sheldon, and Pitcavage, Mark, 'Militia – History and Law FAQ: Parts 1–7', http://militia-watchdog.org/

Sim, Stuart, ed., *Post-Marxism: A Reader*, Edinburgh: Edinburgh University Press, 1998.

— *Irony and Crisis: A Critical History of Postmodern Culture*, Cambridge: Icon Books, 2002.

Simmons, Harvey G., *The French National Front: The Extremist Challenge to Democracy*, Boulder, CO and Oxford: Westview Press, 1996.

Singer, Peter, ed., *Applied Ethics*, Oxford: Oxford University Press, 1986.

'Slain Fortuyn's Influence Is Still at Work', *The Guardian*, 24 January 2003, p. 21.

Smith, Adam, *The Wealth of Nations, Books I–III* (1776), ed. Andrew Skinner, Harmondsworth: Penguin, 1986.

Soros, George, *The Crisis of Global Capitalism: Open Society Endangered*, New York: BBS/Public Affairs, 1998.

Stiglitz, Joseph E., *Globalization and its Discontents*, New York and London: W.W. Norton, 2002.

— 'There is No Invisible Hand', *The Guardian*, 20 December 2002, p. 17.

Strange, Susan, *Casino Capitalism*, Oxford: Blackwell, 1986.

Thurlow, Richard, *Fascism in Britain: From Oswald Mosley's Blackshirts to the National Front*, London and New York: I.B. Tauris, 1998.

Warraq, Ibn, 'Honest Intellectuals Must Shed their Spiritual Turbans', *The Guardian*, Review, 10 November 2001, p. 12.

Weber, Max, *The Protestant Ethic and the Spirit of Capitalism* (1920), trans. Talcott Parsons, London: George Allen and Unwin, 1930.

Wighton, David, 'Mandelson Plans a Microchip Off the Old Block', *Financial Times*, 23 October 1998, p. 8.

Wilcox, William Clyde, *God's Warriors: The Christian Right in Twentieth-Century America*, Baltimore and London: Johns Hopkins University Press, 1992.

Winstanley, Gerrard, *The Law of Freedom and Other Writings*, ed. Christopher Hill, Harmondsworth: Penguin, 1973.

Yates, Frances, *The Occult Philosophy in the Elizabethan Age* (1979), London and New York: Routledge, 2001.

Žižek, Slavoj, *The Sublime Object of Ideology*, London and New York: Verso, 1989.

# Notes

## Chapter 1

1 See Jean-François Lyotard, *The Postmodern Condition: A Report on Knowledge*, trans. Geoff Bennington and Brian Massumi, Manchester: Manchester University Press, 1984.

2 See Francis Fukuyama, *The End of History and the Last Man*, London: Hamish Hamilton, 1992.

3 Zygmunt Bauman, *Intimations of Postmodernity*, London: Routledge, 1992, p. 175.

4 Nancy Tatom Ammerman, *Bible Believers: Fundamentalists in the Modern World*, Brunswick, NJ and London: Rutgers University Press, 1987, pp. 1–2.

5 Ahmed Rashid, *Jihad: The Rise of Militant Islam in Central Asia*, New Haven, CT and London: Yale University Press, 2003, p. xii.

6 See Akbar S. Ahmed, *Postmodernism and Islam: Predicament and Promise*, London and New York: Routledge, 1992; and Joseph E. Stiglitz, *Globalization and its Discontents*, New York and London: W.W. Norton, 2002.

7 Naomi Klein, 'The Daily War', *The Guardian*, 17 March 2003, p. 20.

8 William E. Connolly, *The Ethos of Pluralization*, Minneapolis, MN: University of Minnesota Press, 1995, p. 106.

9 Ahmed Rashid, *Jihad*, p. 3.

10 See Chapter 7 of Malise Ruthven, *The Divine Supermarket: Travels in Search of the Soul of America*, London: Chatto and Windus, 1989.

11 Quoted ibid., p. 223.

12 This issue is discussed in Gilles Kepel, *The Revenge of God: The Resurgence of Islam, Christianity and Judaism in a Modern World*, trans. Alan Braley, Cambridge: Polity Press, 1994. Like

many other commentators on Islam, Kepel prefers to speak of 're-Islamisation' rather than fundamentalism.

13 A.C. Dixon, ed., *The Fundamentals* (1910–15), New York and London: Garland, 1988.

14 Quoted in George M. Marsden, *Fundamentalism and American Culture: The Shaping of Twentieth-Century Evangelism: 1870–1925*, New York and Oxford: Oxford University Press, 1980, p. 159.

15 Ibid., p. 117.

16 James M. Gray; quoted ibid., p. 122.

17 Malise Ruthven, *The Divine Supermarket*, p. 198.

18 George M. Marsden, *Reforming Fundamentalism: Fuller Seminary and the New Evangelicalism*, Grand Rapids, MI: William B. Eerdmans, 1987, p. vii.

19 John Bunyan, *The Pilgrim's Progress* (1678), ed. Roger Sharrock, Harmondsworth: Penguin, 1965, p. 39.

20 For the diversity of postmodern thought itself, see my *Irony and Crisis: A Critical History of Postmodern Culture*, Cambridge: Icon Books, 2002.

21 See T.W. Adorno, Else Frenkel-Brunswik, Daniel J. Levinson and R. Nevitt Sandford, *The Authoritarian Personality*, New York, Evanston, IL and London: Harper Row, 1950.

### Chapter 2

1 See, for example, Donna Haraway, *Simians, Cyborgs, and Women: The Reinvention of Nature*, London: Free Association Books, 1991; and Sadie Plant, *Zeros + Ones: Digital Women and the New Technoculture*, London: Fourth Estate, 1998.

2 T.W. Adorno, et al., *The Authoritarian Personality*, p. 973.

3 Ibid., p. 976.

4 Max Horkheimer, Preface to ibid., p. ix.

5 John Horgan, *The End of Science: Facing the Limits of Knowledge in the Twilight of the Scientific Age*, London: Little, Brown, 1997, p. 266.

6 T.W. Adorno, et al., *The Authoritarian Personality*, p. 1.

7 Ibid., p. 975.

8 William Clyde Wilcox, *God's Warriors: The Christian Right in Twentieth-Century America*, Baltimore and London: Johns Hopkins University Press, 1992, p. 224.

9 Ibid., p. 222.

10 Ibid., p. 232.

11 Ibid., p. 26. The survey can be found in Kenneth Wald, Dennis Owen and Samuel Hill, 'Habits of the Mind?: The Problem of

Authority in the New Christian Right', in *Religion and American Political Behavior*, ed. Ted Jelen, New York: Praeger, 1989.

12 William Clyde Wilcox, *God's Warriors*, p. 26

Chapter 3

1 Peter Gay, *The Enlightenment: An Interpretation. The Rise of Modern Paganism*, New York and London: W.W. Norton, 1977, p. 8.

2 Dorinda Outram, *The Enlightenment*, Cambridge: Cambridge University Press, 1995, p. 34.

3 Quoted in John Horgan, *The End of Science*, p. 76.

4 Dorinda Outram, *The Enlightenment*, p. 45.

5 Roland Jacquard, *In the Name of Osama Bin Laden: Global Terrorism and the Bin Laden Brotherhood*, trans. George Holoch, Durham, NC and London: Duke University Press, 2002, p. 1.

6 Malise Ruthven, *Islam: A Very Short Introduction*, Oxford: Oxford University Press, 1997, p. 114.

7 Jonathan Riley-Smith, *The Crusades: A Short History*, London: Athlone Press, 1987, pp. xxviii–xxix.

8 Ibid., p. 16.

9 Quoted in Jill Kilsby, *Spain: Rise and Decline, 1474–1643*, London: Hodder and Stoughton, 1986, p. 7.

10 Ibid., pp. 21, 19.

11 Jonathan Riley-Smith, *The Crusades*, p. 4.

12 G.R. Elton, *Reformation Europe, 1517–1559*, London: Fontana, 1963, p. 22.

13 Norman Cohn, *The Pursuit of the Millennium: Revolutionary Millenarians and Mystical Anarchists of the Middle Ages*, London: Secker and Warburg, 1957, p. 272.

14 Carter Lindberg, *The European Reformations*, Oxford and Malden, MA: Blackwell, 1996, p. xii.

15 As Lindberg points out, various commentators have preferred the term 'bibliocracy' to describe Geneva under Calvin (ibid., p. 263).

16 Ibid.

17 Quoted ibid., p. 249.

18 Ibid., p. 272.

19 John Milton, *Lycidas* (1637), lines 125–9; in *Poetical Works*, ed. Douglas Bush, Oxford: Oxford University Press, 1966, p. 146.

20 John Bunyan, 'A Vindication of Some Gospel-Truths Opened' (1657), in *Miscellaneous Works*, I, eds T.L. Underwood and Roger Sharrock, Oxford: Clarendon Press, 1980, p. 161.

21 Christopher Hill, *The Century of Revolution, 1603–1714*, 2nd edn, Wokingham: Van Nostrand Reinhold, 1980, p. 144.

22 'The Declaration of Breda' (1660), in *Seventeenth-Century England: A Changing Culture. Volume I: Primary Sources*, ed. Ann Hughes, London: Ward Lock Educational, 1980, pp. 248–50 (p. 250).

23 John Bunyan, *The Holy War* (1682), eds Roger Sharrock and James F. Forrest, Oxford: Clarendon Press, 1980, p. 247.

24 Malise Ruthven, *The Divine Supermarket*, p. 307.

25 Paul Hayes, *Fascism*, London: George Allen and Unwin, 1973, p. 19.

26 Ibid., p. 20.

27 Ibid., p. 51.

28 See Alex Callinicos, *An Anti-Capitalist Manifesto*, Cambridge: Polity Press, 2003.

29 A.A. Zhdanov, 'Soviet Literature – The Richest in Ideas, The Most Advanced Literature', in Maxim Gorki, et al., *Soviet Writers' Congress 1934: The Debate on Socialist Realism and Modernism in the Soviet Union* (1935), ed. H.G. Scott, London: Lawrence and Wishart, 1977, pp. 15–24 (p. 21).

## Chapter 4

1 Ziauddin Sardar and Merryl Wyn Davies, *Why Do People Hate America?*, 2nd edn, Cambridge: Icon Books, 2003.

2 Malise Ruthven, *The Divine Supermarket*, p. 254.

3 The Runnymede Trust, *Islamophobia: A Challenge For Us All: Report of the Runnymede Trust Commission on British Muslims and Islamophobia*, London: The Runnymede Trust, 1997, p. 4.

4 Quoted in Johannes J.G. Jansen, *The Dual Nature of Islamic Fundamentalism*, London: Hurst and Co., 1997, p. 106.

5 Ibn Warraq, 'Honest Intellectuals Must Shed their Spiritual Turbans', *The Guardian*, Review, 10 November 2001, p. 12.

6 Ziauddin Sardar, *The Future of Muslim Civilisation*, London: Croom Helm, 1979, pp. 57, 56.

7 Tariq Ali, *The Clash of Fundamentalisms: Crusades, Jihads and Modernity*, London and New York: Verso, 2002, pp. 312–13.

8 Youssef M. Choueiri, *Islamic Fundamentalism*, London: Pinter, 1990, p. 120.

9 Johannes J.G. Jansen, *The Dual Nature of Islamic Fundamentalism*, p. xi.

10 See Roland Jacquard, *In the Name of Osama Bin Laden*.

11 Rohan Gunaratna, *Inside Al Qaeda: Global Network of Terror*, London: Hurst and Co., 2002, p. 52.

12 Ahmed Rashid, *Jihad*, p. 2.

13 Quoted in Roland Jacquard, *In the Name of Osama Bin Laden*, p. 73.

14 John Gray, *Al Qaeda and What it Means to be Modern*, London: Faber and Faber, 2003, p. 117.

15 Ibid., p. 1.

16 Ibid., p. 81.

17 Youssef M. Choueiri, *Islamic Fundamentalism*, p. 94.

18 Annie Proulx, *That Old Ace in the Hole*, London: Fourth Estate, 2002, p. 196.

19 See Richard Hofstadter, *The Paranoid Style in American Politics, and Other Essays*, London: Jonathan Cape, 1966.

20 Malise Ruthven, *Islam in the World*, 2nd edn, Harmondsworth: Penguin, 1991, p. 317.

21 Malise Ruthven, *The Divine Supermarket*, p. 158.

22 Chris Arnot, 'What Makes a Martyr?', *The Guardian*, Education, 29 April 2003, p. 14.

23 Mark Harrison, 'The Logic of Suicide Terrorism', http://makeashorterlink.com/?C4AC12334

24 Chris Arnot, 'What Makes a Martyr?', p. 14.

25 Frances Yates, *The Occult Philosophy in the Elizabethan Age* (1979), London and New York: Routledge, 2001, p. 130.

26 Johannes J.G. Jansen, *The Dual Nature of Islamic Fundamentalism*, p. 118.

27 Malise Ruthven, *Islam in the World*, p. 307.

28 Salman Rushdie, *The Satanic Verses*, London: Vintage, 1988.

29 Anouar Abdallah, 'Why Is It Necessary to Defend Salman Rushdie?', in *For Rushdie: Essays by Arab and Muslim Writers in Defense of Free Speech*, trans. Kevin Anderson and Kenneth Whitehead, New York: George Braziller, 1994. Originally published in French, the collection mounts a spirited defence of Rushdie's right to engage in a critique of Islam, even by those who disagree with his motives.

30 Roland Jacquard, *In the Name of Osama Bin Laden*, p. 41.

31 Ahmed Rashid, *Taliban: The Story of the Afghan Warlords*, 2nd edn, London, Basingstoke and Oxford: Macmillan, 2001, p. 82.

32 Nancy Hatch Dupree, 'Afghan Women Under the Taliban', in *Fundamentalism Reborn?: Afghanistan and the Taliban*, ed. William Maley, London: Hurst and Co., 1998, pp. 145–66 (p. 158).

33 Roland Jacquard, *In the Name of Osama Bin Laden*, p. 42. For a selection of some of the relevant decrees, see Ahmed Rashid's *Taliban*, Appendix 1.

34 Quoted in Ahmed Rashid, *Taliban*, Appendix 1, p. 217.

35 Roland Jacquard, *In the Name of Osama Bin Laden*, p. 38.

36 Ahmed Rashid, *Jihad*, pp. 3–4.

37 Quoted in Malise Ruthven, *The Divine Supermarket*, p. 223.

38 *The Oxford Encyclopaedia of the Modern Islamic World*, I–IV, ed. John L. Esposito, Oxford: Oxford University Press, 1995, II, p. 32.
39 Quoted in Malise Ruthven, *The Divine Supermarket*, p. 227.
40 Margaret Lamberts Bendroth, *Fundamentalism and Gender, 1875 to the Present*, New Haven, CT and London: Yale University Press, 1993, p. 5.
41 Jim Woodall; quoted in Didi Herman, *The Antigay Agenda*, p. 89.
42 Martin Amis, 'The Palace of the End', *The Guardian*, 4 March 2003, p. 23.
43 George M. Marsden, *Reforming Fundamentalism*, p. 152.
44 William Clyde Wilcox, *God's Warriors*, p. 2.
45 David A. Hubbard on Harold Lindsell; quoted in George M. Marsden, *Reforming Fundamentalism*, p. 277.
46 George M. Marsden, *Fundamentalism and American Culture*, p. 62.
47 Hal Lindsey, with C.C. Carlson, *The Late Great Planet Earth*, Grand Rapids, MI: Zondervan, 1970, p. 137.
48 Tim LaHaye and Jerry B. Jenkins, *Left Behind*, Wheaton, IL: Tyndale House, 1995.
49 Margaret Lamberts Bendroth, *Fundamentalism and Gender*, p. 6.
50 Quoted in George M. Marsden, *Fundamentalism and American Culture*, p. 101.
51 Margaret Lamberts Bendroth, *Fundamentalism and Gender*, p. 99.
52 Ibid., p. 79.
53 Malise Ruthven, *The Divine Supermarket*, p. 2.
54 Haideh Moghissi, *Feminism and Islamic Fundamentalism: The Limits of Postmodern Analysis*, London and New York: Zed Books, 1999, p. 70.
55 Ibid., p. viii.
56 Ibid., p. 2.
57 Ibid., p. 73.
58 Ziauddin Sardar, *The Future of Muslim Civilisation*, p. 39.
59 Didi Herman, *The Antigay Agenda*, p. 4
60 Quoted ibid., p. 29.
61 Ibid., p. 140.
62 Quoted ibid., p. 145.
63 Ibid., p. 169.
64 Andrew Marvell, 'To His Coy Mistress', in James Reeves and Martin Seymour-Smith, eds, *Poems of Andrew Marvell*, London: Heinemann, 1969, p. 33.
65 Frances Yates, *The Occult Philosophy*, p. 215.

66 Matthew Engel, 'Meet the New Zionists', *The Guardian*, G2, 28 October 2002, pp. 2–3 (p. 2).

67 Ibid.

68 Ibid.

69 Philip Melling, *Fundamentalism in America: Millennialism, Identity and Militant Religion*, Edinburgh: Edinburgh University Press, 1999, pp. 7–8.

70 Ibid., p. 5.

71 Ritchie Ovendale, *The Origins of the Arab–Israeli Wars*, 2nd edn, London and New York: Longman, 1992, p. 229.

72 John Brockington, *Hinduism and Christianity*, Basingstoke and London: Macmillan, 1992, pp. 184, 185.

73 A.L. Herman, *A Brief Introduction to Hinduism: Religion, Philosophy, and Ways of Liberation*, Boulder, CO and Oxford: Westview Press, 1991, pp. 27, 28.

74 Shyam Bhatia, 'Bombay's McCarthyite Terror', *The Observer*, 23 April 1995, p. 16.

75 Ibid.

76 Salman Rushdie, 'Religion, As Ever, Is the Poison in India's Blood', *The Guardian*, Review, 9 March 2002, p. 12.

77 Nancy Tatom Ammerman, *Bible Believers*, p. 42.

78 Terry Eagleton, 'Pedants and Partisans', *The Guardian*, Review, 22 February 2003, p. 36.

79 Ibid.

Chapter 5

1 George Soros, *The Crisis of Global Capitalism: Open Society Endangered*, New York: BBS/PublicAffairs, 1998, p. xx.

2 John Gray, *Al Qaeda*, p. 46.

3 Ernest Gellner, *Postmodernism, Reason and Religion*, London and New York: Routledge, 1992, p. 72.

4 See Mark Harrison, 'The Logic of Suicide Terrorism'.

5 Akbar S. Ahmed, *Postmodernism and Islam*, p. 260.

6 Johannes J.G. Jansen, *The Dual Nature of Islamic Fundamentalism*, p. 172.

7 Joseph E. Stiglitz, 'There is No Invisible Hand', *The Guardian*, 20 December 2002, p. 17.

8 Ibid.

9 Joseph E. Stiglitz, *Globalization and its Discontents*, p. 126.

10 Jonathan C. Brown, *A Brief History of Argentina*, New York: Facts on File, 2003, p. ix.

11 Ibid., p. 270.

12 Quoted ibid., p. 271.

13 Joseph E. Stiglitz, *Globalization and its Discontents*, p. 215.

14 Stephen Byers, 'I Was Wrong. Free Market Trade Policies Hurt the Poor', *The Guardian*, 19 May 2003, p. 18.

15 Naomi Klein, *No Logo*, London: HarperCollins, 2001, p. xvii.

16 Ibid., p. xxi.

17 Kenichi Ohmae, *The End of the Nation State: The Rise of Regional Economies*, London: HarperCollins, 1995, pp. 1, 41.

18 Naomi Klein, *No Logo*, p. xxi.

19 Ibid., p. xix.

20 See Alex Callinicos, *An Anti-Capitalist Manifesto*.

21 John Gray, *False Dawn: The Delusions of Global Capitalism*, 2nd edn, London: Granta, 1999, p. 235.

22 Ibid., pp. 120, 235.

23 Ibid., p. 78.

24 Will Hutton, *The State To Come*, London: Vintage, 1997, p. 2.

25 John Gray, *False Dawn*, p. 81.

26 Ibid., p. 82.

27 Ibid., p. 116.

28 See Michel Foucault, *Madness and Civilization: A History of Insanity in the Age of Reason*, trans. Richard Howard, London: Tavistock, 1967; and *Discipline and Punish: The Birth of the Prison*, trans. Alan Sheridan, Harmondsworth: Penguin, 1979.

29 John Gray, *False Dawn*, p. 70.

30 Jean-François Lyotard, *Libidinal Economy*, trans. Iain Hamilton Grant, London: Athlone Press, 1993, p. 111.

31 Slavoj Žižek, *The Sublime Object of Ideology*, London and New York: Verso, 1989, p. 33.

32 John Gray, *False Dawn*, p. 235.

33 Anthony Giddens, *Runaway World: How Globalisation is Reshaping Our Lives*, 2nd edn, London: Profile Books, 2002, p. xxvii.

34 Ibid., p. 19.

35 David Held, Anthony McGrew, David Goldblatt, and Jonathan Perraton, *Global Transformations: Politics, Economics and Culture*, Cambridge: Polity Press, 1999, p. 444.

36 Thomas Hobbes, *Leviathan*, ed. C.B. Macpherson, Harmondsworth: Penguin, 1968, p. 186.

37 Adam Smith, *The Wealth of Nations, Books I–III* (1776), ed. Andrew Skinner, Harmondsworth: Penguin, 1986, p. 515.

38 Quoted in Tariq Ali, *The Clash of Fundamentalisms*, pp. 260–1.

39 James Gleick, *Chaos: Making a New Science*, London: Cardinal, 1988, p. 150.

Chapter 6

1 Tariq Ali, *The Clash of Fundamentalisms*, p. 281.

2  Ibid., p. 5.
3  Ibid., p. 199.
4  Ibid., p. 201.
5  Gilles Kepel, *The Revenge of God*, p. 195.
6  Ibid., p. 199.
7  David G. Green, *The New Right: The Counterrevolution in Political, Economic and Social Thought*, Brighton: Harvester Wheatsheaf, 1987, p. 1.
8  Adam Smith, *The Wealth of Nations*, p. 119.
9  David G. Green, *The New Right*, p. 177.
10 David Wighton, 'Mandelson Plans a Microchip Off the Old Block', *Financial Times*, 23 October 1998, p. 8.
11 Francis Fukuyama, *The End of History and the Last Man*, London: Hamish Hamilton, 1992, pp. 338–9.
12 Ibid., p. 338.
13 Omar Bakri; quoted in Jon Ronson, *Them: Adventures with Extremists*, London, Basingstoke and Oxford: Picador, 2002, p. 43.
14 Francis Fukuyama, 'The West Has Won', *The Guardian*, 11 October 2001, p. 21.
15 Chantal Mouffe, *The Democratic Paradox*, London and New York: Verso, 2000, pp. 110–11.
16 Ibid., p. 113.
17 William E. Connolly, *The Augustinian Imperative: A Reflection on the Politics of Morality*, Newbury Park, CA and London: Sage, 1993, p. 23.
18 Chantal Mouffe, *The Democratic Paradox*, p. 104.
19 Ibid., p. 140.
20 William E. Connolly, *Identity/Difference: Democratic Negotiations of Political Paradox*, Ithaca, NY and London: Cornell University Press, 1991, p. x.
21 Ibid., p. 66.
22 Ibid., p. 67.
23 Jacques Derrida, *Specters of Marx: The State of the Debt, the Work of Mourning, and the New International*, trans. Peggy Kamuf, New York and London: Routledge, 1994, p. 85.
24 Ibid., p. 79.
25 Ibid., p. 13.
26 Terrell Carver, *The Postmodern Marx*, Manchester: Manchester University Press, 1998, p. 5.
27 Jean-Paul Sartre, *What is Literature?* (1948), trans. Bernard Frechtman, London: Methuen, 1967, p. 190.
28 Ernesto Laclau and Chantal Mouffe, *Hegemony and Socialist Strategy: Towards a Radical Democratic Politics*, London: Verso, 1985, p. 1.

29 For a selection of the responses to Laclau and Mouffe, see Part One of my edited collection *Post-Marxism: A Reader*, Edinburgh: Edinburgh University Press, 1998.

30 Norman Geras, 'Post-Marxism?', *New Left Review*, 163 (1987), pp. 40–82 (p. 43).

31 Ernesto Laclau and Chantal Mouffe, 'Post-Marxism Without Apologies', *New Left Review*, 166 (1987), pp. 79–106 (p. 106).

32 See André Gorz, *Farewell to the Working Class: An Essay on Post-Industrial Socialism*, trans. Mike Sonenescher, London: Pluto Press, 1982.

33 Will Hutton, 'Praise the Lord, Pass the Votes', *The Observer*, 18 May 2003, p. 28.

34 Richard Hofstadter, *The Paranoid Style in American Politics*, pp. viii, xii.

35 Benjamin R. Epstein and Arnold Foster, *The Radical Right: A Report on the John Birch Society and its Allies*, New York: Random House, 1966, pp. 21–2.

36 Tariq Ali, *The Clash of Fundamentalisms*, p. 19.

37 Ibid., p. 274.

38 Ibid., p. 304.

39 Rohan Gunaratna, *Inside Al Qaeda*, p. 221.

40 Tariq Ali, *The Clash of Fundamentalisms*, p. 313.

41 Ibid., p. 198.

## Chapter 7

1 Jonathan Marcus, *The National Front and French Politics: The Resistible Rise of Jean-Marie Le Pen*, Basingstoke and London: Macmillan, 1995, p. 73.

2 Ibid., p. 84.

3 Quoted ibid., p. 87.

4 Quoted ibid., p. 92.

5 Quoted ibid., p. 101.

6 Quoted ibid., p. 102.

7 Ibid., p. 175.

8 Quoted in Harvey G. Simmons, *The French National Front: The Extremist Challenge to Democracy*, Boulder, CO and Oxford: Westview Press, 1996, p. 263.

9 Edward G. Declair, *Politics on the Fringe: The People, Policies, and Organization of the French National Front*, Durham, NC and London: Duke University Press, 1999, p. 234.

10 'Slain Fortuyn's Influence Is Still at Work', *The Guardian*, 24 January 2003, p. 21.

11 Richard Thurlow, *Fascism in Britain: From Oswald Mosley's*

*Blackshirts to the National Front*, London and New York: I.B. Tauris, 1998, p. 234.

12 Quoted in Nick Ryan, *Homeland: Into a World of Hate*, Edinburgh and London: Mainstream, 2003, p. 59.

13 Quoted ibid., pp. 59, 66.

14 Ibid., p. 67.

15 Richard Thurlow, *Fascism in Britain*, p. 268.

16 Ibid., p. 283.

17 This came from my editor at Icon Books, Duncan Heath.

18 Jon Ronson, *Them: Adventures with Extremists*, p. 222.

19 Ibid., p. 81.

20 See the Anti-Defamation League, http://www.militia-watchdog.org/

21 'The Militia Movement – Extremism in America', ibid.

22 Quoted ibid.

23 Ibid.

24 See particularly Sheldon Seps and Mark Pitcavage, 'Militia – History and Law FAQ: Parts 1–7', ibid., 1995.

25 Ibid., Part 1.

26 Ibid.

27 Ted Daniels, ed., *A Doomsday Reader: Prophets, Predictors, and Hucksters of Salvation*, New York and London: New York University Press, 1999, p. 171.

28 Ibid.

29 The Montana Freemen, 'Our De Jure County Government Pursuant to the Word of Almighty God', in ibid., pp. 189–96 (p. 191).

30 Quoted in David Neiwert, 'Patriot Spring: Showdown in Big Sky Country', Pacific Rim News Service, http://www.militia-watchdog.org/contrib.htm/neiwert1.htm

31 Quoted in Ted Daniels, *A Doomsday Reader*, p. 189.

## Chapter 8

1 Leeds Revolutionary Feminist Group, *Love Your Enemy?: The Debate Between Heterosexual Feminism and Political Lesbianism*, London: Onlywomen Press, 1981, p. 7.

2 Ibid., p. 5.

3 Naomi Klein, *No Logo*, p. 105.

4 Ibid., p. 109.

5 Tim Brennan; quoted in ibid., p. 122.

6 See Christopher Manes, *Green Rage: Radical Environmentalism and the Unmaking of Civilization*, London: Little, Brown, 1990.

7 Ziauddin Sardar, *The Future of Muslim Civilisation*, p. 231.

8 Ibid., p. 11.

9  Ibid., p. 230.
10 Rik Scarce, *Eco-Warriors: Understanding the Radical Environmental Movement*, Chicago: Noble Press, 1990, pp. 7, 8.
11 David Brower, Foreword to ibid., p. xii.
12 'Eco-terrorism in Vail, CO', http://www.econedlink.org/lessons/index.cfm
13 James F. Jarboe, 'Congressional Statement, FBI: The Threat of Eco-Terrorism', 12 February 2002, http://www.fbi.gov/congress/congress02/jarboe021202.htm
14 Quoted in 'Ecoterrorism and Ecoterrorists – Acts of Ecoterrorism', http://www.envirotruth.org/ecoterrorism.cfm
15 For a full list of the principles of deep ecology drawn up by Arne Naess and his associate George Sessions, see Bill Devall and George Sessions, *Deep Ecology: Living as if Nature Mattered*, Salt Lake City, UH: Peregrine Smith, 1985, p. 70.
16 Alan Atkisson and Michael E. Zimmerman, 'Introduction to Deep Ecology: An Interview with Michael E. Zimmerman', http://www.context.org/ICLIB/IC22/Zimmrman.htm
17 Quoted in Benjamin R. Barber, *Jihad vs. McWorld*, 3rd edn, London: Corgi, 2003, pp. 212–13.
18 Judith Jarvis Thomson, 'A Defence of Abortion', in Peter Singer, ed., *Applied Ethics*, Oxford: Oxford University Press, 1986, pp. 37–56 (p. 38).
19 Ibid., p. 49.
20 See Michael Tooley, 'Abortion and Infanticide', ibid., pp. 57–85.
21 Elizabeth Adell Cook, Ted G. Jelen, and Clyde Wilcox, *Between Two Absolutes: Public Opinion and the Politics of Abortion*, Boulder, CO and Oxford: Westview Press, 1992, p. xvi.
22 See ibid.
23 Peter Singer, 'All Animals Are Equal', in Peter Singer, ed., *Applied Ethics*, pp. 215–28 (p. 216).
24 Ibid., p. 222.
25 Ibid., p. 227.
26 Ibid., p. 223.

Chapter 9

1 Ziauddin Sardar, *The Future of Muslim Civilisation*, p. 11.
2 Etel Adnan, 'On the Subject of Rushdie', *For Rushdie*, p. 16.
3 David Held, et al., *Global Transformations*, p. 444.
4 See, for example, Roger Lewin, *Complexity: Life on the Edge of Chaos*, London: Phoenix, 1993.
5 Ziauddin Sardar, *The Future of Muslim Civilisation*, p. 215.

# Index